REVELATIO...
LOST CONT...

This truly staggering work unlocks the mysteries
of an amazing civilisation – and
represents the biggest historical bombshell since
Velikovsky unleashed his prophetic theories on
the world.

This was the lost island-continent where a
super-race grew up, thousands of years before
Christ – whose descendants still live among us,
dispersed and unrecognised. In 2193 B.C. it was
destroyed by an enormous cataclysm of the
type suggested by Velikovsky – collision with
a runaway asteroid – that shook the entire globe.

But some of its inhabitants – along with its
many colonists throughout the world – escaped,
and a rare, almost forgotten record of their
birth, history, adventures, laws and daily life
was preserved. First translated from the ancient
Frisian script in the 1870s, the *Oera Linda
Book* (here reproduced in full) caused a storm
of controversy . . . but was then discarded and
forgotten. Now, in the light of more modern
archaeological, geological and scientific
advances – along with revised occult knowledge
– the secrets of Atland cry out for re-appraisal.

The Other Atlantis

ROBERT J. SCRUTTON
Edited by KEN JOHNSON

SPHERE BOOKS LIMITED
30/32 Gray's Inn Road, London WC1X 8JL

First published in Great Britain by
Neville Spearman (Jersey) Ltd 1977
Copyright © Robert J. Scrutton 1977
First Sphere Books edition 1979

TRADE
MARK

Set in Intertype Times

Printed in Great Britain by
Hazell Watson & Viney Ltd
Aylesbury, Bucks

To my wife Norah
whose patience and help
made this book possible

CONTENTS

ACKNOWLEDGEMENTS

My first thanks must go to Ken Johnson who took great pains to edit my historical, technical and legendary material and present it in an easily readable form. I have also to thank him for many useful suggestions which has resulted in two books rather than one large volume. As a result of his suggestions I present *The Other Atlantis* as a history of a forgotten land remembered only in legends; a forgotten people to whom we owe many of our finest ideals of good government, justice, morality and social security which to-day are beginning to lose meaning; and a forgotten Europe Community of nations and tribes where individual and social freedom, security and justice was the ideal, the religion and the common law.

Secrets of Lost Atland, the second volume to follow, tells of the mystical yet highly practical sciences which these ancient people gave to the whole world and which was developed in Britain by our forebears of long ago with astonishing skills and applications which were peculiarly their own.

I would also like to acknowledge my indirect debts to many people living and dead, without whose investigations into ancient mysteries and modern science this book could not have been written. The names of these people are given in the text.

R.J.S.

INTRODUCTION

When Darwin put back the geological clock and it became abundantly clear that the world was not created in 4004 B.C., myth, legend and religion suffered a crisis of credibility. Subconsciously the West was driven to accept that 'feelings' – the software of history – were fallible, misleading and untrue. Only *facts* mattered.

But simultaneously, or nearly so, a trend was being established in just the opposite direction. 'Facts', like the history of Greece, were turning out to be wrong, and myth and legend were being proved right. Legend described Troy and – lo and behold! – Troy turned out to be fact and has been joined by Knossos and the Gilgamesh story.

At present the scientific standpoint is uncomfortably unstable. Official science is now prepared to recognise that myth and folklore, fairy tale and legend, may indeed be remembered fact and not merely poetic imagination. But it does reserve the right to draw the line somewhere.

Where it draws the line is on the borderland between 'respectable' legend and occult tradition: thus, Troy is O.K., but Atlantis is 'bunk'. And as no aquatic Schliemann is likely to dig up the bed of the Atlantic and uncover Rutya, Detya and Poseidon, the defence rests, so to speak – perhaps a little uneasily.

But suppose, just suppose, that evidence of some unimaginable prehistory were suddenly to appear, not in the form of debatable artifacts, but as an actual written record...

In the view of the present writer this has happened – *and has gone unnoticed*.

In February, 1871, a Frisian antiquarian revealed the existence of a very strange manuscript which had apparently been in the possession of a local family for generations and had been handed down from father to son as a holy obligation. The writing appeared to be in an unknown language

1

but this was presently established as a very ancient dialect of the Frisian tongue.

When translated, the contents were startling enough to cause a sensation in academic circles, but historians hastened to assure everybody that the manuscript was a hoax, a sort of literary Piltdown Man. Sensitives and those who feel that occult traditions hold the real key to history, pleaded for further investigation. Articles appeared in London newspapers but, after a brief notoriety, interest died down and the *Oera Linda Book* has been virtually forgotten.

But the *Oera Linda Book* – here re-discovered and re-interpreted – has strange qualities, in particular certain correspondences with the common ground of all occult traditions, which would seem to entitle it to much deeper investigation than it has received.

In short summary, the proposition of those who support the veridical nature of the *Oera Linda Book* is as follows:

A large, semi-circular land mass, a sort of silhouette halo around the north and east of the British Isles, was contemporary with the conjectured Atlantis. It survived the traditional Atlantis, however, by many thousands of years.

Its name was Atland, and there may be reason to suppose that Atland was the archetype of the Hyperborean tradition.

Although situated between what are now the storm-stricken Hebrides and the Greenland permafrost, Atland was no .mpoverished continent. On the contrary, its climate was sub tropical, yielding abundance of everything for full and happy human existence.

This alleged Golden-Age climate of Atland is entirely in keeping with known geological fact. Greenland is recognised as having had a sub-tropical climate in the geological past.

In the year 2193 B.C., some cosmic calamity struck Mother Earth; perhaps some imbalance of the kind suggested by Immanuel Velikovsky, author of the controversial *Worlds in Collision* (1950). Perhaps an asteroid collided with the earth. At any rate, from descriptions in the *Oera Linda Book*, something consistent with a tilting of the earth's axis took place and, within about three days, climatic changes of overwhelming severity took place. Atland was submerged and her history lost ... or nearly so.

According to the *Oera Linda Book*, the Atlanders were a maritime nation who had charted the seas of the world and sailed to the Mediterranean and colonists were already established in Scandinavia and Northern and Southern Europe, Africa and Greece.[1]

Was this the catastrophe which the priests of Egypt reported to Solon, the catastrophe which has possibly been wrongly confused with the much earlier destruction of Atlantis itself?

Was this the enormous upheaval which sent an Atlantic tidal wave through the Pillars of Hercules and flooded the Middle East, giving rise to the legends of the Deluge, the Ark and Mount Ararat? However that may be, the *Oera Linda Book* suggests a quite exact date of the catastrophe – 2193 B.C.

The implications of the *Oera Linda Book* are that some refugees from the stricken and sinking Atland reached the general area of the Low Countries and Denmark, already populated by Atland colonists since around 4000 B.C. at least. They established themselves there and presently made contact with their other kinsfolk who, as sea-rovers and traders, had maintained communication with the Motherland, and the many Atland-colonised corners of the world.

After a time, the Frisian descendants wrote down accounts of the Motherland, its people, its history, its religion, its law. As generation succeeded generation, some older records were lost, while others were summarised, new chapters of the history of the people added. It became thus the diary of a people renewed and updated as a sacred trust by the family which held it.

This summarisation and addition continued through one line of the Atland descendants until the year A.D. 1256 and thus, provided the authenticity of the manuscripts be accepted, gives an unbroken testament of one people's history for just under three-thousand, five-hundred years – a *document unparalleled in human history.*

1. See Appendix C, *Maps of the Ancient Sea Kings.*

3

Nothing was added after the year 1256 when Hiddo Over de Linda of Friesland recopied all the existing material on to the new cotton-based paper which the Arabs had brought to Spain and which was coming into use throughout Europe.

This final copying was passed to the care of each further generation of the family until 1848 when an old woman, Aafjie Meylhof (*née* Over de Linden), handed it to her nephew, Cornelius Over de Linden. The latter, who became a master shipwright at the Royal Netherlands Dockyards at the Helder, finally decided to allow a copy of the document to be made by Dr. Eelco Verwijs, librarian at the Provincial Library at Leeuwarden, Friesland.

Suddenly the record – with all its implications – entered the public domain.

And the implications are truly incredible. For instance:

That the Tex, the law of Atland, was the origin of democracy, and that subsequent laws became the basis of old English Common Law.

That the Roman goddess Minerva was originally a real person – a Frisian princess who founded the Athenian state.

That the Roman Temple of Vesta, with its attendant virgins indirectly derived from Atland's first 'Earth-Mother' Fasta, a high-priestess who tended a perpetually-burning lamp with magical qualities.

That the Druids – called Golen by the Frisian adventurers – were missionaries from Sidon.

That a Frisian admiral, Inka, sailed west and founded the Inca dynasty in Peru.

That the Greek hero Ulysses visited Europe after the siege of Troy to try to wrest the 'magic' lamp of the Frisians from the priestess Kalip (Calypso).

That the great Indian epic, the *Mahabharata*, was compiled by Frisian colonists who settled in the Punjab fifteen-and-a-half centuries before Christ.

That the Norse god Odin, or Wodan, was a deification of a Frisian adventurer named Wodin.

That the legend of the Golden Fleece derived from

4

the practice of Frisian dwellers on the Rhine, who used sheep's fleeces to sift for gold.

That the Cretan law-giver Minos was none other than a Frisian sea-king named Minno.

That the Roman sea-god Neptune was originally Neef-Teunis, a Frisian adventurer who led his people to Phoenicia in 2000 B.C.

That the Greeks learned their form of writing indirectly through the Phoenicians from the Frisians.

That modern numerals derive not, as is believed, from the Arabic, but from Ancient Frisian.

That Ancient Britain was Atland's equivalent of Botany Bay – a penal colony.

Nonsense? Absurd speculation? Fantasy? The Frisian scholar who first began to decipher the archaic language of the *Oera Linda Book* thought so. But he went on translating. And step by step, incredible implication after incredible implication, he found his disbelief fading. He finally became totally convinced that the *Oera Linda Book* was not fiction, not hoax, but the actual, historical record of a people who had escaped from a land known to myth but unknown to the modern West, and whose descendants live, dispersed and unrecognised all over the world to this very day.

THE WRITERS OF THE OERA LINDA BOOK

1. Adela (Writing c. 559–557 B.C.). Incorporating *Frya's Tex*, (Laws); the writings of *Minno*; the history of *Frya's* people; and the inscriptions on the Citadels.
2. Adelbrost and Apollonia (c. 530 B.C.). Incorporating the Elegy of the Burgtmaagd; the Oldest Doctrine; and a description of the Citadel of Liudgaarde.
3. Frethorik and Wiljow (c. 303 B.C.). Incorporating the return of the Greertmen; the diary of the admiral of Wichhirt; the writings of Hellenia; and the last will of the Eeremoeder Frana.
4. Konerêd.

5

5. Beeden. (c. 70 B.C.–11 A.D.). Incorporating the history of Friso and his son Adel; the advice and counsel of Gosa; the letter of Rika the Oudmaagd, the story of Black Adel or Askar, and an unsigned fragment.

THE CUSTODIANS

Liko Over de Linda – 803 A.D.
Hiddo Over de Linda – 1256 A.D.

CHRONOLOGY

B.C.

2193: The destruction of Atland.
2092: Magyars and Finns colonise Scandinavia from the East.
2012: Magyars invade Friesland.
2000: Colonisation of Phoenicia by the Frisians.
1550: Colonisation of the Punjab by the Frisians.
1188: Ulysses visits Kalip, high-priestess of Walcheren.
591: Denmark lost to the Frisians.
589: The murder of Frana, Eeremoeder of Texland.
559: Accession of Adela.
557: Death of Adela in surprise attack of Texland by the Finns.
540–530: Apollonia's writings, covering the history of Friso, Asega, and Askar, kings of Friesland.
303: Writings of Frethorik and Wiljo.
70: Writings of Konered.

A.D.

11: Writings of Beeden.
803: Liko Over de Linda preserves the *Oera Linda* manuscripts.
1256: Hiddo Over de Linda saves and re-copies the *Oera Linda* manuscripts.

1848 : Aafjie Meylhof hands over the MSS to Cornelius Over de Linden.

1867 : Cornelius Over de Linden allows Dr. Eelco Verwijs to copy and translate the MSS.

ATLAND: THE LAND
THAT TIME FORGOT

THE STORY OF THE OERA LINDA BOOK

By its very nature, a work such as this requires three separate and distinct phases: First, an explanation of the origin of the *Oera Linda Book* itself and the comparatively short-lived controversy that it caused. Secondly, verbatim extracts from the manuscripts themselves, so that the reader can become familiar with its narrators, its characters and its styles. Thirdly, an interpretation of those narratives in the light of modern scientific knowledge, archaeological evidence and, in the case of the more esoteric passages, occult traditions. This is what I have attempted to do.

ORIGINS

Cornelius Over de Linden was a master shipwright of the Royal Netherlands Dockyards at the Helder, opposite the West Frisian Island of Texel. In April, 1820, his grandfather, Andries Over de Linden, died, aged 61. An ancient manuscript, owned by the family for generations beyond memory, was found among his effects. It was then placed in the custody of Cornelius's aunt, Mrs. Aafjie Meylhof (*née* Over de Linden), until the grandson came of age. But in fact, Mrs. Meylhof for some unknown reason did not hand over the manuscript to her nephew until August, 1848.

The manuscript was written in a strange, undecipherable script which Cornelius could neither read nor understand. It was not until 19 years later, in 1867, that Cornelius showed the manuscript to a Dr. Eelco Verwijs, of the Leeuwarden Provincial Library in Friesland. After studying some fragments, Dr. Verwijs came to the conclusion that the writing was an ancient form of Frisian dialect. He persuaded Cornelius to allow him to make a copy of the entire writings.

11

Dr. Verwijs then approached the Frisian Society, a body devoted to the study of Frisian history and philology, with the hope that they might offer to finance the cost of translating, editing, printing and publishing of the book. But they refused. Clearly, they believed the documents to be a hoax or a forgery.

However, a deputy states alderman of Friesland commissioned Dr. Verwijs to edit a copy of the book, without any agreement being made as to where the expenses were to come from. Eventually, a Dr. J. G. Ottema, who became fascinated by the manuscript, footed the bill for the publication of the controversial documents. Its Frisian title was *Thet Oera Linda Bok*.

Almost immediately upon its publication historians, archaeologists, antiquarians and other scholars – the majority of them without even bothering to study the original – dismissed it out of hand as a forgery. Newspapers all over Europe printed articles, letters and reviews (See Appendix) about the book, and for a while it was a subject for heated discussion in academic circles. But eventually, the interest faded as scepticism prevailed and the book became virtually forgotten, neither fully authenticated as a genuine record of a forgotten race of ancient and highly-civilised peoples, nor totally repudiated as an elaborate and artful hoax.

During the Twenties and Thirties an occasional author referred to the book, tending to hold it at a kind of verbal arm's length. Others published their own particular versions of the 'mystery' of the *Oera Linda Book*, most of which amounted to theories purporting to be irrefutable evidence that the book was a fake. Thus, in 1927, a M. de Jong produced *The Secret of the Oera Linda Book*, in which he claimed to prove that Dr. Verwijs was the forger. The following year J. F. Hof, in a volume published at Leeuwarden, asserted that Cornelius Over de Linden and the Friesland librarian had collaborated in inventing the manuscript. R. C. J. A. Boles in 1933 reverted to the idea that Over de Linden was the sole perpetrator of the fraud.

Reviewers, particularly in England, gave the book a mixed

reception, the general concensus being that, if the book were genuine, it was undoubtedly one of the most important historical documentary finds ever. Many, however, remained highly sceptical. And yet, even today, the argument has still not been satisfactorily resolved.

Readers of the present volume can get an idea of the *Oera Linda Book*'s impact on contemporary media by studying the review and the paper read to the Frisian Society in February, 1871. (See Appendix A and B.)

One conveniently anonymous critic of *The Morning Post*, for example, based the sum total of his argument against the book's authenticity on his somewhat show-off mastery of old Frisian grammatical style armed, as he or she admits, with a copy of Richtofen's *Old Frisian Dictionary*. Yet his rigid, copper-plate standards are barely plausible. Anyone who cared to attack the King James Authorised Version of the Bible using a dictionary of Hebrew in the same manner would have little trouble demolishing the Old Testament as 'a blatant forgery'. What, for example, I wonder, would the same *Morning Post* critic, with his perfectionist ideals of grammar, have made of, say, one of today's popular dailies, or even the average person's informal letter to a relative, containing such sentences as:

'... whent to Bingo on Saterday, but know luck as usuel. Mavis' his husband is still on nites'?

The Morning Post critic concentrated on only one aspect of the manuscript and said little or nothing of validity about, for example, the divergent styles of the writers, the content of the narratives, the paper on which the manuscript was transcribed. Besides, there are many other haunting qualities about the book which, in my opinion, point to its authenticity: its apparent occasional naivety which, upon closer scrutiny, appears to conceal deeper truths and occult wisdom; its incompleteness – there are pages missing and the manuscript ends abruptly in mid-sentence; the emergent personalities of its various authors; its rich detail and logic; its affirmation of modern theories about the distribution of culture; its feasibility in the light of recent theories of Continental Drift and the possibility of cosmic cataclysms and

13

its confirmation by a mass of archaeological, mythological, geological, linguistic and geographical evidence which I intend to present later.

The other important factor in considering the possibility of a forgery is, of course, motive. For what purpose? None of our 'suspects' – Cornelius Over de Linden, Dr. Verwijs, and the benefactor Dr. Ottema – stood to gain much. None was shown to have made any large amounts of money from the book's publication. Indeed, under the barrage of criticism and scepticism which they unleashed, nor did they accrue any academic kudos from the unveiling of the private family heirloom. Quite the opposite, in fact.

Perhaps the most significant contemporary comment on the book's credibility was begrudgingly made by one of its original critics, a Professor Vitringa. In a letter to the *Devanter Courant*, he wrote:

'I cannot find but that the facts related in the *Oera Linda Book*, so far as they can be controlled by regular history, are not untruthful.'

Today, the early Frisian and Dutch versions, along with the English translation published by William R. Sandbach in 1876, and the various commentaries, are long out of print. Simply for this reason, in re-examining what I believe is a most important and valuable document shedding light on hitherto unknown facts of early Western civilisation, I give verbatim extracts from the *Oera Linda Book*. The reader may judge for himself. Sandwiched between these extracts are my own comments and interpretations, co-relating the text to modern scientific knowledge, archaeology and traditional mythology and occult doctrine.

CHAPTER ONE

WHAT THE BOOK CONTAINS:
IN THE BEGINNING...

The *Oera Linda Book* begins with two introductory letters,
each intended for its subsequent custodians. I give them
here in full. The first, is by Hiddo Over de Linda and is
dated A.D. 1256:

OKKE MY SON –
   You must preserve these books with body and soul.
They contain the history of all our people, as well as of
our forefathers. Last year I saved them in the flood, as
well as you and your mother; but they got wet, and therefore began to perish. In order not to lose them, I copied
them on foreign paper.
   In case you inherit them, you must copy them likewise,
and your children must do so too, so that they may never
be lost.
   Written at Liuwert, in the three thousand four hundred
and forty-ninth year after Atland was submerged – that
is, according to the Christian reckoning, the year 1256.
                     Hiddo, surnamed Over de Linda – Watch.

It is this first letter which establishes clearly the date of
the sinking of the Atland continent – 2193 B.C. (3449 – 1256
= 2193). The second, much earlier letter, dated A.D. 803, is
signed by Liko Over de Linda, and suggests that at the
time the Frisians were subject to some religious persecution.
In fact, at the time it was written, the Emperor Charlemagne
had been waging a war for almost thirty years against the
Saxons and drafting them by the thousand into Flanders
and Northern France. Assisted by Pope Leo III, Charlemagne was planning to exhume the spectre of the Roman
empire under the mantle of the Holy Roman Church. Note
the difference in style from the later letter:

Beloved successors, for the sake of our dear forefathers, and of our dear liberty, I entreat you a thousand times never let the eye of a monk look on these writings. They are very insinuating, but they destroy in an underhand manner all that relates to us Frisians. In order to gain rich benefices, they conspire with foreign kings, who know that we are their greatest enemies, because we dare to speak to their people of liberty, rights and the duties of princes. Therefore they seek to destroy all that we derive from our forefathers, and all that is left of our old customs.

Ah, my beloved ones! I have visited their courts! If Wralda permits it, and we do not shew ourselves strong to resist, they will altogether exterminate us.

                    LIKO, Surnamed OVER DE LINDA.
Written at Liudwert,
Anno Domini 803.

The *Oera Linda Book*, after these two letters, then consists of five main sections, each by various writers and, containing within them, extracts from the work of other chroniclers. (See Table: The Writers.) The first and main section of the text, however, is called *The Book of Adela's Followers*. Adela, writing around 559–557 B.C., was regarded as a great leader by her people, although, when she was offered the official title of *Volksmoeder* – literally 'Mother-of-the-People' – she turned it down because she wanted to marry and, traditionally, the female leaders of her people remained celibate and unattached. She did, however, by her own admission, 'keep an eye' on the people and the various comings and goings throughout their lands in Northern Europe, as if, she says, 'I had really been your Volksmoeder'.

In summary, *The Book of Adela's Followers*, gives first a list of *Grevetmen*, or aldermen, burghers, and sea-kings, under whose direction the book was composed. It describes the earliest oral history of Adela's people – originally Atlanders – including their own story of the Creation of earth's three root races, white, black and yellow. It outlines the code

16

of laws given to the white races by their goddess-mother, *Frya*, the subsequent laws expounded by the first *Eere-moeder*, or Earth-Mother, Fasta, and various other laws evolved for navigators, warriors etc., and for the election of *Burgtmaagden*, chiefs of each borough's Council of Virgins. It tells the story – in the words of the sea-king Minno – of the princess Min-erva, who journeyed to Greece. It describes the degeneration of the other two root races and the various wars fought between their descendants and Frya's people. And, most important of all, it describes the destruction of Atland in some cataclysm that caused the once-idyllic continent to sink without trace.

Initially, the place-names, titles and names of various characters in the *Oera Linda* texts will be totally unfamiliar and, possibly, somewhat confusing to the reader. For this reason, a simple glossary has been compiled for easy reference and guidance.

It is perhaps best, in giving extracts from the book, to begin at The Beginning. Not the physical beginning of the book, but at The Beginning of Creation, as the Atlanders and their descendants had been taught to conceive it. It should then be easier for the reader to understand the morality, philosophies and attitudes of the white, Frisian, or Frya's people as the story of their development, adventures and contacts with other peoples evolves.

Here, then, from *The Book of Adela's Followers*, is their concept of both cosmogenesis and anthopogenesis:

'This is our earliest history.

Wr-alda, who alone is eternal and good, made the beginning. Then commenced time. Time wrought all things, even the earth. The earth bore grass, herbs, and trees, all useful and all noxious animals. All that is good and useful she brought forth by day, and all that is bad and injurious by night.

After the twelfth Juulfeest she brought forth three maidens:

Lyda out of fierce heat.
Finda out of strong heat.
Frya out of moderate heat.

When the last came into existence, Wr-alda breathed his spirit upon her in order that men might be bound to him. As soon as they were full grown they took pleasure and delight in the visions of Wr-alda.

Hatred found its way among them. They each bore twelve sons and twelve daughters – at every Juul-time a couple. Thence come all mankind.

Lyda was black, with hair curled like a lamb's; her eyes shone like stars, and shot out glances like those of a bird of prey.

Lyda was acute. She could hear a snake glide, and could smell a fish in the water.

Lyda was strong and nimble. She could bend a large tree, yet when she walked she did not bruise a flower-stalk.

Lyda was violent. Her voice was loud, and when she screamed in anger every creature quailed.

Wonderful Lyda! She had no regard for laws; her actions were governed by her passions. To help the weak she would kill the strong, and when she had done it she would weep by their bodies.

Poor Lyda! She turned grey by her mad behaviour, and at last she died heart-broken by the wickedness of her children. Foolish children! They accused each other of their mother's death. They howled and fought like wolves, and while they did this the birds devoured the corpse. Who can refrain from tears at such a recital?

Finda was yellow, and her hair was like the mane of a horse. She could not bend a tree, but where Lyda killed one lion she killed ten.

Finda was seductive. Her voice was sweeter than any bird's. Her eyes were alluring and enticing, but whoever looked upon them became her slave.

Finda was unreasonable. She wrote thousands of laws,

but she never obeyed one. She despised the frankness of the good, and gave herself up to flatterers.

That was her misfortune. Her head was too full, but her heart was too vain. She loved nobody but herself, and she wished that all should love her.

False Finda! Honey-sweet were her words, but those who trusted them found sorrow at hand.

Selfish Finda! She wished to rule everybody, and her sons were like her. They made their sisters serve them, and they slew each other for the mastery.

Treacherous Finda! One wrong word would irritate her, and the cruellest deeds did not affect her. If she saw a lizard swallow a spider, she shuddered; but if she saw her children kill a Frisian, her bosom swelled with pleasure.

Unfortunate Finda! She died in the bloom of her age, and the mode of her death is unknown.

Hypocritical children! Her corpse was buried under a costly stone, pompous inscriptions were written on it, and loud lamentations were heard at it, but in private not a tear was shed.

Despicable people! The laws that Finda established were written on golden tablets, but the object for which they were made was never attained. The good laws were abolished, and selfishness instituted bad ones in their place. O Finda! Then the earth overflowed with blood, and your children were mown down like grass. Yes Finda! those were the fruits of your vanity. Look down from your watch-star and weep.

Frya was white like the snow at sunrise, and the blue of her eyes vied with the rainbow.

Beautiful Frya! Like the rays of the sun shone the locks of her hair, which were as fine as spiders' webs.

Clever Frya! When she opened her lips the birds ceased to sing and the leaves to quiver.

Powerful Frya! At the glance of her eye the lion lay down at her feet and the adder withheld his poison.

Pure Frya! Her food was honey, and her beverage was dew gathered from the cups of the flowers.

Sensible Frya! The first lesson that she taught her children was self-control, and the second was the love of virtue; and when they were grown she taught them the value of liberty; for she said, "Without liberty all other virtues serve to make you slaves, and to disgrace your origin."

Generous Frya! She never allowed metal to be dug from the earth for her own benefit, but when she did it, it was for the general use.

Most happy Frya! Like the starry host in the firmament, her children clustered around her.

Wise Frya! When she had seen her children reach the seventh generation, she summoned them all to Flyland, and there gave them her Tex, saying, "Let this be your guide, and it can never go ill with you."

Exalted Frya! When she had thus spoken the earth shook like the sea of Wr-alda. The ground of Flyland sunk beneath her feet, the air was dimmed by tears, and when they looked for their mother she was already risen to her watching star; then at length thunder burst from the clouds, and the lightning wrote upon the firmament: "Watch!"

Far-seeing Frya! The land from which she had risen was now a stream, and except her Tex all that was in it was overwhelmed.

Obedient children! When they came to themselves again, they made this high mound and built this citadel upon it, and on the walls they wrote the Tex, and that every one should be able to find it they called the land about it Texland. Therefore it shall remain as long as the earth shall be the earth.'

Commentary

All great civilisations received their initial impulse from the teachings and examples of men who claimed to speak with divine authority. But the great teacher of the people of Atland was a woman – Frya – who spoke with the authority of her universal God, Wr-alda.

What else do we know about the eternal Wr-alda?

In a later section of the *Oera Linda Book – The Writings of Adelbrost and Apollonia* – and under the heading of *The Oldest Doctrine*, we are told:

'Learn and announce to the people Wr-alda is the ancient of ancients, for he created all things. Wr-alda is all in all, for he is eternal and everlasting. Wr-alda is omnipresent but invisible, and is therefore called a spirit. All that we can see of him are the created beings who come to life through him and go again, because from Wr-alda all things proceed and return to him. Wr-alda is the beginning and the end. Wr-alda is the only almighty being, because from him all other strength comes, and returns to him. Therefore he alone is the creator, and nothing exists without him. Wr-alda established eternal principles, upon which the laws of creation were founded, and no good laws could stand on any other foundation. But although everything is derived from Wr-alda, the wickedness of men does not come from him. Wickedness comes from heaviness, carelessness and stupidity; therefore they may well be injurious to men, but never to Wr-alda. Wr-alda is wisdom, and the laws that he has made are the books from which we learn, nor is any wisdom to be found or gathered but in them. Men may see a great deal, but Wr-alda sees everything. Men can learn a great deal but Wr-alda knows everything. Men can discover much, but to Wr-alda everything is open. Mankind are male and female, but Wr-alda created both. Mankind love and hate, but Wr-alda alone is just. Therefore Wr-alda is God, and there is no good without him. In the progress of time all creation alters and changes, but goodness alone is unalterable; and since Wr-alda is good, he cannot change. As he endures, he alone exists; everything else is show.'

It would appear then, from this later piece of Frisian theology, that Wr-alda has much in common with the eternal and almighty Being of the earth's major monotheistic religions of today: Judaism, Islam, Zoroastrianism, the

21

Baha'i Faith and Christianity. Also, the final phrase, 'he alone exists, everything else is show', has some affinity with the Hindu and Buddhist principles of everything earthly being illusion, or *maya*.

It is similarly interesting to note the similarity between Wr-alda and the Timeless Essence which, say modern sciences, was the primal force from which our universe of space and time was derived.

'Then commenced Time,' says the *Oera Linda Book*. And, after the appearance of grasses, herbs, trees and animals: 'All that is good and useful she (Irtha, the Earth) brought forth by day, and all that is bad and injurious by night.'

Ancient sages used the terms 'day' or 'light' to denote primordial spirit – that which gives life; and 'night' or 'darkness' to denote material or destructive forces. (Compare *Genesis*, I, iii, iv.)

After the 'twelfth Juulfeest' we are told, there appeared the 'mothers' of the earth's three major root-races: Lyda, Finda and Frya. But before looking at these root-races and their symbolic 'mothers', let us first examine the term 'Juulfeest'.

This is undoubtedly the Scandinavian Yuletide, the so-called pagan festival when fires were lit on the shortest day of the year to encourage the return or rebirth of the life-giving sun. It was on to this festival that the early Church fathers later grafted the Christian celebration of Christmas.

But it surely must have taken longer than only twelve Juulfeests, or years, for the various races of mankind to evolve, especially in the light of modern theories of evolution. And it undoubtedly did. The ancients divided time into long and short cycles, like wheels within wheels. There was the great Orphic cycle of 120,000 years, during which it was said that ethnological changes in races occurred. There was also the Cassandra cycle of 136,000 years during which there were changes in solar-planetary influences and their correlation with the mental evolution of man.

In the Hebrew testament it is said three times that when a prophet spoke of the past or foretold the future, a 'day' should be taken to mean a year. Like the ancient leaders of Israel, Frya was a great prophetess who spoke of the past and foretold the future. She did not speak of 'days' but Juulfeests, each of which represents a solar year. In the old mystical sense a solar year is the time taken by the sun to make one cycle through the twelve constellations of the zodiac. Twelve of these cycles is about 310,416 years which is, I believe, the period of time indicated in the Frisian Creation Legend during which the three root races made their appearance on earth. First, the black race, then the yellow and, lastly, the white.

In the account of Finda, mother of the yellow race, it is said that the laws she established were written on golden tablets. The writer of the Scandinavian epic poems, *The Edda*, tells of the finding of such golden tablets:

> *Then again*
> *The wonderful*
> *Golden tablets*
> *Are found in the grass:*
> *In time's morning,*
> *The leader of the gods*
> *And the Odin's race*
> *Possessed them.*

The Edda are believed to have been composed around the 13th century. Could this reference be a kind of race-memory of the finding of Finda's tablets of law?

When Frya summoned her 'children' to the holy Island of Flyland – the text is not specific, but we may conjecture that it was somewhere west of Atland – to give them her laws (Tex), before she disappeared, she said:

'Prosperity awaits the free. *At last they shall see me again.* Though him only can I recognise as free who is neither a slave to another nor to himself.'

Like all prophets of God of whom history and ancient scriptures relate, Frya promised that the free in mind, body and spirit would see her again. Thus the *Oera Linda Book*, whose traditions pre-date the Bible, the Hindu Vedas and

Buddhist scriptures by many thousands of years, is the first known reference to the succession of the great prophets of God, each a manifestation of the same Spirit, each founding a new religion suitable to the people of that time and establishing a new, progressive culture.

Jesus indicated this Spirit manifesting in a succession of prophets when he said that the Spirit in him had existed before the earth was made, and afterwards Abraham was 'glad to see his day' in Melchezedic. Shortly before his death and before his people entered the Promised Land, Moses said: 'The Lord thy God will raise up unto thee a prophet from the midst of thee, of thy brethren, like unto me; unto him shall ye hearken'. (*Deuteronomy*, XVIII, xv–xviii). He then reminded them of the laws he had given which, if faithfully followed, would ensure their prosperity and peace among the nations.

When Frya had given her laws, her holy island foundered; her children had reached their seventh generation. Evidently her life had been a long one, like the lives of the founders of many other races. The lists of the legendary kings of China, Persia, pre-Diluvian Sumer, the god-men of Egypt and the forefathers of Abraham were all said to have lived from 500 to 1,000 years. Were all the chroniclers of the early history of ancient races romancers? It would seem unreasonable so to assume.

Turning to the root-races that sprang from Lyda, Finda and Frya, we learn from other parts of the *Oera Linda Book* that Frya's children were tall, some of them more than seven feet. The book later tells how they spread from Atland all over Europe, even to Egypt, where a mixture of the yellow and black peoples of Finda and Lyda were established.

The ancestors of Frya's white race may have been the tall Cro-Magnons who left evidence of their skills in Europe. Archaeological evidence suggests that Cro-Magnon man was well over six feet tall, intelligent and good-looking. Dressed in modern clothes, he would be virtually indistinguishable from a tall man of today. He is said to have replaced the shorter, broad-chested, muscular Neanderthal Man, with the small forehead and little chin.

24

The Cro-Magnons dressed themselves in sewn and embroidered skin clothes. The flounced dresses of some of their women, whose pictures adorn caves in Spain, are strikingly similar in design to those worn by Minoan ladies of Ancient Crete where, as we shall learn later, Frya's people travelled.

Cro-Magnon cave-art, beautifully painted in vivid colour and realistic perspective, is full of action and astounded modern discoverers, causing anthropologists to revise their opinions somewhat about our so-called 'apelike' ancestors. Delicately-carved mammoth tusks, showing the phases of the moon, provided Cro-Magnon with his calendar.

Contrary to general belief, ancient calendars were not used solely to enable men to keep track of the seasons and important events. Only during the last thousand years of human history has the purpose of the calendar been so limited. The religious and social motives of ancient humanity will not be properly appreciated until the esoteric purposes of their calendars are understood. The symbolic Earth-Mother and the Solar deity were representative also of the underground water-courses and the 'life-energy' which emanates from the earth's telluric lines. These radiations vary in strength and effect with the phases of the moon, day and night, the seasons and the positions of the sun. They influence the growth of vegetation, the habits of both animals and men, according to the beliefs of both the ancients and many modern scientific investigators. For these reasons, all ancient religions were closely associated with the forces of the earth, sun and moon, a subject I shall examine more fully later in the second volume, *Secrets of Lost Atland*.

Thus it was the Cro-Magnon man paid homage to the Mother of Life, possibly a deification of Frya herself. More than 20,000 years ago, Cro-Magnon took a piece of limestone and carved a figure of the Earth-Mother, holding the horn of plenty. It is now in the Bordeaux Museum, where it is known as the Venus of Laussel. There is also a similar Cro-Magnon carving, equally ancient, in the Musée de l'Homme, in Paris, known as the 'Venus of Lespouge'.

Yet another Earth-Mother figure – possibly the world's first free-standing statue – was discovered in excavations on the banks of the Danube, in the gorge of the Iron Gate, where the river twists and whirls between the Yugoslav, Rumanian and Bulgarian mountains. There, a small town of some twenty houses was unearthed, on a ledge overlooking the river. The archaeologist Dragoslav Srejovic commented: 'We have what looks like town planning, thousands of years before the Mesopotamians and Egyptians invented it.'

Could these people – whose diet consisted of berries, tubers and fish – also be descendants of Frya's children? Perhaps because fish were abundant they gave their Earth-Mother a somewhat fishy appearance. Bones excavated showed that they were well-nourished, healthy and lived to a ripe old age. Each of their houses had a cement floor, walls of stone slabs, a hearth and a shrine or alcove, where one of the many little Earth-Mother statuettes stood. The community continued for about 2,500 years. There was no room for further houses on the ledge so, presumably, the young had to seek sites for their own homes elsewhere.

In fact, the remains of large villages of two-storey houses have been found on the banks of rivers throughout the same general area. One was discovered after a map, like a street-guide, was found scratched on a rock. So accurately was it drawn that archaeologists used it to guide their 'digs'. As in the case of the townlet overlooking the Danube, the houses were carefully arranged around a central market-place.

There were workshops, storehouses and places of worship. The people had domesticated animals, cultivated the land and built fishing-boats. They paid devotion to the Earth-Mother and worshipped the Solar deity. This community thrived for thousands of years from the early Stone Age until the coming of Roman invaders.

It is just to the south of this area, in Bulgaria, that more recent excavations have unearthed yet another half-forgotten culture that mined, smelted and worked metals – including gold, bronze and copper – as long ago as 4200 B.C. and possibly even earlier. These were the warrior-horsemen known as Thracians who inhabited the land to the north of Ancient Greece and who were mentioned by Homer. Among many priceless objects found was an ornamental shinguard of silver and gold from Vratza. It bears the face of a goddess. She has golden hair and large eyes and is distinctly Caucasian. Could this be yet another stylised representation of Frya, the Earth Mother?

The Thracians buried their dead in long *tumuli* or barrows, like those of Ancient Britain. They practised agriculture and celebrated fertility rites like those associated with the bountiful Earth-Mother – those of Orpheus and Dionysus.

Among the many finds of recent times was that at Ezerovo of a seal-ring, dated to the fifth century B.C. On it are characters of one of the few Thracian inscriptions ever found. It has been suggested that the letters are Greek, but the actual writing – still undeciphered – is assumed to be Thracian. However, the so-called 'Greek' characters also strongly resemble the 'runic' script of Frya, a subject I shall explore later in this book. (See Fig. 3, p. 76). Like their northern neighbours, the Thracians flourished for thousands of years, eventually coming under Roman domination around the second century B.C.

Apart from the better-known black races of mankind, there are several strains which could have been offshoots of Lyda's children. For example, there are the small, black dwarfs who, legend says, built great stone structures for a taller people in the Pacific, such as those of Easter Island. A similar, diminutive black people carved out tiny rooms and passages under the foundations of ancient cities in South America, and helped to build the mysterious stone temples of Malta and were afterwards persecuted by the priests.

As for Finda's short, yellow people, one branch of them could have been the tiny folk who left the imprints of their feet all over Europe in sacred caves whose walls they covered with wonderfully-executed drawings and paintings of animals. These little people belonged to the same stock as the diminutive honey-coloured Bushmen of South Africa, exceedingly skilled artists who, apparently, had the same permanently-erect penis depicted in European rock etchings. Likewise their women, shown in the carefully-executed

27

Fig. 1

Aurignacian ivory figurine of a female, showing the strange natural apron of the little people. After Piette, L'Anthr.

carvings of Europe, displayed the same folds of flesh which cover the vaginas of the South African Bushwomen. (See Fig. 1.) Mention of these natural female 'aprons' in ancient Egyptian papyruses indicates that these small people may also have been the first inhabitants of Egypt.

CHAPTER TWO

THE GOLDEN AGE OF ATLAND

What kind of a place was Atland? To find out, let us first allow the *Oera Linda Book* to speak for itself. *The Book of Adela's Followers* contains the following description:

THIS STANDS INSCRIBED UPON ALL CITADELS

Before the bad time came our country was the most beautiful in the world. The sun rose higher, and there

28

was seldom frost. The trees and shrubs produced various fruits, which are now lost. In the fields we had not only barley, oats and rye, but wheat which shone like gold, and which could be baked in the sun's rays. The years were not counted, for one was as happy as another.

On one side we were bounded by Wr-alda's Sea, on which no one but us might or could sail; on the other side we were hedged in by the broad Twiskland[1] through which the Finda people dared not come on account of the thick forests and the wild beasts.

Eastward our boundary went to the extremity of the East Sea, and westward to the Mediterranean Sea; so that besides the small rivers we had twelve large rivers given us by Wr-alda to keep our land moist, and to show our seafaring men the way to his sea.

The banks of these rivers were at one time entirely inhabited by our people, as well as the banks of the Rhine from one end to the other. Opposite Denmark and Jutland we had colonies and a Burgtmaagd. Thence we obtained copper and iron, as well as tar and pitch, and some other necessaries. Opposite to us we had Britain, formerly Westland, with her tin mines.

Britain was the land of the exiles, who with the help of their Burgtmaagd had gone away to save their lives; but in order that they might not come back they were tattooed with a B on the forehead, the banished with a red dye, the other criminals with blue. Moreover, our sailors and merchants had many factories among the distant Krekalanders[2] and in Lydia.[3] In Lydia the people are black. As our country was so great and extensive, we had many different names. Those who were settled to the east of Denmark were called Jutten, because often they did nothing else than look for amber (*jutten*) on the shore. Those who lived in the islands were called Letten, because they lived an isolated life. All those who lived between Denmark and the Sandval, now the Scheldt, were called

1. Tusschenland, Duitschland, or Germany.
2. Krekalanders – Greeks.
3. Lydia – Libya.

Stuurlieden,[4] Zeecampers[5] and Angelaren.[6] The Angel-aren were men who fished in the sea, and were so named because they used lines and hooks instead of nets. From there to the nearest part of Krekaland the inhabitants were called Kadhemers, because they never went to sea but remained ashore.

Those who were settled in the higher marches bounded by Twiskland – were called Saxmannen, because they were always armed against the wild beasts and the savage Britons. Besides these we had the names Landzaten,[7] Marzaten,[8] and Woud or Hout zaten.[9]

Commentary

It is highly likely that when the Ancient Greeks wrote of fair Hyperborea, beyond the north winds – a land of happy dancing to the strains of lutes and cithara – they referred to Atland. As Adela's book says, 'The years were not counted, for one was as happy as another'.

Legends of practically all climes and places on earth tell of a Golden Age, when mankind lived in peace, happy and contented. The legendary Atlantis may at one time have been one of the sources of these folk memories and, un-doubtedly, Atland was another. But despite the various legends – of the Greek Hyperborea and Ogygia, the Fortu-nate Isles and the Isles of the Blessed – the *Oera Linda Book* would appear to be the only written record of a people who actually knew and enjoyed such a Golden Age of content-ment. Queen Adela's picture of her pleasant and peaceful antediluvian homeland is particularly vivid. The sun, she says, rose higher in those days and there was seldom frost. There were trees and shrubs bearing fruit which now no longer exist. She even claims that wheat, which 'shone' like gold, could be baked in the strong rays of the sun – a testa-

4. Stuurlieden – pilots.
5. Zeecampers – Naval men.
6. Angelaren – Fishermen.
7. Landzaten – Natives of the land.
8. Marzaten – Natives of the fens.
9. Woud or Hout zaten – Natives of the woods.

ment to the much warmer climate that the northern hemisphere must have enjoyed many centuries ago.

It is interesting to note, in this latter connection, that St. John, in his *Gospel of Peace*, gives Jesus's description of this ancient way of baking Passover bread by the rays of the sun.

It is quite clear, reading Adela's description, that the great continent of Atland, north-east of Scotland, enjoyed a climate that was at least semi-tropical. As we shall hear later, only a terrible cosmic disaster could have changed the angle of the earth's axis so that the once-warm region became the storm-stricken and ice-bound sea that it is today.

The phrase about Wr-alda's Sea 'on which no-one but us could sail' gives an idea of the esteem in which the Atlanders held themselves as mariners. They must have been the finest shipwrights in the ancient world. In those days, thousands of years before Christ, only their sailors had the skills, instruments and courage required to sail to lands as far away as India and, as we shall eventually hear, possibly America. These long voyages and adventures were recorded and will be quoted later.

Although the *Oera Linda Book* does not contain any examples, the Atlanders must have possessed accurate maps to navigate the oceans of the world and exchange merchandise with distant countries. During the Middle Ages, mariners in Europe and around the Mediterranean coasts used accurate navigation charts which had been copied from very ancient maps. No ships were supposed to have sailed to the American continent before the sixteenth century and yet the Hadji Ahmed map, dated A.D. 1559, discovered in Turkey, shows in almost perfect outline the Pacific and Atlantic coasts of America. Then there is the wonderful Oronteus Map, dated A.D. 1532. It shows the whole of the Antarctic continent, which no ship was known to have explored until 1770. Oronteus Finaeus, a French cartographer, is said to have produced this heart-shaped map in the 16th century. He dedicated it to Francis I. He had neither the high mathematical skills nor the instruments required to draw this map. He could not have known the shape of the Antarctic coast, with its estuaries and indications of great rivers, because the whole continent was hidden beneath great glaciers. It is only comparatively recently, with the help of modern instruments used from the air, that the shape of the continent has been detected. It is significant, though, that both American and British cartographers have found some of the ancient maps useful in the correction of modern maps.

The Oronteus map shows the southern point of the American Continent too close to the Antarctic land mass. In an otherwise astonishingly accurate world map, it is difficult to accept that this is a mistake. It is quite possible, especially in view of modern theories about the tectonic plates upon which the earth's continents rest, and move about in the phenomenon known as Continental Drift, that the two great land masses are shown in a position they once occupied at the time the map was made. Some great shock may have tilted our planet, disturbing the positions of the continents significantly.

Recent investigations indicate that around 180 million years ago, India, Australia and Antarctica formed one great land mass which, in ancient legends, is called Gondwanaland. The occultist and founder of the Theosophical Society, Madame H. P. Blavatsky, claimed that when Gondwanaland broke up, it divided into three parts and formed Lemuria. These masses then separated further and formed the great arc of the early Atlantis, which curved from the southern hemisphere to the northern. Apparently, the Atlantis of which Plato wrote was a northern part of this land mass, which had broken up to form the present continents.

In fact, a scientific confirmation of the break-up of two giant super-continents – dubbed Gondwanaland and Laurasia – and the shifting of these fragments on tectonic plates came in 1968. Geologists aboard the U.S. research ship, *Glomar Challenger*, by drilling cores up to three-and-a-half miles deep into the ocean floors, established the past and likely future movements of the earth's land masses.

Similar investigations in the floor of the Indian ocean have revealed how India was rafted northwards for 5,000 kilometres before it collided with Asia. The impact created the

Himalayas. Africa and South America are still being pushed apart with an overall northward direction at the rate of about three centimetres a year. (*Scientific American*, May, 1973.)

It is thus possible that the early maps showing Antarctica's coastlines were made before the great continent was ice-bound – possibly in the same period of which Adela writes, when Atland was warm and pastoral.

Sediments taken from the bottom of the Antarctic Ross Sea by the Byrd Expedition of 1949 showed that warm conditions prevailed there for a long period up to about 4000 B.C. Similar conditions must have prevailed in the northern hemisphere.

In his *Maps of the Ancient Sea Kings*, (Turnstone Press, London), Professor Charles H. Hapgood, who examined the ancient charts referred to, came to the conclusion that they were all derived from a single world map of great antiquity, from a civilisation older than any yet known.

It is my contention that this civilisation was Atland, whose peoples, as we shall see in later extracts from the *Oera Linda Book*, sailed practically all over the world, trading and forming colonies.

Why then, it may be asked, did the ancient maps come later to be replaced by much more inaccurate versions? Professor Hapgood suggests that later cartographers, who did not understand spherical trigonometry, used a square grid in map-making. He found distortions similar to those of maps of the Middle Ages, in a Chinese map dated some time before the twelfth century.

He wrote: 'The square grid imposed on the map is evidence of the same decline of science we have observed in the West, when an advanced cartography, based on spherical trigonometry and on effective instruments for determining latitudes and longitudes, gave way to the vastly inferior cartography of Greece – and when, later in the Middle Ages, even the geographical science known to the classical world was lost ... It seems to me that the evidence of this map points to the existence in very ancient times of a worldwide civilisation, the map-makers of which mapped virtually the entire globe with a uniform general level of technology, with similar methods, equal knowledge of mathematics and probably the same sort of instruments.'

Nowadays a chronometer is used to determine longitudes. By measuring the altitudes of heavenly bodies, distances east or west can be calculated of some fixed meridian like that of Greenwich. This can only be done when the observer knows the exact time on that meridian. There may not have been chronometers in the ancient world, but longitudes could have been measured by a navigator near a strange coast, observing the eclipses of the moon. An observatory at home – and, we shall discover, the Atlanders had such observatories – would note the position of a particular star when the eclipse took place. The navigator at the distant coast would make a similar observation and when he returned home the two records would be compared. Accurate computation by this method would require many years of observations and calculations before perfect maps could be drawn, unless the ship's navigators possessed complex instruments which could give the positions of stars and planets at any given time.

One of the many devices used in those far-off times was one of the minerals which polarised light. Even when the sun was hidden by thick clouds or fog, the colour of such a stone changed or there was a shifting of colour when the stone indicated the position of the sun. I have a friend in British Honduras who owns one of these simple devices. Her grandfather found it on the site of a ruined Maya temple. It is in the form of a dolphin twisted in a spiral so that it could be worn as a thumb-ring. The body is of stone plated with gold, which indicates its extreme age. The head is crowned with a large blue-green stone, the colours of which change and shift when held towards the sun. I have tested it on wet, dull days and find it operates as efficiently as it must have done thousands of years ago. Perhaps it was left in Central America by a mariner of old Atland, or its Frisian descendants.

Another and more complex contrivance is now in the National Archaeological Museum of Greece. It is an ancient orrery, or model of the solar system, and was found by fishermen in the Mediterranean in 1900. By turning a small crank so that the position of the sun and moon indicated by the device correspond with their actual observed positions, other heavenly bodies are moved into their correct positions on the device. With the use of such an instrument the exact positions at sea could be determined after a few minutes' calculation. One archaeologist remarked of the orrery: 'Finding a thing like this is like finding a jet plane in the tomb of King Tut.'

According to Cicero, a similar device, a celestial sphere of very ancient origin, was displayed in the Temple of Virtue in Rome.

The star-computer found in the Mediterranean is very, very old and too delicate to touch. If a working copy of it were made, it could prove extremely useful in our own time.

As for the other great navigational aid, the compass, it was used by the Chinese in very ancient times. Greeks said that Bards from Britain carried an 'arrow' which always pointed the way back to their homeland. If the magnetic compass was used by these people in 500 B.C., it is possible that Atland mariners, who traded both with the Greeks and the yellow races of 'Finda's people', may have had similar aids.

Going back to Adela's text, it is extremely interesting to note that Britain was an island penal colony. Later references in the *Oera Linda Book* refer to the exiles there working in tin mines, presumably those of Cornwall.

Note also the practice of marking the foreheads of the exiles with the letter B – red for the banished and blue for criminals. Red and blue on a white skin: three colours which, with the Frisian sun-cross, were to become the emblems of Scotland and England in the Union Jack. Even in those days, Britons were great travellers who displayed their marked foreheads far and wide. The signs – like the mark of Cain – eventually became signs of distinction and pride. Britons might even have visited Crete, like the Frisians. A fresco of a so-called prince found in the Palace of Knossos shows a similar mark on the nobleman's forehead. The red religious, or caste, mark worn on the forehead of some women of India may have its origin in a custom of the Frisian people who settled in that country.

Although the *Oera Linda Book* gives us no further detailed description of Britain before the sinking of Atland, I shall have much to say in my forthcoming companion volume of the Britain of that period.[10]

CHAPTER THREE

THE END OF A GOLDEN AGE

It is now time to examine what the *Oera Linda Book* says of the destruction of Atland. Although Adela gives no actual indication, it is fair to assume that the idyllic Golden Age lasted for many centuries. But then, suddenly, in what is referred to as the 'Bad Time', all was swiftly and irretrievably lost. The *Oera Linda Book* describes what happened in one brief passage:

HOW THE BAD TIME CAME

During the whole summer the sun had been hid behind the clouds, as if unwilling to look upon the earth. There was perpetual calm, and the damp mist hung like a wet sail over the houses and the marshes. The air was heavy and oppressive, and in men's hearts was neither joy nor cheerfulness. In the midst of this stillness the earth began to tremble as if she was dying. The mountains opened to vomit forth fire and flames. Some sank into the bosom of the earth, and in other places mountains rose out of the plain. Aldland, called by the seafaring people Atland, disappeared, and the wild waves rose so high over hill and dale that everything was buried in the sea. Many

10. *Secrets of Lost Atland.*

people were swallowed up by the earth, and others who had escaped the fire perished in the water.

It was not only in Finda's land that the earth vomited fire, but also in Twiskland. Whole forests were burned one after the other, and when the wind blew from that quarter, our land was covered with ashes. Rivers changed their course, and at their mouths new islands were formed of sand and drift.

During three years this continued, but at length it ceased, and forests became visible. Many countries were submerged, and in other places land rose above the sea, and the wood was destroyed through the half of Twiskland. Troops of Finda's people came and settled in the empty places. Our dispersed people were exterminated or made slaves. Then watchfulness was doubly impressed upon us, and time taught us that union is force.

And so, in this calm, straightforward, matter-of-fact way, the *Oera Linda Book* describes the end of a once great and peaceful land. What could have caused such a calamity? To find out, we shall have to examine what science and other traditions of similar cataclysms tell us.

Science maintains that the Ice Ages, covering a great part of Europe with a thick sheet of ice, came slowly and with equal tardiness melted, leaving glaciers in the high Alps and in the polar regions. But there are many vague and contradictory dates concerning the coming of the ice and its Disappearance.

According to the scientific view, an Ice Age consisting of three long interglacial periods began about one million years ago and ended about 10,000 B.C. A fluctuating glacial period of Europe called the Wurm was thought to have ended about 30,000 years ago, was later dated as 10,000 years ago and more recently re-dated as 6,000 years ago. The fact is, no-one is sure when the supposed Ice Ages began and ended. In fact, many scholars wonder if a European Ice Age ever occurred at all.

The ice theory was invented primarily to account for huge blocks of stone which are scattered over Europe in regions where the rock formations are quite different. To explain the presence of these rocks, a myth was invented; sheets of ice crept from the North Pole and pushed the great boulders across Europe and, when the ice melted, the rocks were left behind to puzzle geologists. If anyone had suggested at the time the myth was invented that the rocks fell from the sky, this would have been greeted by scientists with derision and laughter – there *were* no rocks in the sky to fall, said the scholars of those days. Yet now we know that millions of rocks varying in size from peas to mountains whirl around the sun in many different orbits. We are told that great rocks *have* fallen to earth, some with a force equal to the explosion of many nuclear bombs. The Meteor Crater in Arizona, 4,000 feet across and 170 feet deep, is believed to have been made by a meteoroid weighing about 180,000 tons, which exploded with a force equal to that of a 20-megaton nuclear bomb.

If there had been an age of ice which pushed stones across Europe, why did the ice only move stones and leave behind the trunks of the millions of great trees and the animals which flourished in the previously warm north? How could the creeping walls of ice leave millions of animals lying where they died? Some surely would have become fossils and would have been found piled in heaps when the glaciers began to retreat from Europe.

In his thought-provoking book, *Colony Earth* (Souvenir Press), Richard Mooney says:

'If we look at the last Ice Age, the Wurm, we see the extent of this alleged ice field. At its maximum extent it covered the British Isles as far south as the Thames Valley, North America as far south as the Mississippi Delta, and in the mainland of Europe, parts of Scandinavia, France, Germany and parts of Russia. However, it missed Jutland (Denmark) and spread no further west over continental Europe than Mecklenburg in East Prussia. A large part of Siberia escaped.

'Why did the ice appear in such an odd patchy manner?

'Why is there no evidence of a similar spread of ice at the South Pole? By the same token, why are these geological

38

conditions, which have been associated with glaciations in the past, totally absent in the present arctic regions?

'Another rationale for the ice-sheet hypothesis was the presence of striations, or scratches, on rock surfaces over which the ice moved. Strangely, in the Highlands of Scotland, where the evidence for the "glaciation" is more noticeable than anywhere else in the British Isles, the striations exist on the north-facing slopes, but not on the south-facing slopes. If the ice, moving down from the north, ascended the hill slopes causing these scratches, they should have been even deeper on the descent of the southern side. Yet they are missing altogether on the downward slopes.'

If a tremendous cosmic projectile struck the earth, say, north of Atland, the impact would have been sufficient to rock the earth and possibly change the angle of its axis. It might also have slowed down the revolution of the earth and moved the planet further from the sun. In either event, the tilting of the axis or the movement away from the sun could have drastically lowered the temperature of the northern hemisphere. A slowing down of revolution would certainly have increased the length of the year.

Now, without exception, all the records of ancient civilisations show that this probably did happen. The year once consisted of only 360 days. Then, after some great cosmic calamity, it became necessary to add five extra days (silent or dead days) to the ancient calendars, because the length of the year had increased to 365 days.

The *Ephemerides of Minor Planets for 1965* lists 1,651 asteroids that range in diameter from one mile to about five-hundred miles. Most of these minor planets travel around the sun in orbits between those of Mars and Jupiter. However, about a dozen have comet-like orbits that periodically bring them near to the orbit of the earth. A few years ago the asteroid *Icarus* – about sixth-tenths of a mile in diameter – came within four million miles of the earth. In 1932 the asteroid *Apollo* came within two million miles of our planet. *Adonis* came within less than a million miles in 1936 and in the following year *Hermes* approached within 485,000 miles, which is about twice the distance of the moon from the earth.

In 2193 B.C. – the year that Atland sank – a minor planet could have passed inside the orbit of the moon and become a captive of the earth's gravitational field. If this actually happened, the asteroid would circle the earth in an ever-decreasing spiral orbit. The conflicting gravitational forces of the earth, moon and the intruder from space would cause increasing disturbances in the electromagnetic and gravitational fields of the earth, and these could have caused the atmospheric and enervating conditions which the people of Atland experienced during its fateful last summer: the thick clouds which hid the sun, the damp, oppressive mist and the earth-tremors as powerful gravitational forces pulled and thrust at the earth's crust.

A celestial object sufficiently large to move the planet from its orbit, or to tilt its axis, would, had it struck Atland, have destroyed it and would also have wiped out the greater part of Greenland, Iceland, the British Isles and islands within one or two-hundred miles of the Arctic Circle in a tremendous explosion. Yet the impact must have been at a great distance from Atland and the explosion must have left behind a colossal crater, the rim of which would be visible to this day. The most likely point of impact could have been the region which is now the Arctic Ocean. Here, the polar ice floes float in a tremendous crater-like sea, edged around with hundreds of rock-torn islands and the northern extremities of continents, broken and rent into a confusing variety of violently-fissured land. If the waters of the Arctic Sea were drained away it would look like one of the enormous craters of the moon, with similar far-flung evidence of radial blasts of destruction.

On a much lesser scale, the Santorini islands form the rim of such a crater after volcanic violence blasted to dust the beautiful Minoan civilisation of Strongulê in the Mediterranean; tidal waves hundreds of feet high were hurled over the sea, inundating the low lands as far as the delta of the Nile and the southern coastlands of Europe. Earthquakes

40

tilted the island of Crete, destroyed its palaces and cities and buried them in ashes.

The blast from the great explosion of an asteroid in the Arctic could have thrust the earth from its orbit with an action similar to a mighty ram-jet, turning over the planet's axis. The major evidence of the catastrophe which submerged Atland is to be found in the present Arctic lands, in Siberia, Scandinavia and Alaska, and in the crumbled coasts of Scotland and northern Europe.

Many of the coastlands and cities of northern Europe were submerged for ever and the disturbance of the earth's crust continued intermittently and violently for a further thousand years. All this was recorded in books by the Frisian descendants of the Atlanders and inscribed on the walls of their public buildings in Europe.

Stones and great rocks hurled from the north would only score the northern slopes of the mountains and hills of Scotland, while others would be flung high into the air to crash down hundreds of miles away. *They were not moved by ice.*

Only a few of the sites of submerged cities have been found, such as the walls of buildings some three miles off the coast of Holland and the paved roads and walls of a lost city beneath the sea off the Azores. The remains of a number of towns and villages once covered by the frozen seas have also been found on the coasts of Alaska.

One of the outstanding archaeological discoveries was the site of a large town at Toiutak on Hope Point in Alaska. The few remains indicate that the buildings were laid out in long, broad streets. The advanced town planning and artifacts found are those of a people of a pronounced culture, who were certainly not ancestors of the modern Eskimo.

The reader must not for one moment doubt that there were advanced cultures and cities thousands of years before Atland was submerged. Both the peoples of Frya and Finda built towns and cities in Europe as long ago as 8,000 years. This statement would have been ridiculed at the time the *Oera Linda Book* was first published. But not any more.

In 1964 archaeologists discovered a culture which was

already flourishing in 7000 B.C., on the Macedonian plain of northern Greece. It was flooded by an arm of the Aegean Sea, about the time that Atland was submerged. At the time of its discovery it was thought to have been the oldest culture in Europe. The villagers tended sheep, goats and cattle and grew wheat, barley and lentils. The first houses were rectangular structures with mud walls on a framework of wood. Some structures were 40 ft. square, consisting of three main rooms with cement floors, plaster walls painted red or cream, a fenced-in porch, out-buildings and storage pits. Figurines of the Earth-Mother were found in some of the houses.

Returning to the subject of the cataclysm, it is interesting to note that in parts of Scotland are the remains of large stone buildings of extreme age which have been subjected to intense heat. The stone blocks of the walls of these 'vitrified forts' have been compacted together by heat. No satisfactory explanation has been found to account for this phenomenon.

Vitrified stone buildings have also been found in Western Europe, in North Africa, the Middle East, the Gobi Desert and in the Peruvian Andes.

They are unmistakable evidence, which scientists have been loath to accept, of an almost worldwide conflagration and of temperatures so hot that rocks melted and ran like treacle. Many rocks show evidence of both vitrification and striations. The evidence is overwhelming that an ancient world was destroyed not by cold and ice, but by great floods and fire.

In the Gobi Desert, deep below the ruins of Khara Khota, a Professor Koslov found a tomb dated at about 12,000 B.C. A sarcophagus held the bodies of two men. The sign of a dissected circle, like the Frisian sun-cross, was inscribed on the sarcophagus. Nearby were strange sand vitrifications, caused by a tremendous heat, thousands of years after the bodies were entombed.

Unfortunately, the *Oera Linda Book* does not describe in detail the mass terror, the animals that died, nor the deeds of heroism that must have taken place during the holocaust when Atland sank, in some world-shaking cataclysm.

We do know, however, of the many hundreds of mammoths that died in Siberia. They have been found sealed in ice, their bodies unharmed and with fresh food in their mouths and stomachs. They had every appearance of having died suddenly while peacefully grazing on lush vegetation that grew in semi-tropical regions. No one has been able to explain satisfactorily how and why they died. C. H. Hapgood and other writers say that millions of animals were suddenly destroyed in North America. With equal suddenness animals which had been flourishing in regions which are now bitterly cold, perished.

Slow, creeping ice and cold could not have killed them in that way. If the temperature had begun to fall the animals would have migrated quite naturally to warmer climes. These creatures died instantly while grazing.

I suggest that – like the victims of an atomic holocaust – people and animals were killed instantly by the blast, shock waves and, possibly, intense radiation when some extra-terrestrial body, such as an asteroid, struck the Arctic. Seas were blasted into vapour, which cooled and fell as snow, covering the bodies and the devastated lands. The resultant tilting of the earth's axis caused once-temperate or semi-tropical lands to freeze over suddenly, putting the mammoths and other creatures into deep freeze. So fresh was the meat of the Siberian mammoths that it has been served up as steaks at Russian State banquets.

Scientists have invented many different theories to explain the causes of the Ice Age. Clouds of interstellar dust shut off the sun's radiations; a thinning out of hydrogen clouds which feed the sun damped down solar energies; a change in solar gravitation caused the earth to move further from its parent-star . . . and so on.

Yet I believe that the theory which I have put forward is much more factual, based on tangible evidence and far less improbable than those of the scientists. The Ice Age must have begun somewhere around 2100 B.C. – *and we are still living in it.*

In his *Colony Earth*, author Richard Mooney quotes the

following article by a well-known scientist, from a 1968 edition of the *Saturday Evening Post*:

'About a seventh of the entire land surface of our earth, stretching in a great swathe around the Arctic Circle, is permanently frozen ... the greater part of it is covered with a layer of ice, varying in thickness from a few feet to more than a thousand feet, composed of different substances. It includes a high proportion of earth or loam, and often also masses of bones or even whole animals in various degrees of preservation or decomposition.

'The list of animals thawed out of this mass would cover several pages ... the greatest riddle, however, is when, why and how did all these creatures, and in such absolutely countless numbers, get killed, mashed up and frozen into this horrific indecency?

'These animal remains are not in deltas, swamps or estuaries, but are scattered all over the country. Many of these animals were perfectly fresh, whole and undamaged, and still either standing, or at least kneeling upright.

'Vast herds of enormous, well-fed beasts, beasts not specifically designed for extreme cold, were (apparently) placidly feeding in sunny pastures at a temperature in which we would probably not even have needed a coat. Suddenly they were all killed without any visible sign of violence and before they could so much as swallow a last mouthful of food, and then they were quick-frozen so rapidly that every cell in their bodies is perfectly preserved.'

Later in the *Oera Linda Book* we are told that many of Frya's (white) people who survived the terrible destruction – the Frisian-Aryans – set up colonies in Ancient India. They would certainly have preserved the story of the great tragedy which destroyed their homeland and brought about this large-scale destruction of humans and animals. They may have been responsible for the collection of Hindu books that form the great epic known as the *Mahabharata*. It says that 'sixty million people perished in one terrible night'. It contains a number of references to radiation sickness and death:

'For many days there were terrible gales and peoples' hair and finger-nails dropped out.

'Food went bad and birds that had been ... [blasted?] turned white and their legs blistered and turned scarlet.

'The elephants made furious trumpeting and sank dead to the ground over a vast area.

'Then, for several years [three years, says the *Oera Linda Book*] the sun and the stars and the sky were hidden by clouds and violent storms. It seemed that the end of the world had come.'

Adela's account of the destruction of Atland and a part of northern Europe and the documents of antiquity which tell of fire from the heavens and great floods which brought devastation and suffering to lands and peoples in many parts of the world, and the Mosaic story of the plagues of Egypt, now take on a new and dramatic meaning. When giant meteorites struck the earth with explosions equivalent to that of nuclear bombs the dust made the land infertile, killed great numbers of people and blacked out the light of the sun, an Egyptian scribe wrote:

'The land is utterly perished and naught remains ... The sun is veiled and shines not in the sight of man ... I show thee the land upside down ... None knoweth that midday is there ... his shadow is not discerned.'[1]

Another wrote of the turning and tilting of the planet:

'Plague is throughout the land ... Blood is everywhere ... The land turns round as does a potter's wheel ... Oh! that the Earth would cease from noise, and tumult be no more.'[2]

There are records of a similar catastrophe in other ancient writings. The *Kalevala*, a Finnish epic said to date

1. Papyrus, Hermitage (Leningrad) No. 1116.
2. Papyrus Ipuwer (Leiden, No. 344).

back to 'enormous antiquity' describes a time when the sun and moon disappeared from the sky and shadows covered the earth:

> *Even birds grew sick and perished,*
> *men and maidens, faint and famished,*
> *perished in the cold and darkness,*
> *from the absence of the sunshine,*
> *from the absence of the moonlight...*
> *But the wise men of the Northland*
> *could not know the dawn of morning,*
> *for the moon shines not in season*
> *nor appears the sun at midday,*
> *from their stations in the sky-vault.*
>
> *(The Kalevala, Rune 49).*

In his preface to the English translation of the poem, Crawford refers the time of the action to a period when the Hungarians (Magyars) and Finns were still united as one people – 'in other words, to a time at least three thousand years ago'.

This, of course, would tie in with the date given for the sinking of Atland – 2193 B.C. And, as the *Oera Linda Book* later relates, the Magyars and Finns did come out of the east as one people.

It is also noteworthy that the brief descriptions of life in Atland and its eventual submergence are similar to those given in Plato's description of Atlantis and its destruction in the *Critias* and *Timaeus*. Although I tend to the belief that each was a different event and about a different people.

CHAPTER FOUR

THE DELUGE OF BRITAIN

Unfortunately, the *Oera Linda Book* does not record what happened in Westland, the old name for Britain, isle of the exiles, when the holocaust that sank Atland struck. If such a cataclysm occurred, Britain's very foundations would have been rent asunder, leaving the dismembered remnants, the Orkneys, Shetlands and the Outer Hebrides. In the west, much land would have been submerged, perhaps forming the present North Channel, making Ireland a separate island. Irish, Celtic and Icelandic legends all tell of this age of fire and flood which ravaged the northern hemisphere, killing all except those who were lucky enough to escape in ships.

My wife, who is what is known as a 'sensitive' can often intuitively sense events of the past when visiting ancient sites. Ten years ago, while we walked among the desolate tors of Dartmoor, she seemed to sense the devastation that must have swept these isles. I had walked on ahead and found an interesting rock formation. I turned, about to draw her attention to it. She stood some way off, as if petrified, her face frozen with fear. When the experience had passed, she told me:

'It seemed that great green waves as high as the hills came curling and howling high above the tors. The ground heaved. Reaching the sky, the great wall of water came towards me . . .'

It was not until eight years later that I first came across legends of the deluge which she had psychically experienced. The legends are gathered principally from the Welsh Triads, collected by the eminent scholar and bard, the Rev. R. W. Morgan. Among them is a story similar to that of Noah:

'Long before the Kmry came into Britain the Llyn Lion broke up and the Great Deep inundated the whole earth. The Island, afterwards known as Britain, shared in the general catastrophe.

'One vessel floated over the waters, the ship of Nevydd Nay Neivion. In it were the wise Dwy and his wife Dwy Vach, man and woman of God.

'This ship of Nevydd Nay Neivion was built in Britain and was one of its three mighty works.'

(The others could, of course, have been the first Stonehenge, Silbury Hill, the greatest man-made earthworks in

47

Europe, or the great Zodiac Circle of Glastonbury, 'Temple of the Stars'.)

The legend continues:

'For a long time after the subsiding of the deluge the Kymry dwelt in the Summer Land, between the sea of Afez and Deffrobani [the peninsular known as the Crimea was once called the Kimria, land of the Kymry]. The land being exposed to sea floods, they resolved, under the guidance of Hu Gadarn, to seek again the White Island of the West, where their father Dwy Van had built the ship of Nevydd Nay Neivion.

'They journeyed westwards towards the setting sun, being many in number and men of great heart and strength.[1] They came in sight of the Alps, and then part of their migration diverged southwards to become the Kymry (Umbro)[2] of Italy. The others, consisting of the three tribes of the Kymry, the Brython and the Lloegrwys, crossed the Alps. Along either side of the Alps, near the sea, part of the Lloegrwys settled; these are the Ligurians of Italy [it became the Ligurian Republic of Genoa in 1797] and Gaul. Pursuing their course still further they crossed the River of Eddies, the Slow River, the Routh River, the Bright River [the Rhone, the Arar, the Garonne, the Loire] till they reached Gwasgwyn [Gascony, the Vine-Land]. Thence they turned northward and part of the Brython settled in a land they named *Llydaw v Mor Ucha*. The Kymry still held on until they saw the cliffs of the White Island (Britain).

'Then they built ships and passed over the Hazy Ocean (Mor Tawch) and took possession of the Island. And they found no living creature on it, but bisons, elks, bears, beavers and water monsters. And they took possession of it not by war, nor by conquest, not by oppression, but by the

1. In his *Prehistorical London*, E. O. Gordon inserts the old word *Cedeir* which indicates that these people were mighty ones, or giants.
2. Umbria: an ancient division of Italy lying between Etruria on the west and the Sabine territory on the south. The original territory of the Umbrians was continually plundered in the sixth century by Gallic and Etruscan invaders, so that they were restricted to the upland tracts of the Apennines.

48

right of man over nature. And they sent to the Brythons in Llydaw and the Lloegrwys on the Continent, and to as many as came they gave the East and North of the Island. And the Kymry dwelt in the West. These three tribes were of one race, origin and speech. These are the three Pacific Tribes of the Isle of Britain because they came in mutual good will, peace and love;[3] and over them Hu the Mighty, the one sovreign of the Island, and the Island of the mighty ones. Its name Britain, or Prydain, was not yet known'.

There are other legends of blood and fire. In his *Mythology and Rites of British Druids* (1808), Edward Davies, not being aware of the Frisian tradition, says:

'The Patriarch, pure in mind, was shut up with a chosen band in an enclosure with a strong door. Here the just ones were safe from injury. *A tempest of fire arose and split the earth to the great deep.* The lake (sea) Llion burst her bounds, the waves of the sea lifted themselves to the skies on high ground around the borders of Britain. Rain fell in torrents. Water covered the earth, washing away the impure to the chasms of the abyss. The lustration purified the polluted earth. The flood raised the Patriarch's ship on high from the ground, and bore it safe on the crest of the waves'. (My italics).

Like the story of the 'Bad time' told by the Frisians, this tradition indicates that the cause of the deluge was a fierce convulsion of the earth.

The convulsions which destroyed Atland also sank land off the coast of Spain. In 1973 Professor Maxine Asher, leader of a team of American archaeologists searching for legendary Atlantis on the southern coast of Spain, reported that they had discovered broken-off columns and a man-made road on the ocean floor. The remains may have belonged to the holy island of Flyland where Frya, the Earth-Mother of the white races, gave her Tex just before the earth trembled and the island sank.

3. It was a high moral characteristic of the Frisians that when they founded colonies abroad they called them by a name which signified peace or friendship. Thus their Greek colony was named 'Athens', meaning 'friends'.

A few miles off the lowlands of Holland the broken walls of a city were found. Some of the intact walls were topped with copper sheets, as in Plato's story of lost Atlantis.

The story of how warm and beautiful Atland sank and the sun sank low, has an affinity with the poem, *The Spoils of Annwn*, attributed to the British bard, Taliesin. In it, a sorrowful youth represents the sun, chained to the horizon in the ice-bound north. He sighs for the land which was lost, which gave comfort and abundance. This translation is by Thomas Stephen, from his *Literature of the Kymry* (P. 192ff):

Praise to the Lord, Supreme Ruler of the high regions,
Who hath extended his domain to the shore of the world,
Complete was the prison of Gwair in Caer Sidi
                (the heavens over the northern mountain).
Through the permission of Pwyll and Pryderi
                (the sun and the earth?)
No one before him went to it;
A heavy blue chain (of the sky) *firmly held the youth*
                (the sun),

And for the spoils of Annwn gloomily he sings,
And till doom shall he continue his lay.
Thrice the fullness of Pridwen we went into it,
Except seven, none returned from Caer Sidi.

The explanatory notes in parentheses are my own. 'Thrice the fullness of Pridwen' refers to the length of time that the chosen ones in Edward Davies's legend remained in the hillside enclosure during the holocaust. The reference to only seven returning, which is repeated many times throughout the poem, emphasizes the terrible loss of life.

Critics have turned away in despair from this abstruse poem. What is its hidden meaning, its purport? 'Could any ancient oracle be more elaborately incomprehensible?' asks Turner. Yet, when we compare the lines of the poem with the legends of deluge and fire, the meaning becomes clear.

The words *Caer Sidi* sometimes mean the Zodiac, and *Annwn* the starry heavens. Thus, the 'prison of Gwair in Caer Sidi' which holds the sun to the horizon becomes intelligible.

The Spoils of Annwn was eventually used in an ancient ritual of initiation, much in the same way that the Last Supper and sorrows of Christ are incorporated and epitomized in the Eucharist.

With opening lines indicating that an asteroid circled the earth four times before crashing down into the region that is the polar sea, the poem goes on (again, with my interpretations in brackets):

. . . In Caer Pedryvan four times revolving!

It will be my first word from the cauldron (of fire) *when it expresses;*

By the breath of nine damsels (the sun, moon and seven known planets) *it is gently warmed.*

Is it not the cauldron of the chief Annwyn (Lord of the heavens) *in its fashion?*

With a ridge round its edge of pearls!

(Possibly a trailing edge of luminous gases as the comet-like asteroid fell towards the earth. Next, the eruption of the earth's crust on impact caused three days of floods, darkness and the 'jet of night').

. . . A bright sword flashing will be brought to him,

And left in the hand of Llemynawg,

And before the portals of hell, the horns of light (fire) *shall be burning.*

And we went with Arthur in his splendid labours,[4]

Except seven, none returned from Caer Vidiwid (the enclosure of the chosen ones).

. . . In the quadrangular enclosure, in the island of the strong door,

Where the twilight and the jet of night moved together,

Bright wine (fire, or radiations of death) *was the beverage of the host,*

Three times the fullness of Prydwen, we went to sea,

Except seven, none returned from Caer Rigor.

. . . Beyond Caer Whdr they beheld not the prowess of Arthur?

4. Arthur, the Celtic hero, was used in the Druid's rites of initiation as a symbolic figure denoting a candidate. It was not, however, used in the Frisian-Briton rites, described here.

Three times twenty-hundred men stood on a wall (a mountain, where they died),

It was difficult to converse with their sentinel (because of the tumult).

Three times the fullness of Prydwen, we went with Arthur,

Except seven, none returned from Caer Colur (the gloomy and riven mountains).

. . . They (the multitude) *know not on what day, or who caused it.*

Nor what hour in the splendid day Cwy (the fiery visitation) *was born,*

Nor who prevented him from going to the meanders of Devwy (the caves or tunnels with sealed entrances in which people sought protection).

They know not the brindled ox, with his thick head-band,
And seven score knobs in his collar.

(The Age of Taurus, the Bull, which was passing away at the time of the submergence of Atland).

And we went with Arthur of mournful memory,

Except seven, none returned from Caer Vandwy (the enclosure, resting on a height).

(When the time of violence and fear ended, the dawn of a new era broke, the Age of Aries, the Ram – the animal with the 'silver head'.)

I will not have merit from men with drooping courage,
They know not what day the chief was caused,
Nor what hour in the splendid day the owner was born;
What animal they keep of silver head,
And we went with Arthur of mournful contention,
Except seven, none returned from Caer Ochren (the enclosure of the shelving side of the mountain.)

There is another ancient record which clearly describes every event given in this poem, also contained in the *Mythology and Rites of the British Druids*:

'When the profligacy of mankind had provoked the great Supreme to send a pestilential wind upon the earth. A pure poison descended, every blast was death. At this time the patriarch distinguished for his integrity, was shut up, together with his select company, in the enclosure with the strong

52

door. Here the just ones were saved from injury. Presently a tempest of fire arose. It split the earth asunder to the great deep. The Lake Llion (the sea) burst its bonds, and the waves of the sea lifted themselves on high around the borders of Britain, the rain poured down from heaven, and the waters covered the earth'.[5]

Here again we are given a regular sequence of events, such as would follow the terrible explosion of a tremendous heavenly body in the air, or when it struck the earth in the northern hemisphere, causing earthquakes and tidal waves which submerged Atland:

1. The pestilential wind may have been a shock wave, produced by the colossal explosion.

2. The pure poison whose blast was instant death sounds like the radiation following the shock front of a nuclear explosion.

3. People take shelter in caves.

4. The earth takes fire as blazing rocks and dust fall from the sky.

5. Volcanoes and earthquakes cleave open the earth; fjords are created, especially around the coasts of Scotland.

6. Rain pours down in torrents.

7. Great waves flood the land.

The tales of these frightening days must have been passed from father to son until the 'Elder Edda' gathered them and wrote them down, as Homer did of the heroic days of his past. Here now, from the *Ragnarok* – meaning 'darkness of the gods' or 'rain of dust' – is a description of the savagery and bloodshed among the tribes of 'Finda's people', before and after the cataclysm. As we shall see it, it tallies closely with Adela's account:

> *There saw she wade*
> *in the heavy streams,*
> *Men – foul murderers,*
> *And perjurers,*

5. All this happened seventeen centuries before the Druids were settled in Britain. Consequently there is no mention of Druids – only the patriarch.

And them who others' wives
Seduce to sin.
Brothers slay brothers;
Sisters' children
Shed each other's blood.
Hard is the world!
Sensual sin grows huge.
There are sword-ages, axe-ages;
Shields are cleft in twain;
Storm-ages, murder-ages;
Till the world falls dead,
And men no longer spare
Or pity one another.
Then happens that which will seem a
 great miracle; that the wolf devours the sun.

(The wolf is the tremendous asteroid which sweeps down between the sun and the earth, darkening the sky so that the sun seemed to be gone:)
The stars shall be hurled down from heaven;
(most likely debris of the shattered asteroid).

The Fenris-wolf advances with wide open mouth;
 the upper jaw reaches to heaven and the lower
 jaw is on the earth.
(This probably signifies that fire and
 debris reached from the heavens to the earth).
Fire flashes from his eyes and nostrils.

Another name for the fiery asteroid is the Midgard-Serpent, which 'vomits forth venom, defiling all the air and the sea; he is very terrible, and places himself side by side with the wolf'.

The meaning is clear, two great masses of the broken asteroid move together and hurtle down upon the earth. The saga goes on to say that there is a great 'clash and din' as the 'heavens are rent in twain and Muspellheim (the Day of Judgement, disaster and death) come riding through the opening'.

The epic continues:

Heroes go the way to Hel,
And heaven is rent in twain . . .
All men abandoned their homesteads
When the warder of Midgard (Bifrost, ice and cold)
In wrath slays the serpent,
The sun grows dark,
The earth sinks into the sea,
The bright stars from heaven vanish;
Fire rages,
Heat blazes,
And high flames play
'Gainst heaven itself.

The sun has sunk to the horizon. The north becomes cold.
Snow and ice cover land and sea. And this 'Fimbul winter'
is 'the mighty, the great, the iron winter':

> *It feeds on the bodies*
> *Of men, when they die;*
> *The seats of the gods*
> *It stains with blood.*
> *The sunshine blackens*
> *In the summers thereafter,*
> *And the weather grows bad.*

Clearly, from all this evidence – that of legend and tradition and that of geological knowledge – some great cataclysm of the type that could sink a continent like Atland,
struck the northern hemisphere. Its repercussions are echoed
around the world in great traditions of a deluge from one
race of antiquity to another – Gilgamesh, Noah, Deucalion
and the folk-memories and annals of the Chinese, the Eski-
mos, the Indians of South and North America, even in the
southern hemisphere among the Polynesians.

A great nation was almost destroyed, but for those of its
descendants who either escaped, or had already colonised
the northern lands of the European continent. Now, we shall
return to the text of the *Orea Linda Book* to learn of their
laws, customs, lives, and adventures.

CHAPTER FIVE

FRYA'S TEX

Next to their religion embracing Wr-alda, the all-pervading spirit, the Atlanders and their Frisian descendants held their laws in great reverence. They inscribed them – along with some of their history and other knowledge – on the walls of their great citadels. These laws are also extensively recorded in the *Oera Linda Book*. Following the Creation Legends already quoted earlier, the book outlines the laws handed down by Frya, the Mother of the white races – Frya's Tex – and subsequent laws. Because they shed a great deal of light on the morals and attitudes of the Frisians and on their actions in dealing with other peoples, I give them here in full.

FRYA'S TEX

Prosperity awaits the free. At last they shall see me again. Though him only can I recognise as free who is neither a slave to another nor to himself. This is my counsel:

1. When in dire distress, and when mental and physical energy avail nothing, then have recourse to the spirit of Wr-alda; but do not appeal to him before you have tried all other means, for I tell you beforehand, and time will prove its truth, that those who give way to discouragement sink under their burdens.

2. To Wr-alda's spirit only shall you bend the knee in gratitude – thricefold – for what you have received, for what you do receive, and for the hope of aid in time of need.

3. You have seen how speedily I have come to your assistance. Do likewise to your neighbour, but wait not for his entreaties. The suffering would curse you, my

maidens would erase your name from the book, and I would regard you as a stranger.

4. Let not your neighbour express his thanks to you on bended knee, which is only due to Wr-alda's spirit. Envy would assail you, Wisdom would ridicule you, and my maidens would accuse you of irreverence.

5. Four things are given for your enjoyment – air, water, land, and fire – but Wr-alda is the sole possessor of them. Therefore, my counsel to you is, choose upright men who will fairly divide the labour and the fruits, so that no man shall be exempt from work or from the duty of defence.

6. If ever it should happen that one of your people should sell his freedom, he is not of you, he is a bastard. I counsel you to expel him and his mother from the land. Repeat this to your children morning, noon, and night, till they think of it in their dreams.

7. If any man should deprive another, even his debtor, of his liberty, let him be to you as a vile slave; and I advise you to burn his body and that of his mother in an open place, and bury them fifty feet below the ground, so that no grass shall grow upon them. It would poison your cattle.

8. Meddle not with the people of Lyda, nor of Finda, because Wr-alda would help them, and any injury that you inflicted on them would recoil upon your own heads.

9. If it should happen that they come to you for advice or assistance, then it behoves you to help them; but if they should rob you, then fall upon them with fire and sword.

10. If any of them should seek a daughter of yours to wife, and she is willing, explain to her her folly; but if she will follow her lover, let her go in peace.

11. If your son wishes for a daughter of theirs, do the same as to your daughter; but let not either one or the other ever return among you, for they would introduce foreign morals and customs, and if these were accepted by you, I could not longer watch over you.

12. Upon my servant Fasta I have placed all my hopes. Therefore you must chose her for Eeremoeder. Follow my advice, then she will hereafter remain my servant as well

57

as all the sacred maidens who succeed her. Then shall the lamp which I have lighted for you never be extinguished. Its brightness shall always illuminate your intellect, and you shall always remain as free from foreign domination as your fresh river-water is distinct from the sea.

This, then, was the original Tex, as outlined by Frya before the holy island of Flyland foundered. But, built upon these basic principles, other laws were evolved and implemented. Next, are the guidelines given by Fasta, the first Eeremoeder, appointed by Frya:

THIS HAS FASTA SPOKEN

All the regulations which have existed a century, that is, a hundred years, may be the advice of the Eeremoeder, with the consent of the community, be inscribed upon the walls of the citadel, and when inscribed on the walls they become laws, and it is our duty to respect them all. If by force or necessity any regulations should be imposed upon us at variance with our laws and customs, we must always return to our own again. That is Frya's will, and must be that of all her children.

FASTA SAID—

Anything that any man commences, whatever it may be, on the day appointed for Frya's worship shall eternally fail, for time has proved that she was right; and it is become a law that no man shall, except from absolute necessity, keep that day otherwise than as a joyful feast.

THESE ARE THE LAWS ESTABLISHED FOR THE GOVERNMENT OF THE CITADELS

1. Whenever a citadel is built, the lamp belonging to it must be lighted at the original lamp in Texland, and that can only be done by the mother.

2. Every mother shall appoint her own maidens. She

may even choose those who are mothers in other towns.

3. The mother of Texland may appoint her own successor, but should she die without having done so, the election shall take place at a general assembly of the whole nation.

4. The mother of Texland may have twenty-one maidens and seven assistants, so that there may always be seven to attend the lamp day and night. She may have the same number of maidens who are mothers in other towns.

5. If a maiden wishes to marry, she must announce it to the mother, and immediately resign her office, before her passion shall have polluted the light.

6. For the service of the mother and of each of the Burgtmaidens there shall be appointed twenty-one townsmen – seven civilians of mature years, seven warriors of mature years, and seven seamen of mature years.

7. Out of the seven three shall retire every year, and shall not be replaced by members of their own family nearer than the fourth degree.

8. Each may have three hundred young townsmen as defenders.

9. For this service they must study Frya's Tex and the laws. From the sages they must learn wisdom, from the warriors the art of war, and from the sea-kings the skill required for distant voyages.

10. Every year one hundred of the defenders shall return to their homes, and those that may have been wounded shall remain in the citadels.

11. At the election of the defenders no burgher or Grevetman, or other person of distinction, shall vote, but only the people.

12. The mother at Texland shall have three times seven active messengers, and three times twelve speedy horses. In the other citadels each maiden shall have three messengers and seven horses.

13. Every citadel shall have fifty agriculturalists chosen by the people, but only those may be chosen who are not strong enough to go to war or to go to sea.

14. Every citadel must provide for its own sustenance,

and must maintain its own defences, and look after its share of the general contributions.

15. If a man is chosen to fill any office and refuses to serve, he can never become a burgher, nor have any vote. And if he is already a burgher, he shall cease to be so.

16. If any man wishes to consult the mother of a Burgtmaid, he must apply to the secretary, who will take him to the Burgtmaster. He will then be examined by a surgeon to see if he is in good health. If he is passed, he shall lay aside his arms, and seven warriors shall present him to the mother.

17. If the affair concerns only one district, he must bring forward not less than three witnesses; but if it affects the whole of Friesland, he must have twenty-one additional witnesses, in order to guard against any deceptions.

18. Under all circumstances the mother must take care that her children, that is, Frya's people, shall remain as temperate as possible. This is her most important duty, and it is the duty of all of us to help her in performing it.

19. If she is called upon to decide any judicial question between a Grevetman and the community, she must incline towards the side of the community in order to maintain peace, and because it is better that one man should suffer than many.

20. If any one comes to the mother for advice, and she is prepared to give it, she must do it immediately. If she does not know what to advise, he must remain waiting seven days; and if she then is unable to advise, he must go away without complaining, for it is better to have no advice at all than bad advice.

21. If a mother shall have given bad advice out of ill-will, she must be killed or driven out of the land, deprived of everything.

22. If her Burgtheeren are accomplices, they are to be treated in a similar manner.

23. If her guilt is doubtful or only suspected, it must be considered and debated, if necessary, for twenty-one weeks. If half the votes are against her, she must be declared innocent. If two-thirds are against her, she must

wait a whole year. If the votes are then the same, she must be considered guilty, but may not be put to death.

24. If any one of the one-third who have voted for her wish to go away with her, they may depart with all their live and dead stock, and shall not be the less considered, since the majority may be wrong as well as the minority.

UNIVERSAL LAW

1. All free-born men are equal, wherefore they must all have equal rights on sea and land, and on all that Wr-alda has given.

2. Every man may seek the wife of his choice, and every woman may bestow her hand on him whom she loves.

3. When a man takes a wife, a house and yard must be given to him. If there is none, one must be built for him.

4. If he has taken a wife in another village, and wishes to remain, they must give him a house there, and likewise the free use of the common.

5. To every man must be given a piece of land behind his house. No man shall have land in front of his house, still less an enclosure, unless he has performed some public service. In such a case it may be given, and the youngest son may inherit it, but after him it returns to the community.

6. Every village shall possess a common for the general good, and the chief of the village shall take care that it is kept in good order, so that posterity shall find it uninjured.

7. Every village shall have a market-place. All the rest of the land shall be for tillage and forest. No one shall fell trees without the consent of the community, or without the knowledge of the forester; for the forests are general property, and no man can appropriate them.

8. The market charges shall not exceed one-twelfth of the value of the goods either to native or strangers. The portion taken for the charges shall not be sold before the other goods.

9. All the market receipts must be divided yearly into a hundred parts, three days before the Juul-day.

10. The Grevetman and his council shall take twenty parts; the keeper of the market ten, and his assistants five, the Volksmoeder one, the midwife four, the village ten, and the poor and infirm shall have fifty parts.

11. There shall be no usurers in the market. If any should come, it will be the duty of the maidens to make it known through the whole land, in order that such people may not be chosen for any office, because they are hard-hearted.

For the sake of money they would betray everybody – the people, the mother, their nearest relations, and even their own selves.

12. If any man should attempt to sell diseased cattle or damaged goods for sound, the market-keeper shall expel him, and the maidens shall proclaim him through the country.

In early times almost all the Finns lived together in their native land, which was called Aldland, and is now submerged. They were thus far away, and we had no wars. When they were driven hitherwards, and appeared as robbers, then arose the necessity of defending ourselves, and we had armies, kings and wars.

For all this there were established regulations, and out of the regulations came fixed laws.

HERE FOLLOW THE LAWS WHICH WERE THUS ESTABLISHED

1. Every Frisian must resist the assailants with such weapons as he can procure, invent, and use.

2. When a boy is twelve years old he must devote one day in seven to learning how to use his weapons.

3. As soon as he is perfect in the use of them they are to be given to him, and he is to be admitted as a warrior.

4. After serving as a warrior three years, he may become a citizen, and may have a vote in the election of the headman.

5. When he has been seven years a voter then he may have a vote for the chief or king, and may be himself elected.

6. Every year he must be re-elected.

7. Except the king, all other officials are re-eligible who act according to Frya's laws.

8. No king may be in office more than three years, in order that the office may not be permanent.

9. After an interval of seven years he may be elected again.

10. If the king is killed by the enemy, his nearest relative may be a candidate to succeed him.

11. If he dies a natural death, or if his period of service has expired, he shall not be succeeded by any blood relation nearer than the fourth degree.

12. Those who fight with arms are not men of counsel, therefore no king must bear arms. His wisdom must be his weapon, and the love of his warriors his shield.

THESE ARE THE RIGHTS OF THE MOTHERS AND THE KINGS:

1. If war breaks out, the mother sends her messengers to the king, who sends messengers to the Grevetmen to call the citizens to arms.

2. The Grevetmen call all the citizens together and decide how many men shall be sent.

3. All the resolutions must immediately be sent to the mother by messengers and witnesses.

4. The mother considers all the resolutions and decides upon them, and with this the king as well as the people must be satisfied.

5. When in the field, the king consults only his superior officers, but three citizens of the mother must be present, without any voice. These citizens must send daily reports to the mother, that they may be sure nothing is done contrary to the counsels of Frya.

6. If the king wishes to do anything which his council opposes, he may not persist in it.

7. If an enemy appears unexpectedly, then the king's orders must be obeyed.

8. If the king is not present, the next to him takes com-

mand, and so on in succession according to rank.

9. If there is no leader present, one must be chosen.

10. If there is no time to choose, any one may come forward who feels himself capable of leading.

11. If a king has conquered a dangerous enemy, his successors may take his name after their own. The king may, if he wishes, choose an open piece of ground for a house and ground; the ground shall be enclosed, and may be so large that there shall be seven hundred steps to the boundary in all directions from the house.

12. His youngest son may inherit this, and that son's youngest son after him; then it shall return to the community.

HERE ARE THE RULES ESTABLISHED FOR THE SECURITY OF ALL FRISIANS

1. Whenever new laws are made or new regulations established, they must be for the common good, and not for individual advantage.

2. Whenever in time of war either ship or houses are destroyed, either by the enemy or as a matter of precautions, a general levy shall be assessed on the people to make it good again, so that no one may neglect the general welfare to preserve his own interest.

3. At the conclusion of a war, if any men are so severely wounded as to be unable to work, they shall be maintained at the public expense, and shall have the best seats at festivals, in order that the young may learn to honour them.

4. If there are widows and orphans, they shall likewise be maintained at the public expense; and the sons may inscribe the names of their fathers on their shields for the honour of their families.

5. If any who have been taken prisoners should return, they must be kept separate from the camp, because they may have obtained their liberty by making treacherous promises, and thus they may avoid keeping their promises without forfeiting their honour.

6. If any enemies be taken prisoners, they must be sent to the interior of the country, that they may learn our free customs.

7. If they are afterwards set free, it must be done with kindness by the maidens, in order that we may make them comrades and friends, instead of haters and enemies.

Finally, in this section of the *Orea Linda Book* dealing with established laws and regulations, comes a series of extracts from the writings of the sea-king Minno:

FROM MINNO'S WRITINGS

If any one should be so wicked as to commit robbery, murder, arson, rape, or any other crime, upon a neighbouring state, and our people wish to inflict punishment, the culprit shall be put to death in the presence of the offended, in order that no war may arise, and the innocent suffer for the guilty. If the offended will spare his life and forgo their revenge, it may be permitted. If the Culprit should be a king, Grevetman, or other person in authority, we must make good his fault, but he must be punished.

If he bears on his shield the honourable name of his forefathers, his kinsmen shall no longer wear it, in order that every man may look after the conduct of his relatives.

LAWS FOR THE NAVIGATORS:

Navigator is the title of those who make foreign voyages

1. All Frya's sons have equal rights, and every stalwart youth may offer himself as a navigator to the Olderman, who may not refuse him as long as there is any vacancy.

2. The navigators may choose their own masters.

3. The traders must be chosen and named by the community to which they belong, and the navigators have no voice in their election.

4. If during a voyage it is found that the king is bad or incompetent, another may be put in his place, and on the return home he may make his complaint to the Olderman.

5. If the fleet returns with profits, the sailors may divide one-third among themselves in the following manner: The king twelve portions, the admiral seven, the boatswains each two portions; the captains three, and the rest of the crew each one part; the youngest boys each one-third of a portion, the second boys half a portion each, and the eldest boys two-thirds of a portion each.

6. If any have been disabled, they must be maintained at the public expense, and honoured in the same way as the soldiers.

7. If any have died on the voyage, their nearest relatives inherit their portion.

8. Their widows and orphans must be maintained at the public expense; and if they were killed in a sea-fight, their sons may bear the names of their fathers on their shields.

9. If a topsailman is lost, his heirs shall receive a whole portion.

10. If he was betrothed, his bride may claim seven portions in order to erect a monument to her bridegroom, but then she must remain a widow all her life.

11. If the community is fitting out a fleet, the purveyors must provide the best provisions for the voyage, and for the women and children.

12. If a sailor is worn out and poor, and has no house or patrimony, one must be given to him. If he does not wish for a house, his friends may take him home; and the community must bear the expense, unless his friends decline to receive it.

USEFUL EXTRACTS FROM THE WRITINGS
LEFT BY MINNO:

Minno was an ancient sea-king. He was a seer and a philosopher, and he gave laws to the Cretans. He was born at Lindaoord, and after all his wanderings he had the happiness to die at Lindahem.

If our neighbours have a piece of land or water which it would be advantageous for us to possess, it is proper that we should offer to buy it. If they refuse to sell it, we must let them keep it. This is Frya's Tex, and it would be unjust to act contrary to it.

If any of our neighbours quarrel and fight about any matter except land, and they request us to arbitrate, our best course will be to decline; but if they insist upon it, it must be done honourably and justly.

If any one comes and says, I am at war, you must help me; or another comes and says, My son is an infant and incompetent, and I am old, so I wish you to be his guardian, and to take charge of my property until he is of age, it is proper to refuse in order that we may not come into disputes about matters foreign to our free customs.

Whenever a foreign trader comes to the open markets at Wyringen and Almanland, if he cheats, he must immediately be fined, and it must be published by the maidens throughout the country.

If he should come back, no one must deal with him. He must return as he came.

Whenever traders are chosen to go to trading stations, or to sail with the fleets, they must be well known and of good reputation with the maidens.

If, however, a bad man should by chance be chosen and should try to cheat, the others are bound to remove him. If he should have committed a cheat, it must be made good, and the culprit must be banished from the land in order that our name may be everywhere held in honour.

If we should be ill-treated in a foreign market, whether distant or near, we must immediately attack them; for though we desire to be at peace, we must not let our neighbours underrate us or think that we are afraid.

In my youth I often grumbled at the strictness of the laws, but afterwards I learned to thank Frya for her Tex and our forefathers for the laws which they established upon it. Wr-alda or Alvader has given me many years, and I have travelled over many lands and seas, and after all that I have seen, I am convinced that we alone are chosen by Alvader to have laws. Lydia's people can neither make laws nor obey them, they are too stupid and uncivilised. Many are like Finda. They are clever enough, but they are too rapacious, haughty, false, immoral, and bloodthirsty.

The toad blows himself out, but he can only crawl. The frog cries 'Work, work'; but he can do nothing but hop and make himself ridiculous. The raven cries 'Spare, spare'; but he steals and wastes everything that he gets into his beak.

Finda's people are just like these. They say a great deal about making good laws, and every one wishes to make regulations against misconduct, but does not wish to submit to them himself. Whoever is the most crafty crows over others, and tries to make them submit to him, till another comes who drives him off his perch.

The word 'Eva' is too sacred for common use, therefore men have learned to say 'Evin.'

'Eva' means that sentiment which is implanted in the breast of every man in order that he may know what is right and what is wrong, and by which he is able to judge his own deeds and those of others; that is, if he has been well and properly brought up. 'Eva' has also another meaning; that is, tranquil, smooth, like water that is not stirred by a breath of wind. If the water is disturbed it becomes troubled, uneven, but it always has a tendency to return to its tranquil condition. That is its nature, just as the inclination towards justice and freedom exists in Frya's children. We derive this disposition from the spirit of our father Wr-alda, which speaks strongly in Frya's children, and will eternally remain so. Eternity is another symbol of Wr-alda, who remains always just and unchangeable.

Eternal and unalterable are the signs of wisdom and rectitude, which must be sought after by all pious people, and must be possessed by all judges. If, therefore, it is desired to make laws and regulations which shall be permanent, they must be equal for all men. The judges must pronounce their decisions according to these laws. If any crime is committed respecting which no law has been made, a general assembly of the people shall be called, where judgement shall be pronounced in accordance with the inspiration of Wr-alda's spirit. If we act thus, our judgement will never fail to be right.

If instead of doing right, men will commit wrong, there will arise quarrels and differences among people and states. Thence arise civil wars, and everything is thrown into confusion and destroyed; and, O foolish people! while you are injuring each other the spiteful Finda's people with their false priests come and attack your ports, ravish your daughters, corrupt your morals and at last throw the bonds of slavery over every freeman's neck.

Commentary

The practice of preserving history, customs, religions and science, and of keeping the laws constantly before the eyes of the people by inscribing them on the walls of citadels and public buildings was a very ancient one. Plato said that the laws and customs of Atlantis were written on the walls of the great citadel in the chief city and that once each year the kings assembled around the citadel to renew their allegiance to the good and just laws. The Pyramid Texts of Egypt – found at Saggara, necropolis of the ancient capital of Memphis – are another example of this custom. The Maya of Mexico had a similar tradition; the glyphs which cover the walls of their temples are said to give their history, customs and laws. The old English practice of announcing new laws, regulations and matters of public interest – nowadays done in newspaper advertisements – on the doors of churches, evolved from this very ancient tradition of public proclamation.

When scholars learn to decipher the meanings hidden in the early pictorial signs of the zodiac – excluding those later introduced by the Greeks – it will be realised that the so-called Babylonian 'milestones' served a purpose similar to the inscription on Frisian citadels.

The laws laid down by Frya, Fasta and their successors specified that kings, nobles, dukes and councillors should be elected by public acclaim and should not inherit titles and positions of authority and power by accident of birth. Every adult man was entitled to land sufficient for a house and out-buildings, with stone and wood provided by the community. Extra land, apart from a rear yard and the common grazing and agricultural land, was only granted by the community in recognition of good deeds and voluntary services.

The Tex was designed to ensure that no person should gain possessions and powers and use them to suppress or otherwise undermine the rights and liberties of others. This, it will be seen, was why the power-hungry Magy, priest-king of the Magyars and Finns who invaded northern Europe, detested the Tex and customs of the Frisians.

The Atland-Frisians established a matriarchy based on the principle that women were the informed conscience of the more practically and physically inclined menfolk – a principle that was thereafter lost sight of for almost three thousand years. At various times in their history, mostly because they feared attack from Finda's people, men did take the initiative in organising and implementing the laws for the mobilisation of their armies and defence of their lands.

In some instances, the laws which advocate capital punishment for various offences, might give the initial impression that the Frisians were unnecessarily cruel and ruthless. However, these laws can clearly be seen as designed to protect and maintain their highly democratic system from undesirable internal and external influence and corruption.

For example, Frya's law – number six – requiring the banishment of a man *and his mother*, should he sell his freedom. Why should the mother, too, be expelled? As the Frisians saw it, it was the mother's bounden duty to train her child to love freedom, honesty, engage himself in remunerative occupation and to help others. A son who sold his freedom indicated that his mother had failed in her duty towards her child. This, to the Frisians, was akin to treason, not against the hierarchy, but against the whole community.

As can be seen, the Frisians also were conscientious conservationists – the cutting down of trees without permission from the community for a specific purpose, was forbidden. Their laws also contained anti-exploitation and profiteering clauses, like those concerning usurers and traders in poor quality goods in the market-places, and discouraged nepotism, favouritism, corruption in high places and land-grabbing.

Their rules for important matters of judgement, affecting those who handed out judgements themselves, were designed to eliminate all forms of malpractice.

The overall result was a highly democratic welfare state in the purest sense, in which every citizen – including the aged, sick and those wounded in service – enjoyed their share in the profits of the community as a whole. It was a system highly reminiscent of the Utilitarianism advocated by the 18–19th-century reformer Jeremy Bentham, whose ideal was the happiness of the greatest number.

The laws relating to marriage outside the Frisian race might today be regarded superficially as inclining towards racialism. Yet in fact, as closer study reveals, these regulations were designed not for some altruistic ideals of keeping the race pure, but simply to preserve the system from external influence. The laws regarding prisoners-of-war, of both sides, were exceptionally sensible and humane.

Even the apparent chauvinism of the Frisians – such as Minno's assessment of Lyda's and Finda's races as uncivilised and inferior – was based upon studied judgement and detached observation. Whenever a tribe or nation invades and overcomes another, it has been noted that the conquering nation usually absorbs more of the culture of the vanquished people than it can impose upon them. The Frisians were apparently well aware of this phenomenon – hence the advice of Fasta to submit to the laws and customs of any successful invaders, but to be ready to revert to their own laws when freed from bondage.

Whenever possible, outsiders were invited and encouraged to see and enjoy for themselves the advantages of Frisian society – a most subtle and, possibly, the only acceptable form of propaganda.

Many of the laws contained in the *Oera Linda Book* form the foundation of true democracy in which political representatives are truly the servants of their electors, rather than their masters. It is a type of democracy unknown in the world today. Under it, the rulers, the people and all departments of social life and commerce, by constitutional law had always to be in accord with the spiritual, moral and humane precepts laid down by Frya.

Many similar laws formed the basis of the old Common Law of England, now sadly rendered ineffective through the changing emphasis of social and commercially-motivated practices.

Indeed, the 'Universal Law' expounded by Fasta, of rights and responsibilities binding upon all Frisian states and colonies throughout Europe and other parts of the world, is the first record of International Law and an international citadel of justice supported by an international peace force. In principle, this is the ideal towards which our United Nations Organisation – particularly its worldwide auxiliary organisations – is striving to attain.

In 1876 a newspaper critic of the *Oera Linda Book* poured scorn on the idea of such international regulations, saying that while they might have been suitable in a primitive civilisation they could hardly be practicable in the complex world of the 19th century (See Appendix A). Yet today, in an even more complex world, with all nations interdependent for the supply of food and raw materials, it is realised that such international measures are vital and necessary towards the continued survival of mankind.

When Baha'u'llah, prophet of the now-worldwide Baha'i Faith, submitted similar principles of law to the kings and rulers of the world little more than a century ago, he was also scorned by those in authority. It was, in fact, Baha'u'llah who in the 19th century astounded and shocked many nations when he proclaimed that women would be equal before the law and should receive sufficient education to enable them to take part in all social activities and to help guide humanity in the ways of peace and security. With the ascendancy of the freedom of women, and their equality before the law, it may be that Baha'u'llah's prophecy that total world peace will not be established until the end of this century, is gradually coming true – thanks to the revival of a

72

tradition practised by a forgotten race of Frisians some 3,000 years ago.

World peace, and human societies shaped nearer to the generally acceptable desire, will be assured when women learn how best to make use of their new-found freedoms. To vie with men in their soul-destroying competitive activities is not worthy of womanhood. These activities do not make for peace and the happiness of the human race – they are the cause of wars, social unrest and the many evils which afflict our world. It was the duty of Frisian women to guide their menfolk along paths of justice, public morality and co-operation for the wellbeing of all – which, if emulated in this age and time, would bring to the human race its greatest blessing.

There are two references in Minno's writings which we may add to the other proofs of the extreme antiquity of the manuscripts from which the *Oera Linda Book* was compiled.

He says the princes in Crete feared they would lose their lands when their people were taught the meaning of freedom. When the manuscript was discovered in 1848 nothing was known about ancient Crete except for the vague references made by Homer and the Greek myth of the Minotaur (a man with the head of a bull) which lived in a maze of underground passages. Nothing was known about the princes of Crete, until Sir Arthur Evans at the beginning of this century delved among the ruins of what came to be known as the Palace of Minos at Knossos. His excavations and those of other archaeologists revealed a forgotten prosperous and beautiful Minoan civilization of city states ruled by the merchant princes of whom Minno wrote. When the Minoan 'A' script has been decoded, and perhaps the mysterious circular clay disk found in the ruins of the Palace of Phaistos, written evidence may be brought to light which support the statement made by the Frisian sea-king.

Then again, when the *Oera Linda Book* was published there was scarcely a scholar in the West who knew the meaning of the name Eve. Minno said the name was not uttered because it was too sacred. It indicated the ability implanted in every person to distinguish between right and wrong,

73

between justice and injustice. In ancient times it was the name given to the conscience of man, indicating the essence which made man a living soul. There are many passages in sacred writings of the East where the word woman is used to indicate the soul of man, which, as Minno said: 'is tranquil, smooth, like water that is not stirred by a breath of wind'.

The symbolic story written to describe the so-called making of Eve from Adam's rib is, to say the least, extraordinary. The intelligence cannot accept it or even imagine it. That Adam's body was made from the earth (matter) is self-explanatory, but not the making of a woman from a man's rib. The meaning concealed in this symbolism, written only for the masses of the people, was forgotten for some 3000 years. The meaning was given only to seers who could comprehend it.

Adam signifies the spirit of man. God breathed into the nostrils of Adam and he became a living soul, then Eve was made from his rib – meaning that Adam became aware of his soul and its liability to fall from grace into temptation and thus stray from the ways of the spirit.

We now see that the story of Adam and Eve was derived from the much earlier Sumerian myth of the creation of man in a Summer Land which came to be known as a garden East of Eden. Here the spiritual Adam is the divine Enlil and Eve is the divine Ninlil. Enlil is sick with various ailments and has a severe pain in his rib. Now the Sumerian word for rib is 'ti'. The world also means 'to give life' and Ninlil's name means 'the Lady of Life'. Enlil had raped Ninlil against her will and because of what he had done his rib (conscience) hurt him. Thereupon Ninlil healed him of his pain. In other words, such as those used by Minno, his soul eventually 'returned to its natural tranquil condition'. In the Sumerian and Genesis account of the creation of man, Ninlel-Eve represents the living soul and the spiritual Enlil-Adam. It is clear that the people of Atland and the Frisians of Europe were fully informed of the sacred meaning of the name Eve and all that it implied. A meaning which came to

74

be forgotten and completely unknown to the 'knowledge-able' scholars who ridiculed the contents of the *Oera Linda Book.*

CHAPTER SIX

MINOS AND MIN-ERVA

It is in the next section of the *Oera Linda Book* – further extracts from the writings of the sea-king Minno – that the story of Min-erva is related. Minno also describes his arrival in Crete where he became the law-giver. Minos, founder of a whole line of kings who bore that name. One of them was undoubtedly the Minos of mythology who built the maze in which Theseus killed the half-human monster, the Minotaur.

When Nyhalennia, whose real name was Min-erva, was well established, and the Krekalanders[1] loved her as well as our own people did, there came some princes and priests to her citadel and asked Min-erva where her possessions lay. Hellenia[2] answered, I carry my possessions in my own bosom. What I have inherited is the love of wisdom, justice and freedom. If I lose these I shall become as the least of your slaves; now I give advice for nothing, but then I should sell it. The gentlemen went away laughing and saying, Your humble servants, wise Hellenia. But they missed their object, for the people took up this name as a name of honour. When they saw that their shot had been missed they began to calumniate her, and to say that she had bewitched the people; but our people and the good

1. Krekalanders – Greeks.
2. Note: Min-erva is variously referred to as Nyhalennia, Hellenia, etc., throughout. Later we are told that Nyhellenia is her surname.

75

DEA E-NE HALENN
AE-IANVARINVS
AM BACTHIVSPRO
SE.E-SVIS.V.R.L.M

Fig. 2

An ancient Roman statue of Nyhellenia, (Min-erva) in Rhineland,
shows her stepping from the ship which had taken her to Greece.
Note the dog, symbol of service, at her side, also the three eggs
she holds in her hands. (See text.) They are another representation
of the lamp, which was no ordinary lamp, as used by the Frisian-
Britons.

Krekalanders understood at once that it was calumny.
She was once asked, If you are not a witch, what is the use
of the eggs that you always carry with you? Min-erva
answered, These eggs are the symbols of Frya's counsels,
in which our future and that of the whole human race lies
concealed. Time will hatch them, and we must watch that
no harm happens to them. The priests said, Well
answered; but what is the use of the dog on your right
hand? Hellenia replied, Does not the shepherd have a

76

sheep-dog to keep his flock together? What the dog is to the shepherd I am in Frya's service. I must watch over Frya's flocks. We understand that very well, said the priests; but tell us what means the owl that always sits upon your head, is that light-shunning animal a sign of your clear vision? No, answered Hellenia; he reminds me that there are people on earth who, like him, have their homes in churches and holes, who go about in the twilight, not, like him, to deliver us from mice and other plagues, but to invent tricks to steal away the knowledge of other people, in order to take advantage of them, to make slaves of them, and to suck their blood like leeches.

Another time they came with a whole troop of people, when the plague was in the country and said: We are all making offerings to the gods that they may take away the plague. Will you not help to turn away their anger, or have you yourself brought the plague into the land with all your arts? No, said Min-erva; I know no gods that do evil, therefore I cannot ask them to do better. I only know one good spirit, that is Wr-alda's; and as he is good he never does evil. Where, then, does evil come from? asked the priests. All the evil comes from you and from the stupidity of the people who let themselves be deceived by you. If, then, your god is so exceedingly good, why does he not turn away from the bad? asked the priests. Hellenia answered: Frya has placed us here, and the carrier, that is, Time, must do the rest. For all calamities there is counsel and remedy to be found, but Wr-alda wills that we should search it out ourselves, in order that we may become strong and wise. If we will not do that, he leaves us to our own devices, in order that we may experience the results of wise or foolish conduct. Then a prince said, I should think it best to submit. Very possibly, answered Hellenia; for then men would be like sheep, and you and the priests would take care of them, shearing and leading them to the shambles. This is what our god does not desire, he desires that we should help one another, but that all should be free and wise. That is also our desire, and therefore our people choose their princes, counts, coun-

77

cillors, chiefs, and masters among the wisest of the good men, in order that every man shall do his best to be wise and good. Thus doing, we learn ourselves and teach the people that being wise and acting wisely can alone lead to holiness. That seems very good judgement, said the priests; but if you mean that the plague is caused by our stupidity, then Nyhellenia will perhaps be so good as to bestow upon us a little of that new light of which she is so proud. Yes, said Hellenia, but ravens and other birds of prey feed only on dead carrion, whereas the plague feeds not only on carrion but on bad laws and customs and wicked passions. If you wish the plague to depart from you and not return, you must put away your bad passions and become pure within and without. We admit that the advice is good, said the priests, but how shall we induce all the people under our rule to agree to it? Then Hellenia stood up and said: The sparrows follow the sower, and the people their good princes, therefore it becomes you to begin by rendering yourselves pure, so that you may look within and without, and not be ashamed of your own conduct. Now, instead of purifying the people, you have invented foul festivals, in which they have so long revelled that they wallow like swine in the mire to atone for your evil passions. The people began to mock and to jeer, so that she did not dare to pursue the subject; and one would have thought that they would have called all the people together to drive us out of the land; but no, in place of abusing her they went all about from the heathen-ish Krekaland to the Alps, proclaiming that it had pleased the Almighty God to send his clever daughter, Min-erva, surnamed Nyhellenia, over the sea in a cloud to give people good counsel, and that all who listened to her should become rich and happy, and in the end governors of all the kingdoms of the earth. They erected statues to her on all their altars, they announced and sold to the simple people advice that she had never given, and related miracles that she had never performed. They cunningly made themselves masters of our laws and customs, and by craft and subtlety were able to explain and spread them

78

around. They appointed priestesses under their own care, who were apparently under the protection of Festa,[3] our first Eeremoeder, to watch over the holy lamp; but that lamp they lit themselves, and instead of imbuing the priestesses with wisdom, and then sending them to watch the sick and educate the young, they made them stupid and ignorant, and never allowed them to come out. They were employed as advisers, but the advice which seemed to come from them was but the repetition of the behests of the priests. When Nyhellenia died, we wished to choose another mother, and some of us wished to go to Texland to look for her; but the priests, who were all powerful among their own people, would not permit it, and accused us before the people of being unholy.

FROM THE WRITINGS OF MINNO:

When I came away from Athenia with my followers, we arrived at an island named by my crew Kreta,[4] because of the cries that the inhabitants raised on our arrival. When they really saw that we did not come to make war, they were quiet, so that at last I was able to buy a harbour in exchange for a boat and some iron implements, and a piece of land. When we had been settled there a short time, and they discovered that we had no slaves, they were very much astonished; and when I explained to them that we had laws which made everybody equal, they wished to have the same; but they had hardly established them before the whole land was in confusion.

The priests and the princes declared that we had excited their subjects to rebellion, and the people appealed to us for aid and protection. When the princes saw that they were about to lose their kingdom, they gave freedom to their people, and came to me to establish a code of laws. The people, however, got no freedom, and the princes remained masters, acting according to their own pleasure.

3. Festa is Fasta; possibly a corruption that led to Vesta.
4. Kreta – Crete.

When this storm had passed, they began to sow divisions among us. They told my people that I had invoked their assistance to make myself permanent king. Once I found poison in my food. So when a ship from Flyland sailed past, I quietly took my departure. Leaving alone, then, my own adventures, I will conclude this history by saying that we must not have anything to do with Finda's people, wherever it may be, because they are full of false tricks, fully as much to be feared as their sweet wine with deadly poison.

Here ends Minno's writing.

Following these brief histories of Min-erva and Minno, the *Oera Linda Book* next lists a further series of laws and principles of behaviour to deal with particular problems. They are as follows:

THESE ARE THE THREE PRINCIPLES ON WHICH THESE LAWS ARE FOUNDED

1. Everybody knows that he requires the necessaries of life, and if he cannot obtain them he does not know how to preserve his life.
2. All men have a natural desire to have children, and if it is not satisfied they are not aware what evil may spring from it.
3. Every man knows that he wishes to live free and un-disturbed, and that others wish the same thing.

To secure this, these laws and regulations are made.

The people of Finda have also their rules and regulations, but these are not made according to what is just – only for the advantage of priests and princes – therefore their states are full of disputes and murder.

1. If any man falls into a state of destitution, his case must be brought before the count by the maidens, because a high-minded Frisian cannot bear to do that himself.
2. If any man becomes poor because he will not work,

he must be sent out of the country, because the cowardly and lazy are troublesome and ill-disposed, therefore they ought to be got rid of.

3. Every young man ought to seek a bride and to be married at five-and-twenty.

4. If a young man is not married at five-and-twenty, he must be driven from his home, and the younger men must avoid him. If then he will not marry, he must be declared dead, and leave the country, so that he may not give offence.

5. If a man is impotent, he must openly declare that no one has anything to fear from him, then he may come or go where he likes.

6. If after that he commits any act of incontinence, then he must flee away; if he does not, he may be given over to the vengeance of those whom he has offended, and no one may aid him.

7. Any one who commits a theft shall restore it three-fold. For a second offence he shall be sent to the tin mines. The person robbed may forgive him if he pleases, but for a third offence no one shall protect him.

THESE RULES ARE MADE FOR ANGRY PEOPLE:

1. If a man in a passion or out of illwill breaks another's limb or puts out an eye or a tooth, he must pay whatever the injured man demands. If he cannot pay, he must suffer the same injury as he has done to the other. If he refuses this, he must appeal to the Burgtmaagd in order to be sent to work in the iron or tin mines until he has expiated his crime under the general law.

2. If a man is so wicked as to kill a Frisian, he must forfeit his own life; but if the Burgtmaagd can send him to the tin mines for his life before he is taken, she may do so.

3. If the prisoner can prove by proper witnesses that the death was accidental, he may go free; but if it happens a second time, he must go to the tin mines, in order to avoid any unseemly hatred or vengeance.

THESE ARE THE RULES CONCERNING BASTARDS:

1. If any man sets fire to another's house, he is no Frisian, he is a bastard. If he is caught in the act, he must be thrown into the fire; and wherever he may flee he shall never be secure from the avenging justice.

2. No true Frisian shall speak ill of the faults of his neighbours. If any man injures himself, but does no harm to others, he must be his own judge; but if he becomes so bad that he is dangerous to others, they must bring it before the count. But if instead of going to the count a man accuses another behind his back, he must be put on the pillory in the market-place, and then sent out of the country, but not to the tin mines, because even there a back-biter is to be feared.

3. If any man should prove a traitor and show to our enemies the paths leading to our places of refuge, or creep into them by night, he must be the offspring of Finda; he must be burnt. The sailors must take his mother and all his relations to a desolate island, and there scatter his ashes, in order that no poisonous herbs may spring from them. The maidens must curse his name in all the states, in order that no child may be called by his name, and that his ancestors may repudiate him.

War had come to an end, but famine came in its place. There were three men who each stole a sack of corn from different owners, but they were all caught. The first owner brought his thief to the judge, and the maidens said everywhere that he had done right. The second owner took the corn away from his thief and let him go in peace. The maidens said he has done well. The third owner went to the thief's house, and when he saw what misery was there, he went and brought a waggon load of necessaries to relieve their distress. Frya's maidens came around him and wrote his deed in the eternal book, and wiped out all his sins. This was reported to the Eeremoeder, and she had it made known over the whole country.

CHAPTER SEVEN

GODS, PHOENICIANS AND DRUIDS

The script in which the *Oera Linda* manuscript is written at first glance looks rather like Old Gothic, with some resemblance also to archaic Greek lettering. It has 34 letters, including three different forms of *a*, two forms each for *e*, *i*, *o* and *y*, and four pairs of double consonants: *ng*, *ks*, *rgs* and *th*.

The Frisian dialect used, which shows considerable changes of pronunciation and structure from the oldest to the newest parts of the book, is believed to be that once spoken between the Vlie and the Scheldt. It is said to be very ancient, much more archaic and pure than that of the *Fries Rjuchtboek*, the code of laws attributed to Charlemagne sometime before the early part of the ninth century A.D.

In the next section of the *Oera Linda Book*, a description is given of how the writing was devised – based on the Juul, or wheel of the sun's apparent motion through the twelve constellations of the zodiac. The letters had to be formed on a circular matrix, and both a set or standing form – for use on stone inscriptions – and a cursive, runic or running form, for ordinary writing, were evolved.

Figures were also devised which, it will be seen, are far more similar to our own, than the Arabian from which our numerals were allegedly evolved.

It is worth noting that the ink used by Hiddo Over de Linda, last of the book's copyists, retained its blackness. When the manuscript was examined in 1857 it was ascertained that this ink has no iron content, while ink used after 1276 often contained iron which tended to make writing eventually fade to a grey or yellow colour.

Here is the book's description of the 'invention' of writing by Frya:

What appears at the top is the signs of the Juul – that is, the first symbol of Wr-alda, also of the origin or beginning from which Time is derived; this is the Kroder, which must always go round with the Juul. According to this model Frya formed the set hand which she used to write her Tex. When Fasta was Eeremoeder she made a running hand out of it. The Witkoning – that is, the Sea-King Godfried the Old – made separate numbers for the set hand and for the runic hand. It is therefore not too much that we celebrate it once a year. We may be eternally thankful to Wr-alda that he allowed his spirit to exercise such an influence over our forefathers.

In her time Finda also invented a mode of writing, but that was so high-flown and full of flourishes that her descendants have soon lost the meaning of it.

Afterwards they learned our writing – that is, the Finns, the Thyriers,[1] and the Krekalanders – but they did not know that it was taken from the Juul, and must therefore always be written round like the sun. Furthermore, they wished that their writing should be illegible by other people, because they always had matters to conceal. In doing this they acted very unwisely, because their children could only with great difficulty read the writings of their predecessors, whereas our most ancient writings are as easy to read as those that were written yesterday.

Here is a specimen of the set hand and of the running hand, as well as of the figures, in both. (See black and white insert.)

Next in the manuscript comes the description of Atland before the deluge and of its destruction, both of which passages I have already quoted. Skipping these, we come to the following:

1. Thyriers: Inhabitants of Tyre on the site of Ancient Carthage, N. Africa. The Frisians called Tyre, Thyrisburgt. But see also, further explanation in Chapter 9, footnote.

The Waraburgt is not a maiden's city, but the place
where all the foreign articles brought by sailors were
stored. It lies three hours south from Medeasblik.

Thus is the Preface

Hill, bow your heads; weep, ye streams and clouds. Yes.
Schoonland[2] blushes, an enslaved people tramples on
your garment, O Frya.

This is the History

One hundred and one years after the submersion of
Aldland,[3] a people came out of the East. That people was
driven by another. Behind us, in Twiskland,[4] they fell into
disputes, divided into two parties, and each went its own
way. Of the one no account has come to us, but the other
came in the back of our Schoonland, which was thinly inhabited, particularly the upper part. Therefore they were
able to take possession of it without contest, and as they
did no other harm, we would not make war about it. Now
that we have learned to know them, we will describe their
customs, and after that how matters went between us.
They were not wild people, like most of Finda's race; but,
like the Egyptians, they have priests and also statues in
their churches. The priests are the only rulers; they call
themselves Magyars, and their headman Magy. He is high
priest and king in one. The rest of the people are of no
account, and in subjection to them. This people have not
even a name; but we call them Finns, because although all
the festivals are melancholy and bloody, they are so for-
mal that we are inferior to them in that respect. But still
they are not to be envied, because they are slaves to their

2. Schoonland – Scandinavia.
3. 2193−101=2092 B.C.
4. Twiskland – Germany.

priests, and still more to their creeds. They believe that evil spirits abound everywhere, and enter into men and beasts, but of Wr-alda's spirit they know nothing. They have weapons of stone, the Magyars of copper. The Magyars affirm that they can exorcise and recall the evil spirits, and this frightens the people, so that you never see a cheerful face. When they were well established, the Magyars sought our friendship, they praised our language and customs, our cattle and iron weapons, which they would willingly have exchanged for their gold and silver ornaments, and they always kept their people within their own boundaries, and that outwitted our watchfulness.

Eighty years afterwards, just at the time of the Juulfest, they overran our country like a snowstorm driven by the wind. All who could not flee away were killed. Frya was appealed to, but the Schoonlanders had neglected her advice. Then all the forces were assembled, and three hours from Godasburgt they were withstood, but war continued. Kat or Katerine was the name of the priestess who was Burgtmaagd of Godasburgt. Kat was proud and haughty, and would neither seek counsel nor aid from the mother; but when the Burgtheeren knew this, they themselves sent messengers to Texland to the Eeremoeder. Minna – this was the name of the mother – summoned all the sailors and the young men from Oostflyland and Denmark. From this expedition the history of Wodin sprang, which is inscribed on the citadels and is here copied.

At Aldergamude there lived an old sea-king whose name was Sterik, and whose deeds were famous. This old fellow had three nephews. Wodin, the eldest, lived at Lumkamakia, near the Eemude, in Oostflyland, with his parents. He had once commanded troops. Teunis and Inka were naval warriors, and were just then staying with their father at Aldergamude. When the young warriors had assembled together, they chose Wodin to be their leader or king, and the naval force chose Teunis for their sea-king and Inka for their admiral. The navy then sailed to Denmark, where they took on board Wodin and his valiant host.

The wind was fair, so they arrived immediately in Schoonland. When the northern brothers met together, Wodin divided his powerful army into three bodies. Frya was their war-cry, and they drove back the Finns and Magyars like children. When the Magy heard how his forces had been utterly defeated, he sent messengers with truncheon and crown, who said to Wodin: O almighty king, we are guilty but all that we have done was done from necessity. You think that we attacked your brothers out of illwill, but we were driven out by our enemies, who are still at our heels. We have often asked your Burgtmaagd for help, but she took no notice of us. The Magy says that if we kill half our numbers in fighting with each other, then the wild shepherds will come and kill all the rest. The Magy possesses great riches, but he has seen that Frya is much more powerful than all our spirits together. He will lay down his head in her lap. You are the most warlike king on the earth, and your people are of iron. Become our king, and we will all be your slaves. What glory it would be for you if you could drive back the savages! Our trumpets would resound with your praises, and the fame of your deeds would precede you everywhere. Wodin was strong, fierce, and warlike, but he was not clear-sighted, therefore he was taken in their toils, and crowned by the Magy.

Very many of the sailors and soldiers to whom this proceeding was displeasing went away secretly, taking Kat with them. But Kat, who did not wish to appear before either the mother or the general assembly, jumped overboard. Then a storm arose and drove the ships upon the banks of Denmark, with the total destruction of their crews. This strait was afterwards called the Kattegat. When Wodin was crowned, he attacked the savages, who were all horsemen, and fell upon Wodin's troops like a hailstorm; but like a whirlwind they were turned back, and did not dare to appear again. When Wodin returned Magy gave him his daughter to wife. Whereupon he was incensed with herbs; but they were magic herbs, and by degrees he became so audacious that he dared to disavow and ridicule

87

the spirits of Frya and Wr-alda, while he bent his free head before the false and deceitful images. His reign lasted seven years, and then he disappeared. The Magy said that he was taken up by their gods and still reigned over us, but our people laughed at what they said. When Wodin had disappeared some time, disputes arose. We wished to choose another king, but the Magy would not permit it. He asserted that it was his right given him by his idols. But besides this dispute there was one between the Magyars and Finns, who would honour neither Frya nor Wodin; but the Magy did just as he pleased, because his daughter had a son by Wodin, and he would have it that this son was of high descent. While all were disputing and quarrelling, he crowned the boy as king, and set up himself as guardian and counsellor. Those who cared more for themselves than for justice let him work his own way, but the good men took their departure. Many Magyars fled back with their troops, and the sea-people took ship, accompanied by a body of stalwart Finns as rowers.

Next comes upon the stage the history of Neef Teunis and Neef Inka.

ALL THIS IS INSCRIBED NOT ONLY ON THE WARABURGT, BUT ALSO ON THE BURGT STAVIA, WHICH LIES BEHIND THE PORT OF STAVRE

When Teunis wished to return home, he went first towards Denmark; but he might not land there, for so the mother had ordered, nor was he to land at Flyland, nor anywhere about there. In this way he would have lost all his people by want and hardship, so he landed at night to steal and sailed on by day. Thus coasting along, he at length arrived at the colony of Kadik,[5] so called because it was built with a stone quay. Here they bought all kinds of stores, but Tuntia, the Burgtmaagd, would not allow them to settle there. When they were ready they began to disagree. Teunis wished to sail through the straits to the

5. Kadik – Cadiz.

88

Mediterranean Sea, and enter the service of the rich Egyptian king, as he had done before, but Inka said he had had enough of all those Finda's people. Inka thought that perchance some high-lying part of Atland might remain as an island, where he and his people might live in peace. As the two cousins could not agree, Teunis planted a red flag on the shore, and Inka a blue flag. Every man should choose which he pleased, and to their astonishment, the greater part of the Finns and Magyars followed Inka, who had objected to serve the kings of Finda's people. When they had counted the people and divided the ships accordingly, the fleet separated. We shall hear of Teunis afterwards, but nothing more of Inka.

Neef Teunis coasted through the straits to the Mediterranean Sea. When Atland was submerged there was much suffering also on the shores of the Mediterranean, on which account many of Finda's people, Krekalanders, and people from Lyda's land, came to us. On the other hand, many of our people went to Lyda's land. The result of all this was that the Krekalanders far and wide were lost to the superintendence of the mother. Teunis had reckoned on this, and had therefore wished to find there a good haven from which he might go and serve under the rich princes; but as his fleet and his people had such a shattered appearance, the inhabitants on the coasts thought that they were pirates, and drove them away. At last they arrived at the Phoenician coast, one hundred and ninety-three years after Atland was submerged.[6] Near the coast they found an island with two deep bays, so that there appeared to be three islands. In the middle one they established themselves, and afterwards built a city wall round the place. Then they wanted to give it a name, but disagreed about it. Some wanted to call it Fryasburgt, others Neeftunia; but the Magyars and Finns begged that it might be called Thyrhisburgt.[7]

Thyr[8] was the name of one of their idols, and it was

6. 2193 − 193 = 2000 B.C.
7. Thyrhisburgt – Tyre.
8. Thyr, in Norse mythology, was the son of Odin.

upon his feast-day that they had landed there; and in return they offered to recognise Teunis as their perpetual king. Teunis let himself be persuaded and the others would not make any quarrel about it. When they were well established, they sent some old seamen and Magyars on an expedition as far as the town of Sidon; but at first the inhabitants of the coast would have nothing to do with them, saying, You are only foreign adventurers whom we do not respect. But when we sold them some of our iron weapons, everything went well. They also wished to buy our amber, and their inquiries about it were incessant. But Teunis, who was far-seeing, pretended that he had no more iron weapons or amber. Then merchants came and begged him to let them have twenty vessels, which they would freight with the finest goods, and they would provide as many people to row as he would require. Twelve ships were then laden with wine, honey, tanned leather, and saddles and bridles mounted in gold, such as had never been seen before.

Teunis sailed to the Flymeer with all this treasure, which so enchanted the Grevetman of Westflyland that he induced Teunis to build a warehouse at the mouth of the Flymeer. Afterwards this place was called Almanaland,[9] and the market where they traded at Wyringen[10] was called Toelaatmarkt. The mother advised that they should sell everything except iron weapons, but no attention was paid to what she said. As the Thyriers had thus free play, they came from far and near to take away our goods, to the loss of our seafaring people. Therefore it was resolved in a general assembly to allow only seven Thyrian ships and no more in a year.

WHAT THE CONSEQUENCE OF THIS WAS

In the northernmost part of the Mediterranean there lies an island close to the coast. They now came and asked to buy that, on which a general council was held.

9. Almanaland – Ameland.
10. Wyringen – Wieringen.

The mother's advice was asked, and she wished to see them at some distance, so she saw no harm in it; but as we afterwards saw what a mistake we had made, we called the island Missellia.[11] Hereafter will be seen what reason we had. The Golen, as the missionary priests of Sidon were called, had observed that the land there was thinly peopled, and was far from the mother. In order to make a favourable impression, they had themselves called in our language *followers of the truth*; but they had better have been called *abstainers from the truth*, or, in short, 'Triuwenden',[12] as our seafaring people afterwards called them. When they were well established, their merchants exchanged their beautiful copper weapons and all sorts of jewels for our iron weapons and hides of wild beasts, which were abundant in our southern countries; but the Golen celebrated all sorts of vile and monstrous festivals, which the inhabitants of the coast promoted with their wanton women and sweet poisonous wine. If any of our people had so conducted himself that his life was in danger, the Golen afforded him a refuge, and sent him to Phonisia, that is, Palmland. When he was settled there, they made him write to his family, friends and connections that the country was so good and the people so happy that no one could form any idea of it. In Britain there were plenty of men, but few women. When the Golen knew this, they carried off girls everywhere and gave them to the Britons for nothing. So all these girls served their purpose to steal children from Wr-alda in order to give them false gods.

Commentary

In the preceding section of the *Oera Linda Book* we are told how offshoots of Finda's yellow race – Magyars and Finns – came out of the East and occupied Scandinavia. It will be remembered that in Adela's account of the Golden Age of Atland it was related how Finda's people had been

11. Marseilles.
12. Triuwenden can be seen as the origin of the name, Druids, while Golen is another form of Galli, or the Gauls of Phoenicia.

91

kept at bay by the 'thick forests and wild beasts' of 'broad Twiskland', or Germany, and beyond. But then, as described in 'How the Bad Time Came', whole forests were destroyed in the fires, floods and upheavals of the cataclysm that sank Atland. Then, troops of Finda's people marched in and either exterminated or enslaved many of the Atland–Frisian survivors in Europe.

It has not been irrefutably established as to where the Finnish-speaking peoples originated, but it is believed they belonged to a transitional sub-race allied to the Mongols. And in fact, the so-called Finno-Ugrian family of languages with which they are associated has, as one of its two main branches, Hungarian, or Magyar. This would, of course, tie in with the *Oera Linda Book*'s account of the arrival together in Scandinavia of the Magyars and Finns around 2092 B.C.

The Frisian account gives the distinct impression that the Magyars, who had copper weapons, were dominant while the Finns, who had only stone implements, were simply tagging along behind.

It is easy to see, in view of the references to 'melancholy and bloody' festivals of these peoples, and the belief that evil spirits could enter men and beasts, how the later legends of the Norse hero, Beserk, evolved. His twelve sons were said to have inherited his martial fury, his 'beserker' rage and his courage. Their enemies were convinced they were possessed by an evil spirit.

Eighty years after their arrival in Scandinavia, where they had been tolerated and befriended by the trusting Frya's people, the Magyars decided to move even further west and overrun the Frisians. That would have been around 2012 B.C., and it is at this time that Wodin – without doubt the real-life prototype of the Norse god Odin – comes on to the scene.

Wodin's prowess as a warrior in driving back the Magyars – he is described as 'strong, fierce and warlike' – is probably the basis upon which he passed into Norse mythology as Odin, the storm-god, his name signifying 'mad', or 'the raging one', and as Wotan, the supreme god of Teutonic tribes. As a brilliant commander of armies, his name came to signify wisdom and valour and Odin was thus a patron of culture and heroes.

The Teutonic tribes adopted him as Woden, and his day became our Wednesday. He was also later identified with the Roman god, Mercury.

Yet according to the story of the real-life warrior Wodin, his reputation exceeded his true character. He was, the *Oera Linda Book* says, 'not clear-sighted' and was easily beguiled by the Magy's praise, offer of wealth, kingship – and his daughter's hand in marriage. And, after the anecdote relating how the narrow strait between Denmark and Sweden, known as the Kattegat, got its name, Wodin is quickly discredited. He was enchanted with 'magic' herbs, disavowed Frya and Wr-alda and, after seven years, mysteriously disappeared. He may well have been conveniently murdered by the power-hungry Magy, after serving his purpose as a 'puppet' king while kept permanently drugged.

Philip Johan von Strahlenberg, in his *Historical and Geographical Descriptions of the North and Eastern Parts of Europe and Asia, Russia, Siberia and Tartary* (1736), describes the long history of the use of a hallucinogenic mushroom called fly agaric (*Amanita muscaria*). Initially used by shamans, or priests, as an inebriant to induce mystico-religious ecstasy, this 'magic herb' produced delusions of grandeur, invisibility in battle, the frenzy of the 'beserker' warrior and insensibility to pain. Archaeological investigations have revealed that warriors used a small, portable, tri-pole tent in which they inhaled fumes of burning herbs and plants to induce similar states of hallucination.

After Wodin's disappearance, the Magy announced that he had been 'taken up' by the gods and still reigned from on high – a claim that was indubitably the foundation of Wodin's deification and elevation to Norse mythology.

When Teunis, seafaring cousin to Inka and Wodin, decided to return westwards, he found he could not land anywhere in Frisian, or former Frisian, territory, by order of the high-priestess. The *Oera Linda Book* does not say as much, but presumably this was under the code of law that forbade

the intermingling of Frya's and Finda's people; it will be
recalled that Teunis had a body of 'stalwart Finns' with
him. Also, it might have been feared that, having been away
among the Magyars so long, Teunis and his men had become tainted by their 'barbarian' ways, as had Wodin.

And so it was that he and Inka finally arrived at the
Spanish port of Cadiz, where Teunis announced that he
wanted to sail into the Mediterranean to enter the service of
the Egyptian king. This did not appeal to Inka, who, after
the red-and-blue-flag ceremony, sailed off to the west to
look for remnants of Atland which he thought might still be
above water. The *Oera Linda Book* has no more to say of
him, although I shall – in the next chapter.

Neef Teunis, or Cousin Teunis, sailed off through the
straits into the Mediterranean. At this point, we are told:

'When Atland was submerged there was much suffering
also on the shores of the Mediterranean, on which account
many of Finda's people, Krekalanders, and people from
Lyda's land, came to us.'

This sentence is merely inserted to explain the wide distribution of peoples – including the Krekalanders (Greeks),
Finda's people (Egyptians) and Lyda's people (Africans) –
throughout the Mediterranean when Teunis arrives there.
But it also helps to clear up a double-mystery that has hitherto confounded readers of certain passages of the Greek historian Herodotus.

According to Herodotus, Egyptian priests told him that
the low delta lands of Egypt were flooded by mighty waves
during the submergence of a great land beyond the Pillars
of Hercules (Straits of Gibraltar). Despite the fact that this
happened before historical Greece, the priests claimed that
the warriors of Athens had repelled invading giants from the
sunken land.

Now the *Oera Linda Book* says that Min-erva founded
Athens, shortly after the Mycenae sacked Troy (probably *c*.
1250 B.C.), and before the Dorians invaded from the north
and founded what has come to be known as historical
Greece. Therefore, the people from the sunken land beyond

the Pillars of Hercules must have been the Frisians who founded Athens.

No doubt Egyptians – a branch of Finda's people – did flee across the Mediterranean to proto-Greece when the Nile delta was flooded.

But stories of (a) the deluge and (b) the tall race of Frya's people who colonised Greece, undoubtedly became muddled over the centuries. The *Oera Linda Book* goes on to relate later how Cecrops, the son of a Frisian girl by an Egyptian priest, brought wild Finda soldiers and drove the Frisians from Athens.

These various events might have become intermingled and by Herodotus's time (*c.* 484–424 B.C.) became the confused account he got from the Egyptians.

Apart from the legend of Deucalion, further evidence of Greek memory of a great deluge was discovered in Rome in 1696. It was an ancient Greek reliquary, shaped like a coffer. In it were thirty-five figurines of people and twenty-one pairs of animals. Their postures suggested that they were trying to escape from a great flood. Struggling men carried women on their shoulders. Others seemed to be trying to save their animals. It is believed that the vessel might have been used in some ancient Greek festival commemorating the deluge.

To return to Teunis. In 2000 B.C. and, to judge by the account of their 'shattered appearance', after many adventures on raging seas, Teunis and his followers landed in Phoenicia, called Palmland later by the Frisians. There, they established Thyrisburgt which, according to the account, must have been one of the first of the so-called Punic settlements in North Africa, long before Carthage became the chief port of the Phoenician empire. Thyrisburgt became known as Tyre, but this is not to be confused with the Tyre (and Sidon) of Palestine Phoenicia in the eastern Mediterranean. Teunis may also have given his name to Tunis to the west of the peninsula upon which Thyrisburgt was built and may also have been the founder of nearby Utica.

In 1975 a British archaeological expedition based at Tunis discovered what was assumed to have been a late Punic naval base on the island of Pantelleria – off the coast of

Tunisia. Now Italian-owned, this volcanic island is undoubtedly the 'island with two deep bays, so that there appeared to be three islands' where Teunis and his men first made landfall. In fact, it is more than likely that the 'Punic' naval base is one built by Teunis, and that its walls and stone slipways are reconstructions of his original harbour facilities. It is believed that, after the Romans took Carthage, they built a lighthouse up through the structure of the earlier Punic buildings. Also found were the remains of a powerful city wall – like the one Teunis built – and the ruins of an extremely ancient temple-like structure in the centre of the island.

It is simply staggering how, as the years go by, fresh archaeological evidence points to the truth of the *Oera Linda Book*. And yet, since it was first revealed to historians in 1869, it has been consistently ignored.

Following Teunis's treasure-laden return to his homeland and the establishment of a large trading port, the book next tells the wry tale of how Marseilles (Missellia) came to be named – after a mistake. And it is here, in the *Oera Linda Book*, that the mysterious origin of the shadowy Druids is cleared up for the first time.

For centuries this arcane sect has puzzled and baffled historians and archaeologists and, to date, no satisfactory account of their background has been forthcoming.

Stuart Piggott, in his study *The Druids* (Thames & Hudson, 1968; Penguin Books, 1974), says:

'As no pre-Christian inscription containing the word "Druid" has so far been discovered, any connection between this body and an archaeological site can only be an unverifiable assumption in our present state of knowledge.'

And later: 'The references in the classical authors on which our knowledge of the Druids is based range in date from around the end of the third century B.C. to the fourth century A.D., and relate to Western Europe (and almost exclusively to Gaul) and to Britain.'

The *Oera Linda Book* lifts the veil. Some time after 2000 B.C., the Frisians sold the island they called Missellia (Marseilles) to the Phoenicians (Thyrians). In the eastern Mediterranean, the Phoenicians established Tyre and Sidon and it was from the latter, we are told, that the Golen came. These were missionary priests whom, because of their experience of them, the seafaring Frisians called *Triuwenden* – 'abstainers from the truth'.

Seeing that the lands around the newly-acquired island were thinly populated, the Golen, or Triuwenden, moved in.

What do the Frisians say of the Triuwenden?

They 'celebrated all sorts of vile and monstrous festivals ...'.

And what do the classical writers say of the Druids? Roughly, the same:

Strabo wrote of 'sacrifices and divinations that are opposed to our usage'. He described how omens were 'read' from the death-throes of a human victim stabbed in the back, how men were impaled, shot to death by arrows and, most horrendous of all, how a writhing mass of human and animal victims were forced into a huge wickerwork figure and burned alive. Caesar gave similar descriptions.

Tacitus wrote of British Druids: 'They deemed it indeed a duty to cover their altars with the blood of captives and to consult their deities through human entrails.'

Beyond that they came from Europe, with Gaul as the favourite place of origin, however, none of the later scholars traced the Druids back to Phoenicia. Although Aylett Sammes, in his *Britannia Antiqua Illustrata* (1676) somehow came very close. He believed that the Druids took over from Phoenician bards in Britain. 'It happened that in continuance of time, the Druids got the upper hand,' he wrote.

According to the *Oera Linda Book*, as well as performing 'vile and monstrous' rites, the Druids specialised in abduction, giving 'refuge' to fugitive Frisians, then forcing them to tempt their friends and families out to Phoenicia by writing letters full of praise for their new 'home'.

Also, it appears, they won over new converts to their religion by supplying kidnapped girls from all over the Continent to Britain, where men were plentiful and women were at a premium.

The next section of the *Oera Linda Book*, in fact, goes on to describe how Frya's people lost all their southern lands and Britain to the Golen, or Druids. But first, we should now examine the possible fate of Inka. His cousin, Neef Teunis, as we have seen, became a veritable 'king' of the Mediterranean, plying between those ports and his homeland, trading and bringing back treasure. It is not difficult to see how such an adventurer might become deified as Neptune, the Roman sea-god, counterpart of the Greek Poseidon. But what of Inka?

CHAPTER EIGHT

WHITE GODS FROM THE PAST

When Inka, along with his faithful following of Frisians, Magyars and Finns, sailed off from Spain to seek out unsubmerged fragments of Atland, it is fairly safe to assume that he did not find any. It is also reasonable to surmise that he kept on going west until eventually he did reach land. Otherwise, had he returned, he would doubtless have been acclaimed by the people of his homeland and the event would almost certainly have been recorded in the history of the Frisians, the *Oera Linda Book*.

Anyway, we have already seen why Inka could not immediately go home and settle – his companions were of Finda's sub-races and Frisian law forbade such intermingling. Also, Frya's people themselves were beginning to dwindle and degenerate, under Magyar and Finnish domination. Home, at this point, was not exactly a desirable place.

We can assume, therefore, that Inka set off with the sole object of somehow finding a suitable place in which to establish an outpost for himself and his mixed followers; somewhere where he could establish and preserve at least a modicum of Frisian life-style and tradition.

And it is my contention that this is exactly what he did – in South America.

But assumption is not sufficient. We must look for evidence, or at least clues, of Inka's presence there.

According to writer-researcher Andrew Tomas, in *Atlantis: From Legend to Discovery* (Robert Hale & Co., 1972; Sphere Books, 1973):

'Aztec priests zealously preserved the memory of *Aztlan, a country in the east,* where Quetzalcoatl had come from *as a culture bearer.*' (My italics.)

Understandably enough, for the purposes of his own thesis and, apparently not being aware of the *Oera Linda Book* and its contents, Tomas takes 'Aztlan' as a possible reference to lost Atlantis. But in fact, it is much closer to the name of Atland. The reference to Quetzalcoatl as a 'culture bearer' is also highly significant. People like Inka and his companions would indeed have been able to introduce a whole new, advanced culture to the primitive Indians of the Yucatan peninsula and the southern reaches of Mexico. That is, had they stayed sufficiently long. Quetzalcoatl, later deified and stylised as a plumed serpent, was regarded as a light-skinned god who had visited the Indians, then sailed off again, promising one day to return.

In addition to the above reference, Tomas also records the following:

'Montezuma, the last king of the Aztecs, told Cortes that "our fathers were not born here, but they came from a distant country called Aztlan, with a high mountain and a garden where the gods lived".'

Montezuma's admission to the Spanish conqueror, with its idyllic overtones, is remarkably reminiscent of the Greek descriptions of Hyperborea. To digress only slightly, let us look more closely at what the Greeks did say of that sought-after land to the north.

In the *Odyssey*, Homer said: '... no snow is there, nor yet any great storm nor any rain ...'

And Pliny, (in Philemon Holland's 1607 translation) wrote: 'Their countrie is open upon the sun, of a blissful and pleasant temperature, void of all noisome wind and hurtful aires. Their habitations be in woods and groves, where they worship the gods both of themselves, and in com-

panies and congregations; no discord know they, no sick-
nesse are they acquainted with.'

It is easy to see how, in telling the early Indians of Yucatan of his lost homeland, Inka's account might eventually
have become distorted to a fabulous isle of the gods.

But back to South America. In yet another passage from
Andrew Tomas's thesis, we are told:

'A white Indian tribe, Paria, used to live in Venezuela,
in a village with so significant a name as *Atlan. They had a
tradition of a calamity which had destroyed their country, a
large island in the ocean.*' (My italics.)

It would appear that Inka and his people, after leaving
Yucatan and Mexico, then sailed south, possibly through
what is now the Gulf of Honduras and on down to
Venezuela, still looking for somewhere to settle. The fact
that the Paria Indians were white seems to suggest that at
least some of his party settled there and inter-married with
local Indians, thus producing the light-skinned strain. But, it
seems, Inka himself moved on, to the south-west into Peru.
Either that or his descendants kept on his name in his
honour.

For it is here, stretching 2,500 miles along the west coast
of South America, that we find one of the most amazing
cultures of the continent. A culture that bore the name of
Inca.

Only an outside influence from a highly-civilised society
could have engendered such an empire which, in only 90
years, grew from a small kingdom at the capital city of
Cuzco, to a vast, rich, diverse nation, stretching from the
hot deserts of northern Chile to the steamy, tropical lowlands of Ecuador, from the fertile Peruvian valleys to the
rarified heights of Bolivia.

It is believed that the original Peruvian Indians were a
primitive tribe who migrated down from the north. Their
ancestors are assumed to have arrived around 30,000 years
ago from Siberia, across the supposed land bridge of the
Bering Strait, to Alaska.

From about 300 B.C. to A.D. 800, the northern coastal
areas of Peru were inhabited by Moche Indians. They built

canals up to 75 miles long, giant platforms of sun-dried clay, and decorated their pottery with realistic pictures of human faces, animals, trees and birds.

Then, between A.D. 500 and 1000, came a totally fresh and alien religious influence – that of Viracocha, represented as a winged god with weeping eyes. He was venerated by the Incas and at Tiahuanaco, in north-west Bolivia, are huge stone figures, terraced courtyards and granite columns, the site of his main shrine. A gateway is embossed with a frieze showing the god weeping copious tears.

It has been suggested that his tears might represent rainfall. But could this not be a stylised representation of Inka, his tears symbolising the deluge that destroyed Atland, or his sad longing for his lost homeland?

No-one has satisfactorily explained what turned the Incas – only one of many Indian tribes in Peru – into the powerful, empire-building nation they became, in such a short time.

I suggest that it was the aggressive drive of an outside influence – of Inka, or more likely his descendants, who journeyed down from Venezuela.

It is significant that, under the Inca dynasty, like that of the Frisians, all boys had organised physical and military training, with slings, spears, star-shaped bronze maces and bronze axes.

The Incas had no horses, nor wheeled vehicles.

But, again like the Frisians, they preferred to expand by persuasion and diplomacy, rather than by violent domination and conquest. To entice other tribes into their empire they offered enemy overlords and chieftains posts in their government. And, provided that Inti, the sun-god and chief deity, was recognised as supreme, all other local gods were accepted and absorbed.

They had no monetary system. All land belonged to the state and, in a similar way to the provisions of Frya's Tex, was divided up on a three-fold basis. The products of one-third went to support the court and governmental administration, another paid for the maintenance of temples, priests and priestesses and their training colleges, and the third part was equally divided among the people.

Again, as in Friesland, taxes were paid by work performed. All those capable were required to work the state-owned lands first, before tilling their own allotted portions.

As in the Burgtmaagd system, girls were specially trained for temple service, were sworn to chastity and became Virgins of the Sun. The Inca regime was not, however, a matriarchy. Presumably, in trying to build a society similar to that of Frya's people, Inka and his descendants had to compromise, because of the diverse attitudes of the Magyars, Finns and native influences.

In the Inca religion, the equivalent of Wr-alda, the creator and all-pervading eternal spirit, was Viracocha. But only one temple, near Cuzco the capital, was dedicated to him. Indeed, the Inca system became so status and class-conscious that eventually only the high nobility were allowed to worship Viracocha.

Inti, represented in temples by enormous golden sun-discs with human features, was the supreme god of the ordinary people, and Quilla, the moon-goddess, was his consort.

In toto, and despite its high-flown and socially-motivated despotism, the Inca system was in fact a highly benevolent and humanitarian welfare state.

It controlled the religion, all administrative officials and protected the interests and natural rights of the common people. Each family was allotted a house and land sufficient to keep its members comfortably fed – as in Frya's system.

On a great festival day each year, the people worked together on the state and 'church' lands. Even the great Inca, or Emperor, as the 'son' of the sun, took part, turning the first sod of crop-planting time with a golden hoe. Once the common work was done the people were free to till their own lands.

The old, sick, crippled and veterans of any battles, along with other non-productive members of society such as administrators, nobles, architects and planners, were supplied with food by the state. Part of the state crop was stashed in warehouses for emergencies, such as poor harvests. Every family was provided with sufficient wool from state herds of alpaca and llama, from which the highly-skilled women wove cloth for garments, or decorated rugs and hangings.

With no money to tempt unscrupulous manipulators, trade was a simple system of fair barter determined by law. Yet a citizen could make a 'deposit' of labour and earn credits by working on the great roads. The 'Royal Road', along which great lorries rumble today, reached from Columbia to Chile – 5,230 kilometres, a stupendous engineering achievement not surpassed by any other people until the Twentieth century.

State officials were responsible for production and distribution in their own areas. Any official who failed to distribute state goods fairly, who was inefficient, unjust, or corrupt, was punished, often with death. Slavery was unknown, as under the Tex. Inca children were taught that work, honesty and obedience to the law were virtues, while laziness, dishonesty and lawlessness were crimes. There were no criminals as such and consequently no jails. So high was the standard of morality that no-one fastened the door of his house when away from home – not, that is, until the Spanish conquistadores arrived.

Agricultural labourers, artisans, doctors, astronomers and engineers – oblivious to worries about paying rates, taxes, rising prices or where the next meal was coming from – were able to give their full attention to their work and to perfecting their craft.

The result was a society whose achievements stagger the imagination. From these people came many of the vegetables, fruit and beneficial drugs of today, evolved from wild plants: the potato in many varieties, the pineapple, the pumpkin, chinchona, from which quinine is derived, coca – source of cocaine.

Their exquisite and delicate works in gold, silver, bronze and semi-precious stones amaze and delight connoisseurs; some of the fine and complex patterns which their weavers produced on hand-looms cannot be reproduced today. The Incas astonished the Western World with their astronomical knowledge and a calendar more accurate than our own leap-year system. They practised trepanning and other medical skills. They carved granite-hard rocks without steel tools and, without any seeming difficulty, transported stone blocks weighing up to 100 tons and fitted them together with the precision of jigsaw puzzle pieces.

Yet although the Inca dynasty largely echoed the Frisian ideal, it bore one blot – that of human sacrifice. But even this was comparatively rare. It was practised only at times of great national crisis, such as the sickness of the emperor or plague and famine. Usually, ten-year-old children had their throats cut or were strangled.

As human sacrifice was a practice of many primitive cultures in South America, it is understandable that it survived even under outside influence from a code as civilised as that of Frya's race. Besides, it is well to remember that the Magyars, who accompanied Inka, also believed in sacrifice to the gods in times of danger and poor crops. Clearly, some concessions were necessary.

While on the subject of human sacrifice, it is worth noting here that the Aztecs practised a ritual that is hauntingly evocative of the eternally-burning lamps of the maidens of Fasta, in which each lamp must be lit from the original at the citadel of Texland. The Aztecs, who had two different calendars, believed that the earth was likely to be destroyed by a cosmic holocaust at the end of every 52-year cycle. On the final day of this cycle their priests would watch the stars from a mountain top near Tenochtitlan. Once the constellation of the Pleiades had climbed to its zenith, they knew the danger was past . . . for another 52 years.

To mark this 'reprieve', a victim would be stretched across an altar, his chest opened with a sacrificial knife with a blade of chalcedony, and the astronomer-priest would light a fire in his chest-cavity. From this flame, messengers would light torches which they would carry to every temple and home. This 'New Fire' was the symbol that life would continue, at least for another fifty-two years.

But, returning to the Incas, we must examine yet more evidence for the outside influence of a race such as that of Inka. It is possible that the Inca monarchy accepted his name because its members were of his blood. If so, and taking into account the tradition that the members of royal families married their brothers and sisters to keep their blood untainted and distinct from that of the native Indian, it would be reasonable to expect some evidence that the blood of the royal line was different to that of the commoner. And in fact, this has been found to be so. Three 'Inca' or Emperor mummies were taken from their golden thrones in the Temple of the Sun at Cuzco and placed in the British Museum. On examination, the blood grouping of the imperial Incas was found to reveal combinations not normally encountered among South American Indians.

The fact that Inca lore had predicted the return one day of the light-skinned god Viracocha, was partly responsible for the downfall of this remarkable empire. This, plus the fact that the Incas had never seen a horse, let alone an armoured soldier mounted upon one, nor experienced the thunder-and-lightning-like effects of firearms, allowed Francisco Pizarro and his Spanish force of only 180 men to kill the Emperor Atahuallpa and conquer his empire of 12 million people, in 1553.

However, for centuries afterwards, there was a legend that some survivors of the fallen dynasty had fled into the Andes on the advent of the Spanish conquistadores. In 1911 Hiram Bingham, an assistant professor in Latin American history at Yale, led an expedition into the mountains – and discovered the 'lost' Inca city of Machu Picchu.

It had a flight of more than 100 terraces, hundreds of feet long. Each had been covered with soil carried up from the valleys below, so that its people could be self-sufficient and grow their own vegetables. It was a network of startling white granite buildings, a city large enough to house 2,000 people. On three sides, 1,000-foot sheer slopes made it almost impregnable to attack.

What happened to its inhabitants is a mystery. No writings were left – not even in the form of knotted cords, or *quipus*, which the Incas used – to explain the fate of its people.

Yet on a later expedition, Bingham found evidence that Machu Picchu had housed a society largely of women – a feature again echoing Frisian tradition. In cave-sepulchres, he found the skeletons of 150 women and only 24 men. It is believed that these 'Chosen Women' – probably Virgins of the Sun – were sent to the secret mountain citadel to escape the Spaniards. The city is thought to have flourished, undetected, for a further 40 years before the last of its sacred virgins died and their male guardians had also either succumbed, or drifted away.

There remains one final puzzle in this account of the Incas. If I am correct that the descendants of Inka founded this civilisation, some explanation must be given for the Inca temples and stepped pyramids. So far as we can discern from the *Oera Linda Book*, the Frisians built neither.

We do, however, know from the book that the Magyars built temples in Europe. But what about pyramids? In fact there is other evidence that these people, who accompanied Inka, did build such structures, at least before they left Russia.

South of Soviet Turkmenistan in the Kara-Koum desert, the ruins of cities have been discovered, the most ancient of which were built 8,000 years ago. There was town-planning, with streets, squares, residential and artisans' quarters, public and religious buildings . . . and evidence of step-pyramids. So it is highly feasible that the Inca practice of building these huge edifices stemmed from the Magyar influence of Inka's culture-bearing inroads into Peru.

CHAPTER NINE

MORE ABOUT MIN-ERVA

The next section of the *Oera Linda Book* flashes back in time, to a period when Min-erva was Burgtmaagd in Middelburg. It describes how the Frisians lost their lands, including Britain, to the Gauls, then goes on to tell of the sea-king Jon and the Frisian colonisation of the Punjab.

*And how we thereby lost all our southern lands and
Britain to the Gauls*

Near the southern mouth of the Rhine and the Scheldt
there are seven islands, named after Frya's seven virgins
of the week. In the middle of one island is the city of
Walhallagara[1] and on the walls of this city the following
history is inscribed. Above it are the words, 'Read, learn,
and watch.'

Five hundred and sixty-three years after the submersion
of Atland – that is, 1,600 years before Christ[2] – a wise
town priestess presided here, whose name was Min-erva –
called by the sailors Nyhellenia. This name was well
chosen, for her counsels were new and clear above all
others.

On the other side of the Scheldt, at Flyburgt, Sijrhed
presided. This maiden was full of tricks. Her face was
beautiful, and her tongue was nimble; but the advice that
she gave was always conveyed in mysterious terms. Therefore the mariners called her Kalta, and the landsmen
thought it was a title. In the last will of the dead mother,
Rosamond was named first, Min-erva second, and
Sijrhed third in succession. Min-erva did not mind that,
but Sijrhed was very much offended. Like a foreign
princess, she wished to be honoured, feared, and worshipped; but Min-erva only desired to be loved. At last
all the sailors, even from Denmark and Flymeer, did homage to her. This hurt Sijrhed, because she wanted to excel
Min-erva. In order to give an impression of her great
watchfulness, she had a cock put on her banner. So then
Min-erva went and put a sheep-dog and an owl on her
banner. The dog, she said, guards his master and his flock,
and the owl watches that the mice shall not devastate the

1. Walhallagara – Middelburg, in Walcheren.
2. In fact, 2193 − 563 = 1630 B.C.

fields; but the cock in his lewdness and his pride is only fit to murder his nearest relations. When Kalta found that her scheme had failed she was still more vexed, so she secretly sent for the Magyars to teach her conjuring. When she had had enough of this she threw herself into the hands of the Gauls; but all her malpractices did not improve her position. When she saw that the sailors kept more and more aloof from her, she tried to win them back by fear. At the full moon, when the sea was stormy, she ran over the wild waves, calling to the sailors that they would all be lost if they did not worship her. Then she blinded their eyes, so that they mistook land for water and water for land, and in this way many a good ship was totally lost. At the first war-feast, when all her country-men were armed, she brought casks of beer, which she had drugged. When they were all drunk, she mounted her warhorse, leaning her head upon her spear. Sunrise could not be more beautiful. When she saw that the eyes of all were fixed upon her, she opened her lips and said:

Sons and daughters of Frya, you know that in these last times we have suffered much loss and misery because the sailors no longer come to buy our paper, but you do not know what the reason of it is. I have long kept silence about it, but can do so no longer. Listen, then, my friends, that you may know on which side to show your teeth. On the other side of the Scheldt, where from time to time there come ships from all parts, they make now paper from pumpkin leaves, by which they save flax and outdo us. Now, as the making of paper was always our principal industry, the mother willed that people should learn it from us; but Min-erva has bewitched all the people – yes, bewitched, my friends – as well as all our cattle that died lately. I must come out with it. If I were not Burgtmaagd, I should know what to do. I should burn the witch in her nest.

As soon as she had uttered these words she sped away to her citadel; but the drunken people were so excited that they did not stop to weigh what they had heard. In mad haste they hurried over the Sandfal, and as night came on

108

they burst into the citadel. However, Kalta again missed her aim; for Min-erva, her maidens, and her lamp were all saved by the alertness of the seamen.

WE NOW COME TO THE HISTORY OF JON

Jon, Jôn, Jhon, Jan, are all the same name, though the pronunciation varies, as the seamen like to shorten everything to be able to make it easier to call. Jon – that is, 'Given' – was a sea-king, born at Alberga, who sailed from the Flymeer with a fleet of 127 ships fitted out for a long voyage, and laden with amber, tin, copper, cloth, linen, felt, otter-skins, beaver and rabbit skins. He would also have taken paper from here, but when he saw how Kalta had destroyed the citadel he became so angry that he went off with all his people to Flyburgt, and out of revenge set fire to it. His admiral and some of his people saved the lamp and the maidens, but they could not catch Sijrhed (or Kalta). She climbed up on the furthest battlement, and they thought she must be killed in the flames; but what happened? While all her people stood transfixed with horror, she appeared on her steed more beautiful than ever, calling to them, 'To Kalta!' Then the other Schelda people poured out towards her. When the seamen saw that, they shouted, 'We are for Min-erva!' from which arose a war in which thousands were killed.

At this time Rosamond the mother, who had done all in her power by gentle means to preserve peace, when she saw how bad it was, made short work of it. Immediately she sent messengers throughout all the districts to call a general levy, which brought together all the defenders of the country. The landsmen who were fighting were all caught, but Jon with his seamen took refuge on board his fleet, taking with him the two lamps, as well as Min-erva and the maidens of both the citadels. Helprik, the chief, summoned him to appear; but while all the soldiers were on the other side of the Scheldt, Jon sailed back to the Flymeer, and then straight to our islands. His fighting men and many of our people took women and children on board, and when Jon saw that he and his people would be punished for their misdeeds, he secretly took his departure. He did well, for all our islanders and the other Scheldt people who had been fighting were transported to Britain. This step was a mistake, for now came the beginning of the end. Kalta, who, people said, could go as easily on the water as on the land, went to the mainland and on to Missellia.[3] Then came the Gauls out of the Mediterranean Sea with their ships to Cadiz, and along all our coasts, and fell upon Britain; but they could not make any good footing there, because the government was powerful and the exiles were still Frisians. But now came Kalta and said: You were born free, and for small offences have been sent away, not for your own improvement, but to get tin by your labour. If you wish to be free again, and take my advice, and live under my care, come away. I will provide you with arms, and will watch over you. The news flew through the land like lightning, and before the carrier's wheel had made one revolution she was mistress of all the Thyriers,[4] in all our southern states as far as the Seine. She built herself a citadel on the high land to the north, and called it Kaltasburgh. It still exists under the name of Kerenak. From this castle she ruled as a true mother, against their will, not *for* her followers, but *over* them, who were thenceforth called Kelts.[5] The Gauls gradually obtained dominion over the whole of Britain, partly because they no longer had any citadel; secondly, because they had there no Burgtmaagden; and thirdly, because they had no real lamps. From all these causes the people could not learn anything. They were stupid and foolish, and having allowed the Gauls to rob them of their arms, they were led about like a bull with a ring in his nose.

3. Missellia – Marseilles.
4. Thyriers – Settlers from Tyre: possibly Phoenician-Frisians; followers of Thyr, son of Odin, who became Thor. But also, possibly, a name given to the tin-miners, and other workers in metal, as Thor was a blacksmith-god like Vulcan.
5. Kelts – Celts.

Ten years after Jon went away, there arrived three
ships in the Flymeer; the people cried Huzza! (What a
blessing!) and from their accounts the mother had this
written.

When Jon reached the Mediterranean Sea, the reports
of the Gauls had preceded him, so that on the nearest
Italian coast he was nowhere safe. Therefore he went
with his fleet straight over to Lybia. There the black men
wanted to catch them and eat them. At last they came to
Tyre, but Min-erva said, Keep clear, for here the air has
long been poisoned by the priests. The king was a des-
cendant of Teunis, as we were afterwards informed; but
as the priests wished to have a king, who, according to
their ideas, was of long descent, they deified Teunis, to the
vexation of his followers. After they had passed Tyre,
the Tyrians seized one of the rearmost ships, and as the
ship was too far behind us, we could not take it back
again; but Jon swore to be revenged for it. When night
came, Jon bent his course towards the distant Kreka-
landen. At last they arrived at a country that looked very
barren, but they found a harbour there. Here, said Min-
erva, we need not perhaps have any fear of princes or
priests, as they always look out for rich fat lands. When
they entered the harbour, there was not room for all the
ships, and yet most of the people were too cowardly to go
any further. Then Jon, who wished to get away, went with
his spear and banner, calling to the young people, to
know who would volunteer to share his adventures. Min-
erva did the same thing, but she wished to remain there.
The greater part stopped with Min-erva, but the young
sailors went with Jon. Jon took the lamp of Kalta and her
maidens with him. Min-erva retained her lamp and her
own maidens.

Between the near and the distant coasts of Italy Jon
found some islands, which he thought desirable. Upon the
largest he built a city in the wood between the mountains.

From the smaller islands he made expeditions for vengeance on the Tyrians, and plundered their ships and their lands. Therefore these islands were called Insulae Piratarum,[6] as well as Johannis Insulae.[7]

When Min-erva had examined the country which is called by the inhabitants Attica, she saw that the people were all goatherds, and that they lived on meat, wild roots, herbs and honey. They were clothed in skins, and had their dwellings on the slopes of the hills, wherefore they were called Hellingers. At first they ran away, but when they found out that we did not attack them, they came back and showed great friendship. Min-erva asked if we might settle there peaceably. This was agreed to on the condition that we should help them to fight against their neighbours, who came continually to carry away their children and to rob their dwellings. Then we built a citadel at an hour's distance from the harbour. By the advice of Min-erva, it was called Athens, because, she said, those who come after us ought to know that we are not here by cunning or violence, but were received as friends (âtha). While we were building the citadel the principal personages came to see us, and when they saw that we had no slaves it did not please them, and they gave her to understand it, as they thought that she was a princess. But Min-erva said, How did you get your slaves? They answered, We bought some and took others in war. Min-erva replied, If nobody would buy slaves they would not steal your children, and you would have no wars about it. If you wish to remain our allies, you will free your slaves. The chiefs did not like this, and wanted to drive us away; but the most enlightened of the people came and helped us to build our citadel, which was built of stone.

This is the history of Jon and of Min-erva.

When they had finished their story they asked respectfully for iron weapons; for, said they, our foes are powerful, but if we have good arms we can withstand them. When this had been agreed to, the people asked if Frya's

6. Islands of the Pirates.
7. John's Islands.

112

customs would flourish in Athens and in other parts or Greece. The mother answered, If the distant Greeks belong to the direct descent of Frya, then they will flourish; but if they do not descend from Frya, then there will be a long contention about it, because the carrier must make five thousand revolutions of his Juul before Finda's people will be ripe for liberty.

THIS IS ABOUT THE GEERTMEN

When Hellenia or Min-erva died, the priests pretended to be with us, and in order to make it appear so, they deified Hellenia. They refused to have any other mother chosen, saying that they feared there was no one among her maidens whom they could trust as they had trusted Min-erva, surnamed Nyhellenia.

But we would not recognise Min-erva as a goddess, because she herself had told us that no one could be perfectly good except the spirit of Wr-alda. Therefore we chose Geert Pyre's daughter for our mother. When the priests saw that they could not fry their herrings on our fire (have everything their own way), they left Athens, and said that we refused to acknowledge Min-erva as a goddess out of envy, because she had shown so much affection to the natives. Thereupon they gave the people statues of her, declaring that they might ask of them whatever they liked, as long as they were obedient to her. By these kinds of tales the stupid people were estranged from us, and at last they attacked us; but as we had built our stone city wall with two horns down to the sea, they could not get at us. Then, lo and behold! an Egyptian high priest, bright of eye, clear of brain, and enlightened of mind, whose name was Cecrops, came to give them advice.

When he saw that with his people he could not storm our wall, he sent messengers to Tyre. Thereupon there arrived three hundred ships full of wild mountain soldiers, which sailed unexpectedly into our haven while we were defending the walls. When they had taken our harbour, the wild soldiers wanted to plunder the village and our ships – one had already ravished a girl – but Cecrops would not permit it; and the Tyrian sailors, who still had Frisian blood in their veins, said, If you do that we will burn our ships, and you shall never see your mountains again. Cecrops, who had no inclination towards murder or devastation, sent messengers to Geert, requiring her to give up the citadel, offering her free exit with all her live and dead property, and her followers the same. The wisest of the citizens, seeing that they could not hold the citadel, advised Geert to accept at once, before Cecrops became furious and changed his mind. Three months afterwards Geert departed with the best of Frya's sons, and seven times twelve ships. Soon after they had left the harbour they fell in with at least thirty ships coming from Tyre with women and children. They were on their way to Athens, but then they heard how things stood there they went with Geert. The sea-king of the Tyrians brought them altogether through the strait which at that time ran into the Red Sea.[8] At last they landed at the Punjab, called in our language the Five Rivers, because five rivers flow together to the sea. Here they settled, and called it Geertmania. The King of Tyre afterwards, seeing that all his best sailors were gone, sent all his ships with his wild soldiers to catch them, dead or alive. When they arrived at the strait, both the sea and the earth trembled. The land was upheaved so that all the water ran out of the strait, and the muddy shores were raised up like a rampart. This happened on account of the virtues of the Geertmen, as every one can plainly understand.

Commentary

Min-erva was encountered for the first time in the writings of the sea-king Minno (See Chapter Six). There, she was already established in Athens and Minno recorded her somewhat cryptic philosophical exchanges with the priests, who at first sought to discredit and ridicule her.

In the foregoing episode, however, although it is placed later in the *Oera Linda Book*, we are taken back to an

8. Now the Suez Canal.

earlier period – 1603 B.C. – when Min-erva was still Burgt-maagd at Middelburg. We find her swapping barbs with the ambitious and unscrupulous Sijrhed, her counterpart across the West Schelde at Flyburgt. Annoyed at being placed only third in line of succession for the title of Eeremoeder, Sijrhed – dubbed Kalta by the mariners because of her 'mysterious' way of giving advice – tries to outdo the popular Min-erva.

What is most interesting here is that we see the origins of Min-erva's chosen symbols – the sheepdog and the owl. The dog, she says, guards both the shepherd and his flocks, while the owl keeps mice from devastating the fields. But, it will be recalled, when quizzed about these symbols much later by the priests of Attica (See Chapter Six), Min-erva gave quite different explanations. The dog, she told the Greeks, was symbolic of her own service to Frya: 'I must watch over Frya's flocks.' And when asked if the owl was a sign of her clear vision, Min-erva answered:

'No ... he reminds me that there are people on earth who, like him, have their homes in churches and holes, who go about in the twilight, not, like him, to deliver us from mice and other plagues, but to invent tricks to steal away the knowledge of other people, in order to take advantage of them, to make slaves of them, and to suck their blood like leeches.'

So we see, from her early days at Middelburg to her development as a philosopher in Athens, the symbol of the owl – in orthodox tradition representing Athena-Minerva's watchfulness and wisdom – in a subtly different light. Like all true mystical thinkers, Min-erva held back more meanings of her symbols than she gave out, and used the variants as it suited her.

As a result of the symbolic 'contest' between the two Burgtmaagden, Kalta, having lost face, turned to the Magyars to teach her conjuring or sorcery, while Min-erva continued her policy of truth and honesty. The *Oera Linda Book* does not say so in so many words – as is often the case throughout its text – but we have here a hint of the development of magic among the pre-historic European races. There is, we observe, magic both of the Left-Hand Path (Kalta), and of the Right-Hand (Min-erva). But more of this later in my forthcoming companion volume, *Secrets of Lost Atland*.

By trickery, treachery, guile and cunning Kalta, despite various setbacks, eventually became mistress of all the Thyriers, as far south as the Seine. She established a citadel of her own somewhere in the north and called it Kaltas-burgh. Her followers, we are told, thus became known as Kelts, or Celts.

The *Oera Linda Book* does not explain the name 'Thyriers', but as I have hinted in footnotes, it is quite likely that these people were Phoenician-Frisian-Magyars from Tyre, where a colony had been established since 2000 B.C. It will be recalled that Tyre was named Thyrhisburgt, on the insistence of the Magyar-Finns, who sailed there with Teunis. Thyr was 'one of their idols' and, in Norse mythology, was the son of Odin (Wodin). He later became Thor, god of thunder. Thor was a blacksmith, closely associated with Vulcan, and it was thought that the ringing and sparking of his hammer on a heavenly anvil caused thunder and lightning. It is quite possible, therefore, that the label 'Thyriers' in addition to signifying the descendants of Teunis's Frisian-Magyar-Finnish colonists in Phoenicia, also included metal-working peoples, like the tin-miners of Britain. For Kalta, it is related, won over the British exiles in the tin mines, by reminding them that, despite their crimes, they were all 'born free'.

Despite this consolidation of her supporters, however, the invading Gauls did eventually manage to wrest Britain from the Frisians. The *Oera Linda Book*'s explanation for their success is that (a) the Britons no longer had a citadel, (b) they were not properly superintended by a *bona fide* Burgt-maagd, having gone over to the renegade Kalta, and (c) 'because they had no *real lamps*'.

Like the allusion to Kalta's initiation into magic, the reference to these sacred lamps is, throughout the whole of the book, cryptic and guarded. I shall deal with the probable nature of the eternally-burning lamps later, in the forthcoming work, when I examine the occult traditions in relation to the Atland-Frisian culture.

It is disappointing, at this juncture, that nothing is said in the *Oera Linda Book* about some of the splendid cities which both the Frisians and the Gauls built in Europe. Some of the Frisian cities, particularly in southern Europe, were taken over by the Gauls and eventually lost to the Romans. I have space here to describe only two such cities.

The sites of two of their towns, Alesia and Bibtractis, have been excavated in France. The ruins are on Frisian foundations, laid down by a Frisian-Gaulish people. As the *Oera Linda Book* relates, there had been much intermarrying between the two peoples; the purity of Frisian science and religion was lost. These mixed people worshipped images of some of the reluctantly-deified priestesses and sea-kings, along with gods 'borrowed' from other nations.

When J. M. Ragon described these cities in *Orthodoxie Meconnique,* he was unaware of the fact that other writers had said the first builders were not pure Gauls. Of Alesia, now called St. Reine or St. Remy, and situated on the banks of the Ose and Oser, and whose destruction is an established fact in Celtic-Gaulish history, he wrote:

'Alesia was renowned for its learning and mysteries. . . . The ancient metropolis, founded two thousand years before Christ, was sacked in 270 and restored 40 years later by Constantine'.

Only a few remains of its ancient splendour may be seen today: the amphitheatre, capitol, and 17-metre high obelisk of granite, a high triumphal arch, catacombs, etc. These ruins throw surprising light upon the Frisian-Gaulish civilisation.

Ragon says: 'Caesar, as a barbarian worthy of Rome, had already accomplished the destruction of the Ancient Mysteries by the sack of the temples and their initiatory colleges, and by the massacre of the Initiates and Druids. Remained Rome; but she never had but the lesser mysteries, shadows of the Secret Sciences. The great Initiation was dead'.

The great *Mystery* was dead. Neither the Gauls, the Romans, nor the Christian elders knew the meaning of the saying that Minerva, the Divine Wisdom, was 'yet in the bosom of the Father when the Universe was given being'. It was an allusion to the fact that every great prophet was a manifestation of the eternal spirit of God – the Frisian Wr-alda – that each was informed by the same power and came to advance human society and enlighten the souls of men with teaching and revelations matched and suited to the particular ages in which they lived.

Ragon indicates in his book how the monotheist religion of the Frisians had become lost in the worship of a pantheon of many gods, of mixed races, when he tells of the city of Bibtractis:

'Bibtractis, the mother of science, the soul of the early nations, a town equally famous for its sacred colleges of Druids [Caesar claimed that the Druids were trained in England], its civilisation, its schools in which 40,000 students were taught philosophy, literature, grammar, jurisprudence, medicine, astrology, occult sciences, architecture, etc . . .'.

Bibtractis rivalled Thebes, Memphis, Athens and Rome:

'It possessed an amphitheatre surrounded by colossal statues, and accommodating 100,000 spectators, a capital, temples of Janus, Pluto, Proserpine, Jupiter, Apollo, Minerva, Cybele, Venus and Anubis; and in the midst of those sumptuous edifices the Naumachy, with its vast basin, an incredible construction, a gigantic work wherein floated boats and galleys devoted to naval games; then a *Champ de Mars*, an acqueduct, fountains, public baths; finally, fortifications and walls, the construction of which dated from the heroic ages'.

The antiquity of these walls – more than one-thousand years before the Druids came to Europe – demonstrates their Frisian origin. The list of temples, meanwhile, illustrates how the later Gaulish-Frisian peoples mixed their religious metaphors: Janus (Roman), Pluto (Greek), Proserpine (Greek), Jupiter (Roman), Apollo (Greek), Minerva (Greek-Frisian), Cybele (Greek), Venus (Roman), and Anubis (Egyptian).

Some of the rolls and manuscripts of these cities were preserved in libraries, but were destroyed by the Romans who sacked them.

In the next section of the *Oera Linda Book* – relating the adventures of Jon – we are given yet another instance of the Frisians' distaste for the deification of their priestesses and sea-kings. Min-erva advises Jon to steer clear of Tyre, where the descendants of Teunis and his mixed followers have deified the sea-king and become corrupt and decadent.

Min-erva is then left ashore at Attica, where she founded the citadel of Athens, while Jon sails on among the Aegean Islands upon some of which he settles. From there he makes raiding parties on the Tyrians who had stolen one of his ships.

Back in Attica, we are given the explanation for the naming of Athens – from *âtha*, the old Frisian word for 'friends'. Following the account of the building of the stone citadel – prototype of the Parthenon – there is a peculiar passage indicating that this history, of Jon and Min-erva, was being related to someone else.

It begins, 'When they had finished their story ...' Before continuing with the account of Geert and the driving out of the Frisians from Athens, this brief interlude contains the first of three prophecies made in the *Oera Linda Book*.

It says 'the people asked if Frya's customs would flourish in Athens and in other parts of Greece'. The 'mother' answers that as long as the Greeks remained direct descendants of Frya they would flourish, but that if they were not, there would be a prolonged struggle. She adds, 'because the carrier must make five thousand revolutions of his Juul before Finda's people will be ripe for liberty'.

As can be seen from the account that follows, after Min-erva's death the Frisian colonists had trouble preserving their monotheistic faith because the priests wanted to deify Min-erva. Eventually, they were attacked by Finda's people – 'wild mountain soldiers' – and driven away.

But, according to the prophecy, Finda's people would not be ripe for liberty for another five thousand years – 'the carrier must make five thousand revolutions of his Juul'. Whether this five thousand year period dates from the time

119

that Kalta made war upon Min-erva (1630 B.C.) or from the (undated) time of the passage in which the prophecy is contained, is not made clear.

It is my guess that it relates to some future time when the human race will have no need of priests, rulers and laws, because truth, honesty of purpose and a sense of worldwide human fellowship will have established themselves. It may refer to the 'Great Peace' forecast by the Baha'i Prophet, Baha'u'llah, who said that another great Prophet would follow him in one thousand years. Baha'u'llah died in 1892. I will return to the subject of this and the other prophecies later.

Upon Min-erva's death, Geert, daughter of one Geert Pyle, was chosen by the Frisians as mother – despite the insistence of the priests upon the deification of Min-erva. The native Atticans, however, to whom Min-erva had shown great affection and kindness, were persuaded that she was indeed a goddess. As a result, the Frisians and their former native proto-Greek friends and allies became estranged.

The Egyptian priest who came upon the scene suddenly – Cecrops – took the side of the attacking natives who were trying to storm the harbour wall that the Frisians had built. It is interesting to note that this wall – 'with two horns down to the sea' – is said by the *Cambridge Ancient History* to have been built in A.D. 431 after the Peloponnesian Wars. It is likely, however, that the original Frisian structure with its 'horns' was the one destroyed during these wars with Sparta and that the new one was built upon the remaining foundations.

Despite his collusion with the natives, Cecrops, enigmatically, commands some respect with the writer of the Frisian narrative, being described as 'bright of eye, clear of brain, and enlightened of mind'. He sent to Tyre for reinforcements and their 'wild mountain soldiers' succeeded in taking the harbour while the Frisians were busy defending the landward side of the fortification.

The humanitarian-minded Cecrops offered Geert and her followers free, unmolested egress from Athens and, eventually, they sailed off, joining up with women and children in

120

Tyrian ships who had originally been heading for Athens. The unnamed sea-king of the Tyrians guided them through a strait leading from the Mediterranean into the Red Sea – an interesting reference to a natural route between the Sinai Peninsula and the Egyptian mainland, on the site of what is now the Suez Canal. The fugitives eventually landed in the Punjab, where they settled, calling it Geertmania, after their 'mother'.

Some time after this – the *Oera Linda Book* is not specific, although it must have been fairly soon after their settlement – some natural calamity occurred, possibly an earthquake, which closed up this natural strait into the Red Sea. For when the King of the Tyrians tried to pursue the Frisians and the Tyrians who had accompanied them, the earth and sea trembled, the water ran out of the strait and he could not get through from the Mediterranean.

The final sentence of this section although at first somewhat oblique, probably signifies that the Geertmen, as the Punjab settlers came to be known, regarded the natural phenomenon that prevented their pursuit as a manifestation of Wr-alda's spirit, looking after Frya's people.

'This happened,' says the text, 'on account of the virtues of the Geertmen as every one can plainly understand.'

Another possible interpretation, however, might be that the Geertmen were, like Moses, imbued with some strange powers, which allowed them to cause the upheaval preventing the Tyrian King's pursuit. Such considerations, however, will best be examined later when we look at the occult aspects of the Frisian's religion and sciences, in the forthcoming sequel.

CHAPTER TEN

THE ADVENT OF ULYSSES

The next section of the *Oera Linda Book* deals with an episode involving the Greek hero Ulysses, whose adventures Homer traced in *The Odyssey*. There also appears in this chapter a Burgtmaagd named Kaat, but nicknamed Kalip, who is undoubtedly the same as the beguiling 'goddess' Calypso who, according to Homer, tried to persuade Ulysses, or Odysseus, to remain with her in her cave sanctuary.

IN THE YEAR ONE THOUSAND AND FIVE[1] AFTER ATLAND WAS SUBMERGED, THIS WAS INSCRIBED ON THE EASTERN WALL OF FRYASBURGT

After twelve years had elapsed without our seeing any Italians in Almanland, there came three ships, finer than any that we possessed or had ever seen.

On the largest of them was a king of the Jonischen Islands,[2] whose name was Ulysses, the fame of whose wisdom was great. To him a priestess had prophesied that he should become the king of all Italy provided he could obtain a lamp that had been lighted at the lamp in Texland. For this purpose he had brought great treasures with him, above all jewels for women more beautiful than had ever been seen before. They were from Troy, a town that the Greeks[3] had taken. All these treasures he offered to the mother, but the mother would have nothing to do with him. At last, when he found that there was nothing to be obtained from her, he went to Walhallagara.[4] There was established a Burgtmaagd whose name was Kaat, but who was commonly called Kalip, because her lower lip stuck out like a mast-head. Here he tarried for years, to the scandal of all that knew it. According to the report of the maidens, he obtained a lamp from her; but it did him no good, because when he got to sea his ship was lost, and he was taken up naked and destitute by another ship. There was left behind this king a writer of pure Frya's

1. 2193−1005=1188 B.C.
2. Jonischen Islands: This could refer to the Aegean Islands, where Jon had established his bases.
3. This undoubtedly refers to the Mycenaeans of different city states: there were no 'Greeks' when Troy was taken.
4. Walcheren,

ALEUTIAN ISLANDS

KURILSKIVE
OSTROVA

ALASKA

CANADA

ARCTIC OCEAN
CRATER

N.P.

ASIA
U.S.S.R.

INVASION
OF THE
MAGY FINNS

GREENLAND

ICELAND

ARCTIC
CIRCLE

NORWAY
SWEDEN

FINLAND

EUROPE

BRITISH ISLES

NETHERLANDS

GERMANY

FRANCE

Arctic Crater caused by the
explosion of a great asteroid
followed by volcanic activity
and earthquakes which sank
Atland and broke up ancient
northern continents.

The Oronteus Finaeus World Map of 1532.

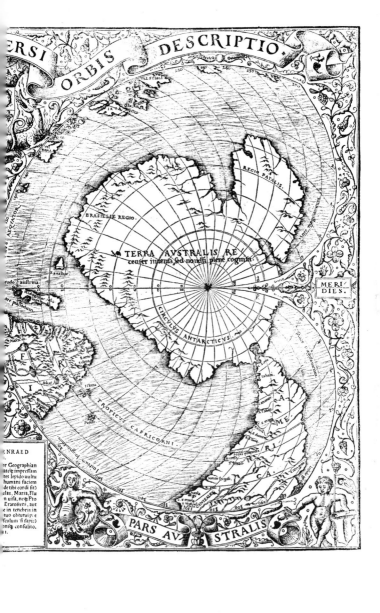

The seven inches high seated terracotta sculpture from Jugoslavia (dated before 4000 B.C.) may have been made to perpetuate the memory of the Great Mother Frya. It is reasonable to suppose that the tall blue-eyed Mother-Founder of the Atland peoples and nations was venerated wherever her Tex and advice were followed in Europe and elsewhere. It is almost a certainty that her image was held in veneration and was in every household shrine. These images were not the plump curves of the Earth Mother of a much earlier time, but small graceful baked-clay figurines, large, very carefully modelled heads and busts, or beautifully executed seated ladies. They have been found in great numbers in settlement debris from 5000 to 2500 B.C. in Jugoslavia, Bulgaria, Romania, on the borders of Russia and elsewhere. The design is repeated again and again, quite obviously from an original pattern which had been carefully followed to perpetuate the memory of a great personage.

In my drawing I have sought to highlight some of the details of one of these master-pieces of prehistoric art. Note the symbolism of the spiral life-force in the elegant helmet coiffure, the convex all-seeing eyes, the prominent nose and arms akimbo in the ancient posture of authority. It may indeed be an impressive remembrance of the Great Mother and the reverence given to her name and the freedom and righteousness enjoyed under her Tex. The brilliant pendant may represent her perpetual light and wisdom.

The Disk of Phaistos

Since going to press notice has been received that this most famous example of ancient picture script has been decoded by Vladimir Georgiev and will appear in the journal *Balkan Linguistics*. In these comments I predicted that when this mysterious disk was deciphered it would confirm what the sea-king Minno said about his visit to the island of Crete. The story it tells does just this. About 1100 B.C. it is believed that a tidal wave of migration swept the Eastern Mediterranean. A sea people from the far North and the Greek-speaking Dorians moved through Greece and Crete. (These were various tribes of Finda's people.) They sacked Troy, destroyed the Hittite empire (a mixed people of Finda folk and Frisians) and forced the Philistines to settle on the coast of Canaan. The migration and the destruction it caused left many unsolved mysteries in its wake, mysteries to which the *Oera Linda Book* provides answers.

The migration began long before 1100 B.C., with the sinking of Atland, and after a few hundred years slowed down to begin again in an intensified form with new upheavals of the earth and the sinking of islands and sea coasts.

Georgiev claims that the disk is written in Luwian, one of the languages of the Hittites. The Luwians were originally on the banks of the Danube, then spread south to settle on the southern coast of Asia Minor. Georgiev's reading of the disk places them in control of part of Crete in 1700 B.C.

Now the 241 signs on the disk in no way resemble the scripts of the Frisians, confirming that when the Magyars overran the banks of the Danube and mixed with the Frisians they invented a new form of writing and used it for secret recording and to confuse the people.

Santadimuwa, whose name is stamped on the disk, may have been a merchant prince of Phaistos when Minno arrived in Crete. When his serfs learned of freedom and the duties of princes from Minno, Santadimuwa's wealth and power was threatened, consequently his recording of Minno's activities gives his own personal point of view. One side of the disk tells of the tribal dissatisfaction and in-fighting and other instances of which Minno tells. His Cretean name is given as Yara. The disk says: When Yara's campaign failed he was banished to a castle. Afterwards he swore he would cause the prince no trouble. 'Yara gathered corn, ensured me an existence without worries, and he would cause me no troubles because it was in his interest.' The friendly words seem like those Minno would have used, but we cannot imagine the prince leaving the banished trouble-maker free to cultivate the land. What actually happened must have been as Minno said. He remained in the land he had bought and the serfs who wanted the same freedom as his people came to his homestead (castle) for help and protection. Then, 'when the princes saw that they were about to lose their kingdoms they went to Minno to establish a code of laws'. But the people got no real freedom and whilst appearing friendly to Minno and his people the princes sowed discord and tried to poison him because he spoke of the duties of princes. So Minno left Crete on a ship from Flyland, perhaps leaving behind some of his crew who were Hittites and who may have agreed to write Santadimuwa's version of the history and the sea-king who gave laws to the people of Crete. Here we have an explanation of the mysterious script being used on the disk; it is quite unlike the A and B script used at that time in Crete. The record of Minno's visit was concealed in secret writings and his name changed, but because Minno was known to be the true maker of the laws, some of the princes made the name their own—that is, if we accept the legends of Greece as containing this grain of truth.

The deciphering of the disk, even in its biased account, is further proof that the *Oera Linda Book* is a true record of 2000 years of lost history. It also proves the truth of the migrations in the second millennium before Christ and those given in the Bible.

In 2000 B.C. the Frisian nations had spread far and wide. The bodies of a man and woman seven feet tall were recently found in a tomb in the Northern Caucasus by Soviet archaeologists. They had lived in the so-called early bronze age. Whether the same can be said of the proudly poised hunters of Sardinia of 1700 B.C. whose little bronze statues have been found, is doubtful. Yet it is interesting to note that these people built interlocking stone houses and broches like those in the Orkneys—a part of the penal island of Atland, and that their proud commanding faces and noses clearly resemble those of the Great Mother and the faces on the maps of the sea-kings mentioned in Appendix C.

As for the geological disturbances which caused the migrations, Dr. Nicholas Fleming of the Institute of Oceanography discovered in 1967 twenty of the sunken cities off the coast of Peloponnese. Some were no doubt on the lost islands shown in the maps of the sea-kings.

ÁTÁIR VNDE STAT IS INUT ÁA WAGAR ÁERE
WÁRA-BURCÁ WRITEN.

ÁWAT ÁIR BOPPA STAT SEND ÁI TÉKNA ÁON
ÁATIOL. ÁAT IS ÁAT FORMA SINNEBILD VVRAL
DAS. AK TON T.ANÁIA ISTÁA T BIIIN VVERUT
TID KEM. ÁAT IS ÁINE KRODER ÁER EVA MIÁ
ÁAT IOL MOROMMEÁLAPE. ÁANA ÁEÁ TRIA
ÁAT STAND SKRIÁT ÁAT ÁIA BRUKTE TO ÁIRA
TEX. ÁA TASTA ERE MODER WERE ÁEÁ ÁIU
.R ÁAT RUN ISTÁA ÁÁ PANDE SKRITE ÁON MAK
AD. ÁER WITKENIA. ÁAT IS SEKENIA. OOD.
TREIÁ. ÁENT ALDA. ÁEÁ ÁER ASVNDER OANA
TEL NOMAR ÁON MAKAD ÁAR STAND AND
RUN SKRIÁT BEDE. TIS ÁERVMBE NAVT TO DROK
ÁAT WI IERLIKS ENIS TEST VR TRIA. WÁ MWO
ON WRALDA EVO ÁANK TOWIA ÁAT ÁIS IN
OAST SA ÁERDE. IN VR VSA EÁLA ÁEÁ TARA
IGÁN. VNDER ÁI TATID ÁEÁ TINDA AKEN SKR
HÁUR TVNDEN. MEN ÁAT WERE SA ÁAGÁÁR
ANDE AND TUL MIÁ TRISLA AND KROLUM
ÁAT ÁA ATERKVMANDA ÁEROÁ ÁIU BITIVD
NESE RIA VR LEREN ÁAVE. ÁERNEI ÁAVON
ÁIA VS SKRIÁT LERED BINOMA ÁA TINNA
ÁA ÁÝPIAR AND ÁA KREKA LANDAR. MEN ÁIA
NISTON NAVT OOD ÁATET ÁON ET IOL MAKAD
WAS AND ÁAT.T ÁERVMBE ALTID SKREVEN
X MAKAD~

Page 45 of the manuscript of the book of Adela's Followers.

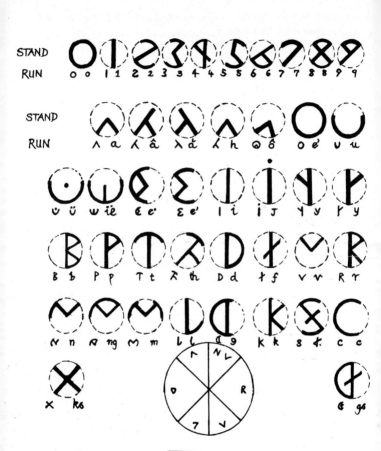

blood, born in the new harbour of Athens, who wrote for us what follows about Athens, from which may be seen how truly the mother Hellicht[5] spoke when she said that the customs of Frya could never take firm hold in Athens.

From the other Greeks you will have heard a great deal of bad about Cecrops, because he was not in good repute; but I dare affirm that he was an enlightened man, very renowned both among the inhabitants and among us, for he was against oppression, unlike the other priests, and was virtuous, and knew how to value the wisdom of distant nations. Knowing that, he permitted us to live according to our own Asegaboek.[6] There was a story current that he was favourable to us because he was the son of a Frisian girl and an Egyptian priest: the reason of this was that he had blue eyes, and that many of our girls had been stolen and sold to Egypt, but he never confirmed this. However it may have been, certain it is that he showed us more friendship than all the other priests together. When he died, his successors soon began to tear up our charters, and gradually to enact so many unsuitable statutes that at long last nothing remained of liberty but the shadow and the name. Besides, they would not allow the laws to be written so that the knowledge of them was hidden from us. Formerly all the cases in Athens were pleaded in our language, but afterwards in both languages, and at last in the native tongue only. At first the men of Athens only married women of our own race, but the young men as they grew up with the girls of the country took them to wife. The bastard children of this connection were the handsomest and cleverest in the world; but they were likewise the wickedest, wavering between the two parties, paying no regard to laws or customs except where they suited their own interests. As long as a ray of Frya's spirit existed, all the building materials were for common use, and

5. This may refer to the prophecies contained in the passage (See Chapter 9) linking the story of Jon and Minerva and that of the Geertmen.

6. Asegaboek – this term is not explained, but in its context would appear to refer to a social and moral code.

no one might build a house larger or better than his neighbours; but when some degenerate townspeople got rich by sea-voyages and by the silver that their slaves got in the silver countries, they went to live out on the hills or in the valleys. There, behind high enclosures of trees or walls, they built palaces with costly furniture, and in order to remain in good odour with the nasty priests, they placed there likenesses of false gods and unchaste statues. Sometimes the dirty priests and princes wished for the boys rather than the girls, and often led them astray from the paths of virtue by rich presents or by force. Because riches were more valued by this lost and degenerate race than virtue or honour, one sometimes saw boys dressed in splendid flowing robes, to the disgrace of their parents and maidens, and to the shame of their own sex. If our simple parents came to a general assembly at Athens and made complaints, a cry was raised, Hear, hear! there is a sea-monster going to speak. Such is Athens become, like a morass in a tropical country full of leeches, toads, and poisonous snakes, in which no man of decent habits can set his foot.

Commentary

It is remarkable to see a classical Greek hero cropping up in the history of a forgotten people of Northern Europe. And what is even more remarkable is the parallel of the names Kalip and Calypso, associated with this hero. In *The Odyssey*, however, there is no mention of Odysseus (Ulysses) going in search of a sacred lamp when he reaches the home of Calypso. The poet Homer simply has Odysseus washed up on the Island of Ogygia – another of the idyllic legendary lands to the north associated with the Hyperborean tradition. Calypso's island home is one of many of Odysseus's ports-of-call during his weary wanderings after the Trojan War.

' "Nine days of drifting followed; but in the night of the tenth the gods washed me up on the Isle of Ogygia, the home of the fair Calypso, that formidable goddess with a woman's voice; and she received me kindly and looked after me",'

Odysseus says. (E. V. Rieu translation: Penguin Classics.)

There, Odysseus sojourned for years with the beautiful goddess, who kept him in her vaulted cave. Eventually, Zeus, chief of the gods, bows to the pleas of Athene and decides it is time for Odysseus to be allowed to leave. The messenger Hermes is sent to order Calypso to let the hero go free. Odysseus has to build his own boat and eventually sets sail again, hoping to return to his kingdom of Ithaca and his beloved wife, Penelope.

In the *Oera Linda* version of the story, Ulysses is not ship-wrecked but arrives in one of three fine ships, to the admiration of the Frisian chronicler. He has been told by some unnamed priestess that if he obtains the eternally-burning lamp at Texland, he will become the King of all Italy. When he gets no co-operation from the Eeremoeder, he then takes up with the Burgtmaagd Kalip and, judging from the disapproving tone of the narrative, lived with her for some years.

There is, however, no mention of what happened to Kalip as a result of her indiscretion in breaking her vows of chastity; we are not told whether she was stripped of her office, banished or punished in some other way. The main concern of the story seems to be that Ulysses did not succeed in his mission. He got a lamp, but it was no use to him. He sailed away, but his ship was lost and he was picked up destitute.

From the Frisian-born writer whom Ulysses left behind, we then hear more of the mysterious Egyptian high-priest Cecrops, whom Geert and her people encountered in Athens. The writer offers some vindication of his character by telling of his tolerant attitude towards the Frisian settlers in Athens. And it is here that we are given the suggestion that Cecrops might have had Frisian blood in his veins – possibly, he is the son of an Egyptian priest and a Frisian girl. At any rate, he is said to have blue eyes.

Next, the unnamed writer paints an unpleasant picture of the degeneration of the Athenians, through the abandonment, or gradual erosion of the Frisian codes of living. It is the kind of thing that Frya's laws were designed to prevent, in insisting that the Frisian race be kept pure and that young men should marry by the age of twenty-five. Homosexuality, incest, greed, gross materialism and slavery are fostered, a way of life that was carried forward to the years of the Greek city states, when the psychological aberrations known as 'Greek love' became the acceptable norm. The intellectual, moral and physical decline made it easier for the Romans to subject the Greeks to domination later.

CHAPTER ELEVEN

THE END OF THE MOTHERS

The next section of the *Oera Linda Book* gives an account of how the Magyars overran Denmark and the ultimate fate of their priest-king, the Magy. It forms the last section of the writings of Adela.

THIS IS INSCRIBED IN ALL OUR CITADELS

How our Denmark[1] was lost to us 1,602 years after the submersion of Atland.[2] Through the mad wantonness of Wodin, Magy had become master of the east part of Scandinavia. They dare not come over the hills and over the sea. The mother would not prevent it. She said, I see no danger in their weapons, but much in taking the Scandinavians back again, because they are so degenerate and spoilt. The general assembly were of the same opinion. Therefore it was left to him. A good hundred years ago Denmark began to trade; they gave their iron weapons in exchange for gold ornaments, as well as for copper and iron-ore. The mother sent messengers to advise them to have nothing to do with this trade. There was danger to their morals in it, and if they lost their morals they would soon lose their liberty. But the Denmarkers paid no attention to her. They did not believe that they could lose

1. Denmark – from Dêna marka, the 'low marches'.
2. 2193 – 1602 = 591 B.C.

their morals, therefore they would not listen to her. At last they were at a loss themselves for weapons and necessaries, and this difficulty was their punishment. Their bodies were brilliantly adorned, but their cupboards and their sheds were empty. Just one hundred years after the first ship with provisions sailed from the coast, poverty and want made their appearance, hunger spread her wings all over the country, dissension marched proudly about the streets and into the houses, charity found no place, and unity departed. The child asked its mother for food; she had no food to give, only jewels. The women applied to the counts; the counts had nothing to give, or if they had, they hid it away. Now the jewels must be sold, but while the sailors were away for that purpose, the frost came and laid a plank upon the sea and the strait (the Sound). When the frost had made the bridge, vigilance ceased in the land, and treachery took its place. Instead of watching on the shores, they put their horses in their sledges and drove off to Scandinavia. Then the Scandinavians, who hungered after the land of their forefathers, came to Denmark. One bright night they all came. Now, they said, we have a right to the land of our fathers; and while they were fighting about it, the Finns came to the defenceless villages and ran away with the children. As they had no good weapons, they lost the battle, and with it their freedom, and Magy became master. All this was the consequence of their not reading Frya's Tex, and neglecting her counsels. There are some who think that they were betrayed by the counts, and that the maidens had long suspected it; but if any one attempted to speak about it, his mouth was shut up by golden chains.

We can express no opinion about it, we can only say to you, Do not trust too much to the wisdom of your princes or of your maidens but if you wish to keep things straight, everybody must watch over his own passions, as well as the general welfare.

Two years afterwards Magy himself came with a fleet of light boats to steal the lamp from the mother of Texland. This wicked deed he accomplished one stormy night, while the wind roared and the hail rattled against the windows. The watchman on the tower hearing the noise, lighted his torch. As soon as the light from the tower fell upon the bastion, he saw that already armed men had got over the wall.

He immediately gave the alarm, but it was too late. Before the guard was ready, there were two thousand people battering the gate. The struggle did not last long. As the guard had not kept a good watch, they were overwhelmed. While the fight was going on, a rascally Finn stole into the chamber of the mother, and would have done her violence. She resisted him, and threw him down against the wall. When he got up, he ran his sword through her: If you will not have me, you shall have my sword. A Danish soldier came behind him and clave his head in two. There came from it a stream of black blood and a wreath of blue flame.

The Magy had the mother nursed on his own ship. As soon as she was well enough to speak clearly, the Magy told her that she must sail with him, but that she should keep her lamp and her maidens, and should hold a station higher than she had ever done before. Moreover, he said that he should ask her, in presence of all his chief men, if he would become the ruler of all the country and people of Frya; that she must declare and affirm this, or he would let her die a painful death. Then, when he had gathered all his chiefs around her bed, he asked, in a loud voice, Frana, since you are a prophetess, shall I become ruler over all the lands and people of Frya? Frana did as if she took no notice of him; but at last she opened her lips, and said: My eyes are dim, but the other light dawns upon my soul. Yes, I see it. Hear Irtha,[3] and rejoice with me. At the time of the submersion of Atland, the first spoke of the Juul stood at the top. After that it went down, and our freedom with it. When two spokes, or two thousand years, shall have rolled down, the sons shall arise who have been bred of the fornication of the princes and priests with the

3. Irtha – the Earth.

128

people, and shall witness against their fathers. They shall all fall by murder, but what they have proclaimed shall endure, and shall bear fruit in the bosoms of able men, like good seed which is laid in thy lap. Yet a thousand years shall the spoke descend, and sink deeper in darkness, and in the blood shed over you by the wickedness of the princes and priests. After that, the dawn shall begin to glow. When they perceive this, the false princes and priests will strive and wrestle against freedom; but freedom, love, and unity will take the people under their protection, and rise out of the vile pool. The light which at first only glimmered shall gradually become a flame. The blood of the bad shall flow over your surface, but you must not absorb it. At last the poisoned animals shall eat it, and die of it. All the stories that have been written in praise of the princes and priests shall be committed to the flames. Thenceforth your children shall live in peace. When she had finished speaking she sank down.

The Magy, who had not understood her, shrieked out, I have asked you if I should become master of all the lands and people of Frya, and now you have been speaking to another. Frana raised herself up, stared at him, and said, Before seven days have passed your soul shall haunt the tombs with the nightbirds, and your body shall be at the bottom of the sea. Very good, said the Magy, swelling with rage; say that I am coming. Then he said to his executioners, Throw this woman overboard. This was the end of the last of the mothers. We do not ask for revenge. Time will provide that; but a thousand thousand times we will call with Frya, Watch! watch! watch!

HOW IT FARED AFTERWARDS WITH THE MAGY

After the murder of the mother, he brought the lamp and the maidens into his own ship, together with all the booty that he chose. Afterwards he went up the Flymeer because he wished to take the maiden of Medeasblik or Stavoren and instal her as mother; but there they were on their guard. The seafaring men of Stavoren and Alderga would gladly have gone to Jon, but the great fleet was out on a distant voyage; so they proceeded in their small fleet to Medeasblik, and kept themselves concealed in a sheltered place behind trees. The Magy approached Medeasblik in broad daylight; nevertheless, his men boldly stormed the citadel. But as they landed from the boats, our people sallied forth from the creek, and shot their arrows with balls of burning turpentine upon the fleet. They were so well aimed that many of the ships were instantly set on fire. Those left to guard the ships shot at us, but they could not reach us. When at last a burning ship drifted towards the ship of the Magy, he ordered the man at the helm to sheer off, but this man was the Dane who had cleft the head of the Finn. He said, You sent our Eeremoeder to the bottom of the sea to say that you were coming; In the bustle of the fight you might forget it; now I will take care that you keep your word. The Magy tried to push him off, but the sailor, a real Frisian and strong as an ox, clutched his head with both hands, and pitched him into the surging billows. Then he hoisted up his brown shield and sailed straight to our fleet. Thus the maidens came unhurt to us; but the lamp was extinguished, and no one knew how that had happened. When those on the uninjured ships heard that the Magy was drowned, they sailed away, because their crews were Danes. When the fleet was far enough off, our sailors turned and shot their burning arrows at the Finns. When the Finns saw that, and found that they were betrayed, they fell into confusion and lost all discipline and order. At this moment the garrison sallied forth from the citadel. Those who resisted were killed, and those who fled found their death in the marshes of the Krylinger wood.

POSTSCRIPT

When the sailors were in the creek, there was a wag from Stavoren among them, who said, Medea may well laugh if we rescue her from her citadel. Upon this, the

130

maidens gave to the creek the name Medea meilakkia.[4] The occurrences that happened after this everybody can remember. The maidens ought to relate it in their own way, and have it well inscribed. We consider that our task is fulfilled. Hail!

THE END OF THE BOOK[5]

Commentary

Once again the *Oera Linda Book* contains a prophecy. Frana, the doomed Eeremoeder of Texland, said that the sons of evil princes and priests would turn against their fathers and many of them would die in the wars they caused, to be followed by others, who would for a thousand years shed their blood over the earth. Then the light of freedom would glimmer, cause more bloodshed, after which 'your children shall live in peace'.

She said the first wars of princes and priests would begin two thousand years after the submergence of Atland. According to the date given by Hiddo Over de Linda, 2193 B.C., this would mean around 193 B.C. This date roughly covers a period when the peoples of Europe, irritated by the encroachments of the Romans upon their lands and the restrictions imposed on their liberties, joined forces and attacked Rome. They were beaten, but with much bloodshed.

At this time also, bad feeling had developed between Rome and Carthage. In 221 B.C., Hannibal was sworn by his father to perpetual enmity with Rome. The Punic Wars followed. Rome was crushed by a series of smashing blows which placed Italy practically at the mercy of Hannibal. After a number of battles, Rome recovered her power. Hannibal, a fugitive, took poison.

Meanwhile Greece, victim of internal strife and decadence, had been in a state of complete anarchy since the death of Alexander the Great and fell an easy prey to Rome.

4. Lake of Medea's laughter.
5. This is the end of Adela's writings, but by no means the end of the *Oera Linda Book*.

131

Rome built her Empire – constantly torn by strife – at home and abroad. Rome lived by the sword and eventually died by a combination of the sword, its own internal evils and corruption. By the year A.D. 268 the empire was shaken and its frontiers threatened on all sides, then was divided into eastern and western empires. Finally, Constantine made himself the sole Emperor of an orientalised empire and adopted Christianity as the state religion, governed from Constantinople.

Time proved the truth of the prophecy. Frisian, Vandal, Goth, Hun, Angle and Saxon never ceased to struggle for freedom, and the remainder of the history of the Roman Empire is chaos. Charlemagne's vast empire, so-called Christendom, was ultimately divided by his grandsons, and the next centuries were occupied by struggles between kings and their feudal lords.

The events which were bearing out the prophecy continued. Scandinavians sailed from their homeland and established themselves in Normandy and south Italy; it was destined that one of these northmen would conquer England. In 1453 the Ottoman Turks captured Constantinople and then spread northward as far as the walls of Vienna.

The two thousand years, plus the further one thousand years of which the Eeremoeder spoke, drew to a close with the Christian monarchs fighting to extend their domains. The last thousand years had carried the nations of Europe 'deeper into darkness in the blood shed by wicked princes and priests', to the prophesied year of 1807. It was the beginning of the end of the old world which the Eeremoeder Frana, the prophet Daniel, Jesus and the sacred writings of Islam had all foretold.

Then, said the wounded Frana, 'the dawn [of freedom and justice] shall begin to glow'.

Note the sequence of events which followed.

'When they perceive this, the false princes and priests will strive and wrestle against freedom; but freedom, love and unity will take the people under their protection, and rise out of the vile pool. The light which at first only glimmered shall gradually become a flame. The blood of

132

the bad shall flow over your surface, but you must not absorb it. At last the poisoned animals [oppressive, warring kings and priests?] shall eat of it, and die of it. All the stories that have been written in praise of the princes and priests shall be committed to the flames. Thenceforth your children shall live in peace.'

And so it came to pass. The French Revolution was merely the labour pains of the old world, about to give birth to the new. Commenting on these prophecies in *Secret Cities of Old South America* (Rider & Co., 1950), Harold T. Wilkins wrote:

'The soldier-liberators of France put paid to the foul dungeons of the Holy Dominican Roman Catholic Inquisition, and prevented the Spanish inquisitors from burning the records of some of the horrible cases of lust and sadism in which these black Inquisitors, blasphemously invoked the name of their Prince of Peace and Charity to all men, had horribly tortured men, women and young children'.

Later, Napoleon was at war with England, but the people whose forefathers were Frisians – men of the North and of Germanic and Saxon blood – whom Frana had said were to take an important part in the birth of the new world, remained undefeated.

In his comments on the prophesies Wilkins points out that Charles II of Spain, late in the Eighteenth Century, expelled from all his dominions the 'subtle, sinister, and dangerous order of the Society of Jesus of Loyola'. This is the extent of his interpretation of historical events in the light of the prophecy. He may have been unaware of what was happening in barbarous Persia, a seed bed from which would blossom a flower of the Spirit whose presence was destined eventually to change the world.

For many years Persian sages had been foretelling the coming of a new Prophet. He came. His name was Ali Mohammed, born in 1819, and He became known as 'the Bab' which means 'the Gate'. When His message was made known and the Baha'i Faith was born in 1844 – as predicted a little more than three thousand years earlier – the earth was stained with the blood of more than two thousand Persians who told of the Bab's message of justice, peace and the unity of man under God. The Baha'i Faith claims to incorporate the best of all religions. Although the Bab claimed He was a manifestation of God and a prophet in His own right, He said His purpose was to announce the coming of an even greater prophet who was already alive at that time. The Bab was imprisoned and, after six years of ministry, died facing a military firing squad.

The Prophet yet to come was a Persian Nobleman who renounced power, position and great wealth to endure forty years of exile, suffering and imprisonment. His name was Bah'u'llah, which means the Glory of God. He said He came to fulfil the promises of all prophets before Him – to cause to be established on earth universal peace, and justice and security for all men. In another forthcoming book, I demonstrate in detail how the work of many prophets over a period of seven thousand years has been fulfilled in the coming of Baha'u'llah. I will repeat here only one of his revelations and a few historical events which are germane to the prophecy of the Frisian Eeremoeder Frana:

'The world's equilibrium hath been upset through the vibrating influence of this most great, this new World Order. Mankind's ordered life has been revolutionised through the agency of this unique, this wondrous System – the like of which mortal eyes have never witnessed'.

Of the new life which Frana foretold, Baha'u'llah announced:

'A new life is, *in this age*, stirring within all the people of the earth; and yet none hath discovered its cause or perceived its motive ... By My Self! *The day is approaching when We will have rolled up the world and all that is therein, and spread out a new order in its stead.* He, verily, is powerful over all things'. (My italics.)

Since He uttered and wrote down these words, a little over a century ago, a new world *has* been laid down before man and few have understood the cause and its motive. Science, knowledge, production, transport and communications have revolutionised the world, new social measures have raised the material standard of living in many nations, new forms

134

of government are being tried. And yet the very foundations of the world tremble, and mankind awaits in fear and trepidation a future which he cannot begin to visualise fully.

The chain of events began when Baha'u'llah wrote to the kings, rulers, leading clergy and peoples of the world, between 1867–73. He advised the kings and the Pope to cease piling up riches and armaments, to stop making war and oppressing their people; He enjoined them to meet in common assembly to work for peace and the relieving of the misery of the world. When they ignored Him He warned them of the calamity which would come; they would be toppled from their thrones, their empires would be broken up and many would lose their lives.

In His own lifetime fourteen kings lost their thrones, many of their kingdoms have vanished from the face of the earth and their empires are now only bad memories. Since Baha'u'llah's time (He died in 1892), ten other kings or emperors have vanished. The Pope who would not acknowledge Baha'u'llah as the One promised by Jesus, Pius IX, lost his empire (the Papal States) and became a prisoner in his own palace until he was given permission to leave by Mussolini during the Second World War. As for the Church, it has lost much of its power, credibility and influence over the people.

The Eeremoeder Frana, it seems, foretold the future correctly.

Although a prisoner for many years of His life, Baha'u'llah wrote works which would fill two hundred volumes, ensuring that no one could misuse His religion or misunderstand the spiritual concepts He pronounced, nor abuse the principles of worldwide social reform He laid down, designed to endure for a thousand years. He said no power on earth could prevent that which He had ordained: a World Assembly, established to maintain world justice; a world code of Human Rights and Responsibilities; a World Police Force, essentially to keep the peace; an International Court of Justice; World Education and Equality of the sexes; a Spiritual Code to determine and control the World Economy for the benefit of all.

135

It should become immediately apparent to the reader that these precepts are a development of those set down by Frya, the great law-maker who founded the Atland-Frisian civilisation.

All the above projected institutions, except the spiritual determinate, have been established or are in advanced stages of development, with of course many faults and failings.

Baha'u'llah foresaw this and, to ensure that His will should prevail, laid down for the Baha'i followers an order of administration, consisting of town and national Assemblies, guided and assisted by an International House of Justice.

These assemblies now form a Baha'i world community in which each member is dedicated to the task of promoting all that their prophet ordained. They are closely involved with the work of the organisations of the United Nations and are represented on some of their councils.

I have made this slight digression from the actual history of the Frisians mainly to indicate that no ideal or law for the benefit of mankind is ever irretrievably lost. It seems to be an immutable, natural law of human society that whatever may happen to people who hold such beliefs and ideals, that for which they lived – or even died – will spring forth again, each time more powerful and worthy.

Both the Eeremoëder Frana and Baha'u'llah said that mankind would enjoy world peace and security either in our own time or in that of our succeeding generation. Baha'u'llah referred to this as the Lesser Peace which should manifest around the end of this century, if I have interpreted His words correctly. The Greater Peace, the peace of the spirit of man with God, which he forecast, would take at least another thousand years. When the thousand years have ended yet another prophet, said Baha'u'llah, would emerge to lead humanity to an even more exalted goal.

CHAPTER TWELVE

ADELA'S ADVICE

Before passing on to the next narrative of the *Oera Linda Book* – the writings of Adelbrost and Apollonia – we turn now to what must have been the final public pronouncement of the Frisians' unofficial leader, Adela. Although in the actual text, this passage is placed at the very beginning of the Book of Adela's followers, chronologically, it comes between the death of the Eeremoeder Frana and the events related in the narrative of Adela's children, Adelbrost and his sister, Apollonia.

Thirty years after the day on which the Volksmoeder was murdered by the commander Magy, was a time of great distress. All the states that lie on the other side of the Weser had been wrested from us, and had fallen under the power of Magy, and it looked as if his power was to become supreme over the whole land. To avert this misfortune a general assembly of the people was summoned, which was attended by all the men who stood in good repute with the Maagden. Then at the end of three days the whole council was in confusion, and in the same position as when they came together. Thereupon Adela demanded to be heard, and said:

You all know that I was three years Burgtmaagd. You know also that I was chosen for Volksmoeder, and that I refused to be Volksmoeder because I wished to marry Apol; but what you do not know is, that I have watched everything that has happened, as if I had really been your Volksmoeder. I have constantly travelled about, observing what was going on. By that means I have become acquainted with many things that others do not know. You said yesterday that our relatives on the other side of the Weser were dull and cowardly; but I may tell you that the Magy has not won a single village from them by force of arms; but only by detestable deceit, and still more by the rapacity of their dukes and nobles.

Frya has said we must not admit amongst us any but free people; but what have they done? They have imitated our enemies, and instead of killing their prisoners, or letting them go free, they have despised the counsel of Frya, and have made slaves of them.

Because they have acted thus, Frya cared no longer to watch over them. They robbed others of their freedom, and therefore lost their own.

This is well known to you, but I will tell you how they came to sink so low. The Finn women had children. These grew up with our free children. They played and gamboled together in the fields, and were also together by the hearth.

There they learned with pleasure the loose ways of the Finns, because they were bad and new; and thus they became denationalised in spite of the efforts of their parents. When the children grew up, and saw that the children of the Finns handled no weapons, and scarcely worked, they took a distaste for work, and became proud.

The principal men and their cleverest sons made up to the wanton daughters of the Finns; and their own daughters, led astray by a bad example, allowed themselves to be beguiled by the handsome young Finns in derision of their depraved fathers. When the Magy found this out, he took the handsomest of his Finns and Magyars, and promised them 'red cows with golden horns' to let themselves be taken prisoners by our people in order to spread his doctrines. His people did even more. Children disappeared, were taken away to the uplands, and after they had been brought up in his pernicious doctrines, were sent back.

When these pretended prisoners had learned our language, they persuaded the dukes and nobles that they should become subject to the Magy – that then their sons would succeed to them without having to be elected. Those who by their good deeds had gained a piece of land in front of their house, they promised on their side should receive in addition a piece behind; those who had got a piece before and behind, should have a rondeel;[1] and

1. Rondeel – a complete circuit.

those who had a rondeel should have a whole freehold. If the seniors were true to Frya, then they changed their course, and turned to the degenerate sons. Yesterday there were among you those who would have called the whole people together, to compel the eastern states to return to their duty. According to my humble opinion, they would have made a great mistake. Suppose that there was a very serious epidemic among the cattle, would you run the risk of sending your own healthy cattle among the sick ones? Certainly not. Every one must see that doing that would turn out very badly for the whole of the cattle. Who, then, would be so imprudent as to send their children among a people wholly depraved? If I were to give you any advice, it would be to choose a new Volksmoeder. I know that you are in a difficulty about it, because out of the thirteen Burgtmaagden that we still have remaining, eight are candidates for the dignity; but I should pay no attention to that.

Teuntia, the Burgtmaagd of Medeasblik, who is not a candidate, is a person of knowledge and sound sense, and quite as attached to our people and our customs as all the rest together. I should farther recommend that you should visit all the citadels, and write down all the laws of Frya's Tex, as well as the histories, and all that is written on the walls, in order that it may not be destroyed with the citadels.

It stands written that every Volksmoeder and every Burgtmaagd shall have assistants and messengers – twenty-one maidens and seven apprentices.

If I might add more, I would recommend that all the respectable girls in the towns should be taught; for I say positively, and time will show it, that if you wish to remain true children of Frya, never to be vanquished by fraud or arms, you must take care to bring up your daughters as true Frya's daughters.

You must teach the children how great our country has been, what great men our forefathers were, how great we still are, if we compare ourselves to others.

You must tell them of the sea-heroes, of their mighty

deeds and distant voyages. All these stories must be told by the fireside and in the field, wherever it may be, in times of joy or sorrow; and if you wish to impress it on the brains and the hearts of your sons, you must let it flow through the lips of your wives and your daughters.

Adela's advice was followed.

So we see how, constantly harrassed and infiltrated by the inroads of the Magyars and Finns, the children of Frya desperately tried to preserve their crumbling culture. Frisian prisoners were enslaved, and, as Adela explains, intermarriage 'denationalised' their long and proud culture and traditions. In an effort to make the most of what remained, Adela reminded her people of the principles upon which their great nation had been founded – the laws of Frya. She implored them to choose for themselves a new Mother, someone who might give them the leadership and drive to re-establish what they once had. As a final resort, she advised them to copy down into histories the accounts of their sea-voyages, to recount these stories to their children as part of a revered heritage. 'Adela's advice was followed,' says the narrative – hence, the *Oera Linda Book* and, we are told elsewhere, other histories which have unfortunately not survived.

We do have, however, following this passage giving Adela's last speech to her people, a list of the officials in charge of the compilation of the book:

These are the Grevetmen under whose direction this book is composed:

Apol, Adela's husband; three times a sea-king; Grevetman of Ostflyland and Lindaoorden. The towns Liudgarda, Lindahem, and Stavia are under his care.

The Saxman Storo, Sytia's husband; Grevetman over the Hoogefennen and Wouden. Nine times he was chosen as duke or heerman. The towns Buda and Manna-garda-forda are under his care.

Abelo, Jaltia's husband; Grevetman over the Zuider-flylanden. He was three times heerman. The towns Aken, Liudburg, and Katsburg are under his care.

Enoch, Dywcke's husband; Grevetman over Westflyland and Texel. He was chosen nine times for sea-king. Waraburg, Medeasblik, Forana, and Fryasburg are under his care.

Foppe, Dunroo's husband; Grevetman over the seven islands. He was five times sea-king. The town Walhalla-gara is under his care.

This was inscribed upon the walls of Fryasburg in Texland, as well as at Stavia and Medeasblik.

It was Frya's day, and seven times seven years had elapsed since Festa was appointed Volksmoeder by the desire of Frya. The citadel of Medeasblik was ready, and a Burgtmaagd was chosen. Festa was about to light her new lamp, and when she had done so in the presence of all the people, Frya called from her watch-star, so that every one could hear it: 'Festa, take your style and write the things, that I may not speak'. Festa did as she was bid and thus we became Frya's children, and our earliest history began.

CHAPTER THIRTEEN

THE DEATH OF ADELA

THE WRITINGS OF ADELBROST AND APOLLONIA

My name is Adelbrost, the son of Apol and Adela. I was elected by my people as Grevetman over the Linda-oorden. Therefore I will continue this book in the same way as my mother has spoken it.

After the Magy was killed and Fryasburgt was restored, a mother had to be chosen. The mother had not named her successor, and her will was nowhere to be found. Seven months later a general assembly was called at Grenaga,[1] because it was on the boundary of Saxa-marken. My mother was chosen, but she would not be the mother. She had saved my father's life, in consequence

1. Grenega – Groningen.

of which they had fallen in love with each other, and she wished to marry. Many people wished my mother to alter her decision, but she said an Eeremoeder ought to be as pure in her conscience as she appears outwardly, and to have the same love for all her children. Now, as I love Apol better than anything else in the world, I cannot be such a mother. Thus spoke and reasoned Adela, but all the other maidens wished to be the mother. Each state was in favour of its own maiden, and would not yield. Therefore none was chosen, and the kingdom was without any restraint. From what follows you will understand Liudgert, the king who had lately died, had been chosen in the lifetime of the mother, and seemingly with the love and confidence of all the states. It was his turn to live at the great court of Dokhem,[2] and in the lifetime of the mother great honour was done to him there, as there were more messengers and knights there than had ever been seen there before. But now he was lonely and forsaken, because everyone was afraid that he would set himself above the law, and rule them like the slave kings. Every headman imagined that he did enough if he looked after his own state, and did not care for the others. With the Burgtmaagden it was still worse. Each of them depended upon her own judgement, and whenever a Grevetman did anything without her, she raised distrust between him and his people. If any case happened which concerned several states, and one maid had been consulted, the rest all exclaimed that she had spoken only in the interest of her own state. By such proceedings they brought disputes among the states, and so severed the bond of union that the people of one state were jealous of those of the rest, or at least considered them as strangers; the consequences of which was that the Gauls or Triuwenden took possession of our lands as far as the Scheldt, and the Magy as far as the Wesara. How this happened my mother has explained, otherwise this book would not have been written, although I have lost all hope that it would be of any use. I do not write in the hope that I shall win back the land

2. Dokhem – Dokkum.

or preserve it: in my opinion that is impossible. I write only for the future generations, that they may all know in what way we were lost, and that each may learn that every crime brings its punishment.

My name is Apollonia. Two-and-thirty-days after my mother's death, my brother Adelbrost was found murdered on the wharf, his skull fractured and his limbs torn asunder. My father, who lay ill, died of fright. Then my younger brother Apol, sailed from here to the west side of Schoonland.[3] There he built a citadel named Lindasburgt,[4] in order there to avenge our wrong. Wr-alda accorded him many years for that. He had five sons, who all caused fear to Magy, and brought fame to my brother. After the death of my mother and my brother, all the bravest of the land joined together and made a covenant, called the Adelbond. In order to preserve us from injury, they brought me and my youngest brother, Adelhirt, to the burgt – me to the maidens, and him to the warriors. When I was thirty years old I was chosen as Burgtmaagd, and my brother at fifty was chosen Grevetman. From mother's side my brother was the sixth, but from father's side the third. By right, therefore, his descendants could put 'overa Linda' after their names, but they all wished to do it in honour of their mother. In addition to this, there was given to us also a copy of *The Book of Adela's Followers*. That gave me the most pleasure, because it came into the world by my mother's wisdom. In the burgt I have found other writings also in praise of my mother. All this I will write afterwards.

These are the writings left by Bruno, who was the writer of this burgt. After the followers of Adela had made copies, each in his kingdom, of what was inscribed upon the walls of the burgt, they resolved to choose a mother. For this purpose a general assembly was called at this farm. By the first advice of Adela, Teuntje was recommended. That would have been arranged, only that my Burgtmaagd asked to speak: she had always supposed

3. Schoonland – Scandinavia.
4. Lindasburgt – Liudasburch, on Cape Lindanaes, Norway.

that she would be chosen mother, because she was at the burgt from which mothers had generally been chosen. When she was allowed to speak, she opened her false lips and said: You all seem to place great value on Adela's advice, but that shall not shut my mouth. Who is Adela, and whence comes it that you respect her so highly? She was what I am now, a Burgtmaagd of this place; is she, then, wiser and better than I and all the others? Or is she more conversant with our laws and customs? If that had been the case, she would have become mother when she was chosen; but instead of that she preferred matrimony to a single life, watching over herself and her people. She is certainly very clear-sighted, but my eyes are far from being dim. I have observed that she is very much attached to her husband, which is very praiseworthy; but I see, likewise, that Teuntje is Apol's niece. Further I say nothing.

The principal people understood very well which way the wind blew with her; but among the people there arose disputes, and as most of the people came from here, they would not give the honour to Teuntje. The conferences were ended, knives were drawn, and no mother was chosen. Shortly afterwards one of our messengers killed his comrade. As he had been a man of good character hitherto, my Burgtmaagd had permission to help him over the frontier; but instead of helping him over to Twiskland, she fled with him herself to Wesara, and then to the Magy. The Magy, who wished to please his sons of Frya, appointed her mother of Godaburgt, in Schoonland; but she wished for more, and she told him that if he could get Adela out of the way he might become master of the whole of Frya's land. She said she hated Adela for having prevented her from being chosen mother. If he would promise her Texland, her messenger should serve as guide to his warriors. All this was confessed by her messenger.

THE SECOND WRITING

Fifteen months after the last general assembly, at the festival of the harvest month, everybody gave himself up

144

to pleasure and merry-making, and no one thought of anything but diversion; but Wr-alda wished to teach us that watchfulness should never be relaxed. In the midst of the festivities the fog came and enveloped every place in darkness. Cheerfulness melted away, but watchfulness did not take its place. The coastguard deserted their beacons, and no one was to be seen on any of the paths. When the fog rose, the sun scarcely appeared among the clouds; but the people all came out shouting with joy, and the young folks went about singing to their bagpipes, filling the air with their melody. But while every one was intoxicated with pleasure, treachery had landed with its horses and riders. As usual, darkness had favoured the wicked, and they had slipped in through the paths of Linda's wood. Before Adela's door twelve girls led twelve lambs and twelve boys led twelve calves. A young Saxon bestrode a wild bull which he had caught and tamed. They were decked with all kinds of flowers, and the girls' dresses were fringed with gold from the Rhine.

When Adela came out of her house, a shower of flowers fell on her head; they all cheered loudly, and the fifes of the boys were heard over everything. Poor Adela! poor people! how short will be your joy! When the procession was out of sight, a troop of Magyar soldiers rushed up to Adela's house. Her father and her husband were sitting on the steps. The door was open, and within stood Adelbrost, her son. When he saw the danger of his parents, he took his bow from the wall and shot the leader of the pirates, who staggered and fell on the grass. The second and third met a similar fate. In the meantime his parents had seized their weapons, and went slowly to Jon's house. They would soon have been taken, but Adela came. She had learned in the burgt to use all kinds of weapons. She was seven feet high, and her sword was the same length. She waved it three times over her head, and each time a knight bit the earth. Reinforcements came, and the pirates were made prisoners; but too late – an arrow had penetrated her bosom! The treacherous Magy had poisoned it, and she died of it.

Yes, departed friend, thousands are arrived, and more are coming. They wish to hear the wisdom of Adela. Truly, she was a princess, for she had always been the leader. O Sorrow, what good can you do!

Her garments of linen and wool she spun and wove herself. How could she add to her beauty? Not with pearls, for her teeth were more white; not with gold, for her dresses were more brilliant; not with precious stones, for her eyes, though soft as those of a lamb, were so lustrous that you could scarcely look into them. But why do I talk of beauty? Frya was certainly not more beautiful; yes, my friends, Frya, who possessed seven perfections, of which each of her daughters inherited one, or at most three. But even if she had been ugly, she would still have been dear to us. Is she warlike? Listen, my friend. Adela was the only daughter of our Grevetman. She stood seven feet high. Her wisdom exceeded her stature, and her courage was equal to both together. Here is an instance. There was once a turf-ground on fire. Three children got upon yonder gravestone. There was a furious wind. The people were all shouting, and the mother was helpless. Then came Adela. What are you all standing still here for? she cried. Try to help them, and Wr-alda will give you strength. Then she ran to the Krylwood and got some elder branches, of which she made a bridge. The others then came to assist her, and the children were saved. The children bring flowers to the place every year. There came once three Phoenician sailors, who began to ill-treat the children, when Adela, having heard their screams, beat the scoundrels till they were insensible, and then, to prove to them what miserable wretches they were, she tied them all three to a spindle.

The foreign lords came to look after their people, and when they saw how ridiculously they had been treated they were very angry, till they were told what had happened. Upon that they bowed themselves before Adela, and kissed the hem of her garment. But come, distant living friend. The birds of the forest fled before the numerous visitors. Come, friend, and you shall hear her wisdom. By the gravestone of which mention has already been made her body is buried. Upon the stone the following words are inscribed:

TREAD SOFTLY, FOR HERE LIES ADELA

The old legend which is written on the outside wall of the city tower is not written in *The Book of Adela's Followers*. Why this has been neglected I do not know; but this book is my own, so I will put it in out of regard to my relations.

THE OLDEST DOCTRINE

Hail to all the well-intentioned children of Frya! Through them the earth shall become holy. Learn and announce to the people Wr-alda is the ancient of ancients, for he created all things. Wr-alda is all in all, for he is eternal and everlasting. Wr-alda is omnipresent but invisible, and therefore is called a spirit. All that we can see of him are the created beings who come to life through him and go again, because from Wr-alda all things proceed and return to him. Wr-alda is the beginning and the end. Wr-alda is the only almighty being, because from him all other strength comes, and returns to him. Therefore he alone is the creator, and nothing exists without him. Wr-alda established eternal principles, upon which the laws of creation were founded and no good laws could stand on any other foundation. But although everything is derived from Wr-alda, the wickedness of men does not come from him. Wickedness comes from heaviness, carelessness, and stupidity; therefore they may well be injurious to men, but never to Wr-alda. Wr-alda is wisdom, and the laws that he has made are the books from which we learn, nor is any wisdom to be found or gathered but in them. Men may see a great deal, but Wr-alda sees everything. Men can learn a great deal, but Wr-alda knows

147

everything. Men can discover much, but to Wr-alda everything is open. Mankind are male and female, but Wr-alda created both. Mankind love and hate, but Wr-alda alone is just. Therefore Wr-alda is good, and there is no good without him. In the progress of time all creation alters and changes, but goodness alone is unalterable; and since Wr-alda is good, he cannot change. As he endures, he alone exists; everything else is show.

THE SECOND PART OF THE OLDEST DOCTRINE

Among Finda's people there are false teachers, who, by their over-inventiveness, have become so wicked that they make themselves and their adherents believe that they are the best part of Wr-alda, that their spirit is the best part of Wr-alda's spirit, and that Wr-alda can only think by the help of their brains.

That every creature is a part of Wr-alda's eternal being, *that* they have stolen from us; but their false reasoning and ungovernable pride have brought them on the road to ruin. If their spirit was Wr-alda's spirit, then Wr-alda would be very stupid, instead of being sensible and wise; for their spirit labours to create beautiful statues, which they afterwards worship. Finda's people are a wicked people, for although they presumptuously pretend among themselves that they are gods, they proclaim the unconsecrated false gods, and declare everywhere that these idols created the world and all that therein is – greedy idols, full of envy and anger, who desire to be served and honoured by the people, and who exact bloody sacrifices and rich offerings; but these presumptuous and false men, who call themselves God's servants and priests, receive and collect everything in the name of the idols that have no real existence, for their own benefit.

They do all this with an easy conscience, as they think themselves gods not answerable to any one. If there are some who discover their tricks and expose them, they hand them over to the executioners to be burnt for their calumnies, with solemn ceremonies in honour of the false

148

gods; but really in order to save themselves. In order that our children may be protected against their idolatrous doctrine, the duty of the maidens is to make them learn by heart the following: Wr-alda existed before all things, and will endure after all things. Wr-alda is also eternal and everlasting, therefore nothing exists without him. From Wr-alda's life sprang time and all living things, and his life takes away time and every other thing. These things must be made clear and manifest in every way, so that they can be made clear and comprehensible to all. When we have learned thus much, then we say further: In what regards our existence, we are a part of Wr-alda's everlasting being, like the existence of all created beings; but as regards our form, our qualities, our spirit, and all our thoughts, these do not belong to the being. All these are passing things which appear through Wr-alda's life, and which appear through his wisdom, and not otherwise; but whereas his life is continually progressing, nothing can remain stationary, therefore all created things change their locality, their form, and their thoughts. So neither the earth nor any other created object can say, I am; but rather, I was. So no man can say, I think; but rather, I thought. The boy is greater and different from the child; he has different desires, inclinations and thoughts. The man and father feels and thinks differently from the boy, the old man just the same. Everybody knows that. Besides, everybody knows and must acknowledge that he is now changing, that he changes every minute even while he says, I am, and that his thoughts change even while he says, I think. Instead, then, of imitating Finda's wicked people, and saying, I am the best part of Wr-alda, and through us alone he can think, we proclaim everywhere it is necessary. We, Frya's children, exist through Wr-alda's life – in the beginning mean and base, but always advancing towards perfection without ever attaining the excellence of Wr-alda himself. Our spirit is not Wr-alda's spirit, it is merely a shadow of it. When Wr-alda created us, he lent us his wisdom, brains, organs, memory, and many other good qualities. By this means we are able to

149

contemplate his creatures and his laws; by this means we can learn and can speak of them always, and only for our own benefit. If Wr-alda had given us no organs, we should have known nothing, and been more irrational than a piece of sea-weed driven up and down by the ebb and flood.

THIS IS WRITTEN ON PARCHMENT – 'SKRIVFILT'. SPEECH AND ANSWER TO OTHER MAIDENS AS AN EXAMPLE

An unsociable, avaricious man came to complain to Troost, who was the maid of Stavia. He said a thunderstorm had destroyed his house. He had prayed to Wr-alda, but Wr-alda had given him no help. Are you a true Frisian? Troost asked. From father and forefathers, replied the man. Then she said, I will sow something in your conscience, in confidence that it will take root, grow, and bear fruit. She continued, When Frya was born, our mother stood naked and bare, unprotected from the rays of the sun. She could ask no one, and there was no one who could give her any help. Then Wr-alda wrought in her conscience inclination and love, anxiety and fright. She looked round her, and her inclination chose the best. She sought a hiding-place under the sheltering lime-trees, but the rain came, and the difficulty was that she got wet. She had seen how the water ran down the pendant leaves; so she made a roof of leaves fastened with sticks, but the wind blew the rain under it. She observed that the stem would afford protection. She then built a wall of sods, first on one side, and then all round. The wind grew stronger and blew away the roof, but she made no complaint upon it. Having found how hard it is to toil alone, she showed her children how and why she had done it. They acted and thought as she did. This is the way in which we became possessed of houses and porches, a street, and lime-trees to protect us from the rays of the sun. At last we have built a citadel, and all the rest. If your house is not strong enough, then you must try and make another. My house was strong enough, he said, but the flood and the wind destroyed it. Where did your house stand? Troost asked. On the bank of the Rhine, he answered. Did it not stand on a knoll? Troost asked. No, said the man; my house stood alone on the bank. I built it alone, but I could not alone make a hillock. I knew it, Troost answered, the maidens told me. All your life you have avoided your neighbours, fearing that you might have to give or do something for them; but one cannot get on in the world in that way, for Wr-alda, who is kind, turns away from the niggardly. Fasta has advised us, and it is engraved in stone all over the doors. If you are selfish, distrustful towards your neighbours, teach your neighbours, help your neighbours, and they will return the same to you. If this advice is not good enough for you, I can give you no better. The man blushed for shame, and slunk away.

Commentary

It is during the foregoing account of the murder of, and lament for, Adela, that we are told twice that she was seven feet tall. Is it possible that a giant race inhabited Europe in pre-historic times? Apart from my earlier reference to the tall, Cro-Magnon race whose fine artwork has been discovered on the Continent, there remain many sites in England, Wales, Scotland and Ireland with such names as 'Giant's Grave', 'Giant's Bed', 'Giant's Chair', 'Giant's Quoiting Stones', 'Giant's Staff', and so on, so-named, no doubt because of legends of exceptionally tall people in the area, or the discovery of extra-large tumuli (burial mounds) or even of huge human remains.

In Tregony-on-the-Fal, Cornwall, in 1761, tin miners found a deeply-buried coffin measuring 11 ft. 3 ins. In it was a huge skeleton which crumbled to dust as soon as it was exposed to the air. Archaeology and tradition have authenticated the discovery of a number of such great skeletons which always crumbled when the graves were opened.

Some of the British burial mounds known as long barrows, especially those which, by the radio-carbon 14 dating method have been established as from the period 4000–3000

B.C., are often known as Giant's Graves. Cornwall is particularly rich in lore and archaeological allusion to a race of huge men. At Trecobbin Hill are to be found the Giant's Cradle, Giant's Spoon and the Giant's Well. And indeed, it will be recalled, the *Oera Linda Book* does tell how exiled men of Atland and Frya's race whom, we may be sure, were tall like Adela, lived and worked in the British tin-mines.

The Scots historian and novelist, the late J. J. Bell, who lived near Dumbarton, claimed that after a violent storm along the Argyllshire coast he was shown a number of giant skulls and bones of considerable size, exposed to view by a fall of cliff. They soon crumbled to dust. There are numerous similar examples.[5]

The famous giants Gog and Magog have a curious connection with ancient British history. Their wooden effigies were preserved for many centuries in the Guildhall, London, until German bombs destroyed them in 1941. Legend says that Gog ruled an ancient city on the site where London now stands. It is said that the White Tower at the Tower of London is the original site of the old settlement's central citadel. Gog's brother was king of Cornwall and Devon. Varying traditions say that invaders from Troy battled with the giants and overthrew them. The Trojan Corinues is supposed to have fought the giant 'Goemagot' and hurled his body over the cliffs at Plymouth.

With the death of Adela and the Gauls and Magyars making increasing encroachments upon their freedom, and their social codes crumbling, an air of hopelessness creeps into the Frisian writings.

Of his chronicle, Adelbrost admits, 'I have lost all hope that it will be of any use. I do not write in the hope that I shall win back the land or preserve it: in my opinion that is impossible. I write only for the future generations, that they may all know in what way we were lost . . .'

Adelbrost is murdered and his sister, Apollonia, who takes over the task of writing down the history, tells of yet another Burgtmaagd – like the renegade Kalta – who goes over

5. *The Riddle of Prehistoric Britain.* (Rider & Co.)

to the enemy. Assemblies are called but no new Volks-moeder is chosen. Then, while the Frisians are celebrating harvest, Magyars attack and, although she puts up a tremendous fight, Adela is killed.

There follows the elegy for her, then the Oldest Doctrine in its entirety, and a parable-style account of the man whose house is destroyed containing the advice urging a give-and-take attitude towards one's neighbours.

CHAPTER FOURTEEN

THE CITADEL OF LIUDGAARDE

NOW I WILL WRITE ABOUT MYSELF. FIRST ABOUT MY CITADEL, AND THEN ABOUT WHAT I HAVE BEEN ABLE TO SEE.

My city lies near the north end of the Liudgaarde. The tower has six sides, and is ninety feet high, flat-roofed, with a small house upon it out of which they look at the stars. On either side of the tower is a house three hundred feet long, and twenty-one feet broad, and twenty-one feet high, besides the roof, which is round. All this is built of hard-baked bricks, and outside there is nothing else. The citadel is surrounded by a dyke, with a moat thirty-six feet broad and twenty-one feet deep. If one looks down from the tower, he sees the form of the Juul. In the ground among the houses on the south side all kinds of native and foreign herbs grow, of which the maidens must study the qualities. Among the houses on the north side there are only fields. The three houses on the north are full of corn and other necessaries; the two houses on the south are for the maidens to live in and keep school. The most southern house is the dwelling of the Burgtmaagd. In the tower hangs the lamp. The walls of the tower are decorated with precious stones. On the south wall the Tex is inscribed. On the right side of this are the formulae, and on the other side the laws; the other things are found upon the three other sides. Against the dyke, near the house of the Burgtmaagd, stand the oven and the mill, worked by four oxen. Outside the citadel wall is the place where the Burgtheeren and the soldiers live. The fortification outside is an hour long – not a seaman's hour, but an hour of the sun, of which twenty-four go to a day. Inside it is a plain five feet below the top. On it are three hundred crossbows covered with wood and leather.

Besides the houses of the inhabitants, there are along the inside of the dyke thirty-six refuge-houses for the people who live in the neighbourhood. The field serves for a camp and for a meadow. On the south side of the outer fortification is the Liudgaarde, enclosed by the great wood of lime-trees. Its shape is three-cornered, with the widest part outside, so that the sun may shine in it, for there are a great number of foreign trees and flowers brought by the seafarers. All the other citadels are the same shape as ours, only not so large; but the largest of all is that of Texland. The tower of the Fryaburgt is so high that it rends the sky, and all the rest is in proportion to the tower. In our citadel this is the arrangement: Seven young maidens attend to the lamp; each watch is three hours. In the rest of their time they do housework, learn, and sleep. When they have watched for seven years, they are free; then they may go among the people, to look after their morals and to give advice. When they have been three years maidens, they may sometimes accompany the older ones.

The writer must teach the girls to read, to write, and to reckon. The elders, or 'Greva', must teach them justice and duty, morals, botany, and medicine, history, traditions and singing, besides all that may be necessary for them to give advice. The Burgtmaagd must teach them how to set to work when they go among the people. Before a Burgtmaagd can take office, she must travel through the country a whole year. Three grey-headed Burgtheeren and three old maidens must go with her. This was the way that I did. My journey was along the Rhine – on this side up, and on the other side down. The higher I went, the poorer the people seemed to be. Everywhere about the Rhine the people dug holes, and the sand that was got out was poured with water over fleeces to get the gold, but the girls did not wear golden crowns of it. Formerly they were more numerous, but since we lost Schoonland they have gone up to the mountains. There they dig ore and make iron. Above the Rhine among the mountains I have seen Marsaten. The Marsaten are people who live on the lakes. Their houses are built upon piles, for protection from the wild beasts and wicked people .There are wolves, bears and horrible lions. Then come the Swiss, the nearest to the frontiers of the distant Italians, the followers of Kalta and the savage Twiskar, all greedy for robbery and booty. The Marsaten gain their livelihood by fishing and hunting. The skins are sewn together by the women and prepared with birch bark. The small skins are as soft as a woman's skin. The Burgtmaagd at Fryasburgt,[1] told us that they were good, simple people; but if I had not heard her speak of them first, I should have thought that they were not Frya's people, they looked so impudent. Their wool and herbs are bought by the Rhine people, and taken to foreign countries by the ship captains. Along the other side of the Rhine it was just the same as at Lydasburcht.[2] There was a great river or lake, and upon this lake also there were people living upon piles. But they were not Frya's people; they were black and brown men who had been employed as rowers to bring home the men who had been making foreign voyages, and they had to stay there till the fleet went back.

At last we came to Alderga. At the head of the south harbour lies the Waraburgt, built of stone, in which all kinds of clothes, weapons, shells and horns are kept, which were brought by the sea-people from distant lands. A quarter of an hour's distance from there is Alderga, a great river surrounded by houses, sheds, and gardens, all richly decorated. In the river lay a great fleet ready, with banners of all sorts of colours. On Frya's day the shields

1. Fryasburgt – Freiburg.
2. Lydasburcht – Leyden.

were hung on board likewise. Some shone like the sun. The shields of the sea-king and the admiral were bordered with gold. From the river a canal was dug going past the citadel Forana,[3] with a narrow outlet to the sea. This was the egress of the fleet; the Fly was the ingress. On both sides of the river are fine houses built, painted in bright colours. The gardens are all surrounded by green hedges. I saw there women wearing felt tunics, as if it were writing felt. Just as at Staveren, the girls wore golden crowns on their heads, and rings on their arms and ankles. To the south of Forana lies Alkmarum. Alkmarum is a lake or river in which there is an island. On this island the black and brown people must remain, the same as at Lydasburcht. The Burgtmaagd of Forana told me that the burgtheeren go every day to teach them what real freedom is, and how it behoves men to live in order to obtain the blessing of Wr-alda's spirit. If there was any one who was willing to listen and could comprehend, he was kept there till he was fully taught. That was done in order to instruct the distant people, and to make friends everywhere. I had been before in the Saxenmarken at the Mannagardaforde castle.[4] There I saw more poverty than I could discover wealth here. She answered: so whenever at the Saxenmarken a young man courts a young girl, the girls ask: Can you keep your house free from the banished Twisklanders? Have you ever killed any of them? How many cattle have you already caught, and how many bear and wolf-skins have you brought to market? And from this it comes that the Saxons have left the cultivation of the soil to the women, that not one in a hundred can read or write; from this it comes, too, that no one has a motto on his shield, but only a misshapen form of some animal that he has killed; and lastly, from this comes also that they are very warlike, but sometimes as stupid as the beasts that they catch, and as poor as the Twisklanders with whom they go to war. The earth and the sea were made for Frya's people. All our rivers run into the sea.

3. Forana – Vroonen.
4. Mannagardaforde – Munster.

The Lydas people and the Findas people will exterminate each other, and we must people the empty countries. In movement and sailing is our prosperity. If you wish the highlanders to share our riches and wisdom, I will give you a piece of advice. Let the girls, when they are asked to marry, before they say yes, ask their lovers: What parts of the world have you travelled in? What can you tell your children about distant lands and distant people? If they do this, then the young warriors will come to us; they will become wiser and richer, and we shall have no occasion to deal with those nasty people. The youngest of the maids who were with me came from the Saxenmarken. When we came back she asked leave to go home. Afterwards she became Burgtmaagd there, and that is the reason why in these days so many of our sailors are Saxons.

END OF APOLLONIA'S BOOK

Commentary

It is a great pity that none of the Frisian citadels have yet been unearthed. But perhaps one day they will. In any event, we have here in Apollonia's words, a vivid description of one such citadel.

They must have been very impressive structures, ninety-foot high hexagonal towers, with an observatory on top, and a thirty-six foot wide moat beneath; the whole, seen from above, representing the shape of the Juul, the sun's apparent circular path. There were beside it, structures three hundred feet long, twenty-one feet wide and high, with domed roofs.

All traces of the fortification and five-mile long wall outside Liudgaurde were destroyed by the second great earthquake and floods which devastated northern Europe. The bastioned fortification walls found at Los Millares and given the new radiocarbon date of 3200 B.C., may well have been built by the Atland colonists. The wall at Frisian Liudgaurde which mounted 300 crossbows may have been similar.

Another bastioned wall of the same period has been found on the Aegean island of Siros: it may be the island which

Adela says was fortified by Jon. The great two-horned fortification walls which Min-erva built from Athens to the harbour five miles away (not the wall built in the fifth century B.C.) were constructed much later in 1250 B.C.

Besides being astronomers and astrologers, the Frisians were also highly versed in the use of herbs, it seems, probably both for medicinal and magical purposes.

There were dwellings for the twenty-one maidens who each took three-hour shifts in teams of seven to tend the perpetually burning lamps of Festa. Cultivated fields, a mill worked by oxen and ovens, either for baking or pottery or possibly both, lay nearby.

The fortification mentioned must have been of staggering length – Apollonia suggests that it took an hour to walk its length, which would, at a normal walking speed of about five miles an hour, make it five miles long. Its causeway was lined with wooden and leather crossbows. These great and formidable weapons were a speciality of the Frisians. They crop up again later in a story of the adventurer Friso. A smaller crossbow was later developed and used in Europe by the Saxons and Normans.

There were thirty-six refuge houses and a field which served both as a meadow for grazing and as an emergency camp in time of attack. A triangular wood of lime-trees sheltered a garden of imported trees and flowers and was positioned so that it got the full benefit of the sun; the Frisians were obviously keen horticulturalists.

The shape of the citadel which, we are told was the standard shape for all citadels, along with the cryptic references to 'formulae' and 'other things' inscribed upon its inner walls, are of great occult significance and I shall deal with this question in due course.

In her description of her journeys along the banks of the Rhine, Apollonia gives what may well be the original tradition underlying the famous legend of Greek mythology in which Jason goes on his quest for the Golden Fleece. The Greek story says that Jason went to Pelias, king of Iolchus, demanding his kingdom. Pelias agreed, on the condition that Jason obtained for him the Golden Fleece. Assisted by the witch Medea, Jason took the Fleece from Colchis, abducted Medea to take her as his wife, along with her young brother Apsyrtus. Their father, King Aeëtes, gave chase and, in a sequence that echoes somewhat the Egyptian legend of Isis and Osiris, Jason killed Apsyrtus, cut his body into pieces and scattered them along the way. This delayed their pursuer who stopped to gather up the remains of his son, while Jason and Medea made off back to Iolchus.

Now Colchis, where Jason is said to have obtained the Fleece, was said to have been somewhere in Asia. But, knowing as we do from the *Oera Linda Book* of the link between Greece and Friesland, it is possible that the hero Jason was based on the voyage of a Greek sailor who, like Ulysses, visited Northern Europe. He probably saw the girls sifting for gold on the banks of the Rhine, possibly even took back with him one of the gold-flecked fleeces – and became the basis of a legend which worked its way into classical Greek mythology.

The gold was obtained by pouring riverbed sand and water into the fleeces. The wool retained the gold dust while the water was poured away. The so-called 'Forty-Niners' of the California gold strike obtained gold from creeks and rivers in much the same way. The Thracians and the later Bulgarians used fleeces in this way and the practice continued along the Rhine, until A.D. 500.

Apollonia's account of the Marsaten, lake-dwellers of Switzerland, is a highly intriguing passage. From various references, we can deduce that Apollonia was writing around 530 B.C. It is highly significant that evidence for these Swiss lake-dwellers was not discovered until the mid-nineteenth century. An abnormal drought and prolonged cold spell in the winter of 1853–4 caused the water levels of Alpine lakes to fall and rivers to shrink. It was then that the first Swiss pile-dwellings was found at Obermeilen. Archaeologists determined that the builders of these dwellings were of the age of polished stone and survived into the Bronze and Iron Ages. Experts found glass and nephrite beads from Egypt, Phoenicia and Asia in some of the dwellings, which confirms the *Oera Linda Book*'s references to the Marsaten people's trade with foreign lands.

As to the reference to wild beasts, including wolves, bears and lions, we know that wolves and bears roamed Europe, but what about lions? In fact, the historian Herodotus wrote of lions in Europe, and of the Swiss lake-dwellers.

CHAPTER FIFTEEN

ALEXANDER AND THE FRISIANS OF INDIA

THE WRITINGS OF FRETHORIK AND WILJOW

My name is Frethorik, surnamed oera Linda, which means over the Linden. In Ljudwardia I was chosen as Asga. Ljudwardia is a new village within the fortification of the Ljudgaarda, of which the name has fallen into disrepute. In my time much has happened. I had written a good deal about it, but afterwards much more was related to me. I will write an account of both one and the other after this book, to the honour of the good people and to the disgrace of the bad.

In my youth I heard complaints on all sides. The bad time was coming; the bad time did come – Frya had forsaken us. She withheld from us all her watch-maidens, because monstrous idolatrous images had been found within our landmarks. I burnt with curiosity to see those images. In our neighbourhood a little old woman tottered in and out of the houses, always calling out about the bad times. I came to her; she stroked my chin; then I became bold, and asked her if she would show me the bad times and the images. She laughed good-naturedly, and took me to the citadel. An old man asked me if I could read and write. No, I said. Then you must first go and learn, he replied, otherwise it may not be shown to you. I went daily to the writer and learnt. Eight years afterwards I heard that our Burgtmaagd had been unchaste, and that some of the burgtheeren had committed treason with the Magy, and many people took their part. Everywhere, disputes arose. There were children rebelling against their parents; good people were secretly murdered. The little old woman who had brought everything to light was found dead in a ditch. My father, who was a judge, would have her avenged. He was murdered in the night in his own house. Three years after that the Magy was master without any resistance. The Saxmen had remained religious and upright. All the good people fled to them. My mother died of it. Now I did like the others. The Magy prided himself upon his cunning, but Irtha[1] made him know that she would not tolerate any Magy or idol on the holy bosom that had borne Frya. As a wild horse tosses his mane after he has thrown his rider, so Irtha shook her forests and her mountains. Rivers flowed over the land; the sea raged; mountains spouted fire to the clouds, and what they vomited forth the clouds flung upon the earth. At the beginning of the Arnemaand[2] the earth bowed towards the north, and sank down lower and lower. In the Welvenmaand[3] the low lands of Fryasland were buried under the sea. The woods in which the images were, were torn up and scattered by the wind. The following year the frost came in the Hardemaand, and laid Fryasland concealed under a sheet of ice. In Sellemaand[4] there were storms of wind from the north, driving mountains of ice and stones. When the spring-tides came the earth raised herself up, the ice melted; with the ebb the forests with the images drifted out to sea. In the Winne, or Minnemaand,[5] every one who dared went home. I came with a maiden to the citadel Liudgaarde. How sad it looked there. The forests of the Lindaoorden were almost all gone. Where Liudgaarde used to be was sea. The waves swept over the fortifications. Ice had destroyed the tower, and the houses

1. Irtha – the Earth.
2. Arnemaand – Harvest month.
3. Welvenmaand – Winter month.
4. Sellemaand – Sprokkelmaand, February;
5. Minnemaand – Bloeimaand, May.

lay heaped over each other. On the slope of the dyke I found a stone on which the writer had inscribed his name. That was a sign to me. The same thing had happened to other citadels as to ours. In the upper lands they had been destroyed by the earth, in the lower lands, by the water. Fryasburgt, at Texland, was the only one found uninjured, but all the land to the north was sunk under the sea, and has never been recovered. At the mouth of the Flymeer, as we were told, thirty salt swamps were found, consisting of the forest and the ground that had been swept away. At Westflyland there were fifty. The canal which had run across the land from Alderga was filled up with sand and destroyed. The seafaring people and other travellers who were at home had saved themselves, their goods, and their relations upon their ships. But the black people at Lydasburgt and Alkmarum had done the same; and as they went south they saved many girls, and as no one came to claim them, they took them for their wives. The people who came back all lived within the lines of the citadel, as outside there was nothing but mud and marsh. The old houses were all smashed together. People bought cattle and sheep from the upper lands, and in the great houses where formerly the maidens were established cloth and felt were made for a livelihood. This happened 1,888 years after the submersion of Atland.[6]

For 282 years we had not had an Eeremoeder, and now, when everything seemed lost, they set about choosing one.[7] The lot fell upon Gosa, surnamed Makonta. She was Burgtmaagd at Fryasburgt, in Texland. She had a clear head and strong sense, and was very good; and as her citadel was the only one that had been spared, every one saw in that her call. Ten years after that the seafarers came from Forana and Lydaasbugt. They wished to drive the black men, with their wives and children, out of the country. They wished to obtain the opinion of the mother upon the subject. She asked them: Can you send them all back to their country? If so, then lose no time, or they will find

6. 2193 — 1888 = 305 B.C.
7. Since 587 B.C.

no relatives alive. No, they said. Gosa replied: They have eaten your bread and salt; they have placed themselves entirely under your protection. You must consult your own hearts. But I will give you one piece of advice. Keep them till you are able to send them back, but keep them outside your citadels. Watch over their morals, and educate them as if they were Frya's sons. Their women are the strongest here. Their blood will disappear like smoke, till at last nothing but Frya's blood will remain in their descendants. So they remained here. Now, I should wish that my descendants should observe in how far Gosa spoke the truth. When our country began to recover, there came troops of poor Saxon men and women to the neighbourhoods of Staveren and Alderga, to search for gold and other treasures in the swampy lands. But the sea-people would not permit it, so they went and settled in the empty village of the West Flyland in order to preserve their lives.

NOW I WILL RELATE HOW THE GEERTMEN AND
MANY FOLLOWERS OF HELLENIA CAME BACK

Two years after Gosa had become the mother[8] there arrived a fleet at Flymeer. The people shouted 'Ho-n-sêen'.[9] They sailed to Staveren, where they shouted again. Their flags were hoisted, and at night they shot lighted arrows into the air. At daylight some of them rowed into the harbour in a boat, shouting again, 'Ho-n-sêen'. When they landed a young fellow jumped upon the rampart. In his hand he held a shield on which bread and salt were laid. After him came a grey-headed man, who said we come from the distant Greek land to preserve our customs. Now we wish you to be kind enough to give us as much land as will enable us to live. He told a long story, which I will hereafter relate more fully. The old man did not know what to do. They sent messengers all round, also to me. I went, and said now that we have a

8. 303 B.C.
9. Ho-n-sâen – What a blessing.

mother it behoves us to ask her advice. I went with them myself. The mother, who already knew it all, said: Let them come, they will help us to keep our lands, but do not let them remain in one place, that they may not become too powerful over us. We did as she said, which was quite to their liking. Fryso remained with his people at Staveren, which they made again into a port as well as they could. Wichhirte went with his people eastwards to the Emude. Some of the descendants of Jon who imagined that they sprang from the Alderga people went there. A small number, who fancied that their forefathers had come from the seven islands, went there and set themselves down within the enclosure of the citadel of Walhallagara. Liudgert, the admiral of Wichhirt, was my comrade, and afterwards my friend. Out of his diary I have taken the following history.

After we had been settled 12 times 100 and twice 12 years[10] in the Five Waters,[11] whilst our naval warriors were navigating all the seas they could find, came Alexander the King, with a powerful army descending the river towards our villages. No one could withstand him; but we sea-people, who lived by the sea, put all our possessions on board ships and took our departure. When Alexander heard that such a large fleet had escaped him, he became furious, and swore that he would burn all the villages if we did not come back. Wichhirte was ill in bed. When Alexander heard that, he waited till he was better. After that he came to him, speaking very kindly – but he deceived, as he had done before. Wichhirte answered: Oh greatest of kings, we sailors go everywhere; we have heard of your great deeds, therefore we are full of respect for your arms, and still more for your wisdom; but we who are free-born Fryas children, we may not become your slaves; and even if I would, the others would sooner die, for so it is commanded in our laws. Alexander said: I do not desire to take your land or make slaves of your people,

10. Since 1551 B.C. Alexander the Great went to the Indus in 327 B.C.
11. Punjab.

164

I only wish to hire your services. That I will swear by both our Gods, so that no one may be dissatisfied. When Alexander shared bread and salt with him, Wichhirte had chosen the wisest part. He let his son fetch the ships. When they were all come back Alexander hired them all. By means of them he wished to transport his people to the holy Ganges, which he had not been able to reach. Then he chose among all his people and soldiers those who were accustomed to the sea. Wichhirte had fallen sick again, therefore I went alone with Nearchus, sent by the king. The voyage came to an end without any advantage, because the Joniers and the Phoenicians were always quarrelling, so that Nearchus himself could not keep them in order. In the meantime, the king had not sat still. He had let his soldiers cut down trees and make planks, with which, with the help of our carpenters, he had built ships. Now he would himself become a sea-king, and sail with his whole army up the Ganges; but the soldiers who came from the mountainous countries were afraid of the sea. When they heard that they must sail, they set fire to the timber yards, and so our whole village was laid in ashes. At first we thought that this had been done by Alexander's orders, and we were all ready to cast ourselves into the sea: but Alexander was furious, and wished his own people to kill the soldiers. However, Nearchus, who was not only his chief officer, but also his friend, advised him not to do so. So he pretended to believe that it had happened by accident, and said no more about it. He wished now to return, but before going he made an inquiry who really were the guilty ones. As soon as he ascertained it, he had them all disarmed, and made them build a new village. His own people he kept under arms to overawe the others and to build a citadel. We were to take the women and children with us. When we arrived at the mouth of the Euphrates, we might either choose a place to settle there or come back. Our pay would be guaranteed to us the same in either case. Upon the new ships which had been saved from the fire he embarked the Joniers and the Greeks. He himself went with the rest of his people along the coast, through the barren wilderness; that is, through the land that Irtha had heaved up out of the sea when she had raised up the strait as soon as our forefathers had passed into the Red Sea.

When we arrived at New Geertmania (New Geertmania is the port that we had made in order to take in water), we met Alexander with his army. Nearchus went ashore, and stayed three days. Then we proceeded further on. When we came to the Euphrates, Nearchus went ashore with the soldiers and a large body of people; but he soon returned, and said, The King requests you, for his sake, to go a voyage up the Red Sea; after that each shall receive as much gold as he can carry. When we arrived there, he showed us where the strait had formerly been. There he spent thirty-one days, always looking steadily towards the desert.

At last there arrived a great troop of people, bringing with them 200 elephants, 1,000 camels, a quantity of timber, ropes, and all kinds of implements necessary to drag our fleet to the Mediterranean Sea. This astounded us, and seemed most extraordinary; but Nearchus told us that his king wished to show to the other kings that he was more powerful than any kings of Tyre had ever been. We were only to assist, and that surely could do us no harm. We were obliged to yield, and Nearchus knew so well how to regulate everything, that before three months had elapsed our ships lay in the Mediterranean Sea. When Alexander ascertained how his project had succeeded, he became so audacious that he wished to dig out the dried-up strait in defiance of Irtha; but Wr-alda deserted his soul, so that he destroyed himself by wine and rashness before he could begin it. After his death his kingdom was divided among his princes. They were each to have preserved a share for his sons, but that was not their intention. Each wished to keep his own share, and to get more. Then war arose, and we could not return. Nearchus wished us to settle on the coast of Phoenicia, but that no one would do. We said we would rather risk the attempt to return to Fryasland. Then he brought us to the new port of Athens, where all the true children of Frya had formerly gone. We went, soldiers with our goods and weapons. Among the many princes Nearchus had a friend named Antigonus. These two had only one object in view, as they told us – to help the royal race, and to restore freedom to all the Greek lands. Antigonus had, among many others, one son named Demetrius, afterwards called 'the City Winner'. He went once to the town of Salamis, and after he had been some time fighting there, he had an engagement with the fleet of Ptolemy. Ptolemy was the name of the prince who ruled over Egypt. Demetrius won the battle, not by his own soldiers, but because we helped him. We had done this out of friendship for Nearchus, because we knew that he was of bastard birth by his white skin, blue eyes, and fair hair. Afterwards, Demetrius attacked Rhodes, and we transported thither his soldiers and provisions. When we made our last voyage to Rhodes, the war was finished. Demetrius had sailed to Athens.[12] When we came into the harbour the whole village was in deep mourning. Friso, who was king over the fleet, had a son and a daughter so remarkably fair, as if they had just come out of Fryasland, and more beautiful than any one could picture to himself. The fame of this went all over Greece, and came to the ears of Demetrius. Demetrius was vile and immoral, and thought he could do as he pleased. He carried off the daughter. The mother did not dare await the return of her *joi* (the sailors' wives call their husbands *joi* or *zoethart*.[13] The men call their wives *troost*[14] and *fro* or *frow*, that is *vreuyde*[15] and frolic; that is the same as *vreugde*.

As she dared not wait for her husband's return, she went with her son to Demetrius, and implored him to send back her daughter; but when Demetrius saw the son he had him taken to his palace and did to him as he had done to his sister. He sent a bag of gold to the mother,

12. The siege of Rhodes was in 305 B.C.
13. Joy, or sweetheart.
14. Comfort.
15. Delight.

which she flung into the sea. When she came home she was out of her mind, and ran about the streets calling out: Have you seen my children? Woe is me! let me find a place to hide in, for my husband will kill me because I have lost his children.

When Demetrius heard that Friso had come home, he sent messengers to him to say that he had taken his children to raise them to high rank, and to reward him for his services. But Friso was proud and passionate, and sent a messenger with a letter to his children, in which he recommended them to accept the will of Demetrius, as he wished to promote their happiness; but the messenger had another letter with poison, which he ordered them to take: But, said he, your bodies have been defiled against your will. That you are not to blame for; but if your souls are not pure, you will never come into Walhalla. Your spirits will haunt the earth in darkness. Like the bats and owls, you will hide yourselves in the daytime in holes, and in the night will come and shriek and cry about our graves, while Frya must turn her head away from you. The children did as their father had commanded. The messenger had their bodies thrown into the sea, and it was reported that they had fled. Now Friso wished to go with all his people to Frya's land, where he had been formerly, but most of them would not go. So Friso set fire to the village and all the royal storehouses; then no one could remain there, and all were glad to be out of it. We left everything behind us except wives and children, but we had an ample stock of provisions and warlike implements.

Friso was not yet satisfied. When we came to the old harbour, he went off with his stout soldiers and threw fire into all the ships that he could reach with his arrows. Six days later we saw the war-fleet of Demetrius coming down upon us. Friso ordered us to keep back the small ships in a broad line, and to put the large ships with the women and children in front. Further, he ordered us to take the crossbows that were in the fore part and fix them on the sterns of the ships, because, said he, we must fight a retreating battle. No man must presume to pursue a single enemy – that is my order. While we were busy about this, all at once the wind came ahead, to the great alarm of the cowards and the women, because we had no slaves except those who had voluntarily followed us. Therefore we could not escape the enemy by rowing. But Wr-alda knew well why he did this; and Friso, who understood it, immediately had the fire-arrows placed on the crossbows. At the same time he gave the order that no one should shoot before he did, and that we should all aim at the centre ship. If we succeeded in this, he said, the others would all go to its assistance, and then everybody might shoot as he best was able. When we were at a cable and a half distance from them the Phoenicians began to shoot, but Friso did not reply till the first arrow fell six fathoms from his ship. Then he fired, and the rest followed. It was like a shower of fire; and as our arrows went with the wind they all remained alight and reached the third line. Everybody shouted and cheered, but the screams of our opponents were so loud that our hearts shrank. When Friso thought that it was sufficient he called us off, and we sped away; but after two days' slow sailing another fleet of thirty ships came in sight and gained upon us. Friso cleared for action again, but the others sent forward a small rowing-boat with messengers, who asked permission to sail with us, as they were Joniers. They had been compelled by Demetrius to go to the old haven; there they had heard of the battle, and girding on their stout swords, had followed us. Friso, who had sailed a good deal with the Joniers, said Yes; but Wichhirte, our king, said No. The Joniers, said he, are worshippers of heathen gods; I myself have heard them call upon them. That comes from their intercourse with the real Greeks, Friso said. I have often done it myself, and yet I am as pious a Frisian as any of you. Friso was the man to take us to Friesland, therefore the Joniers went with us. It seems that this was pleasing to Wr-alda, for before three months were past we coasted along Britain, and three days later we could shout huzza.

169

Commentary

The chronicler Frethorik tells of a second 'bad time' in
the history of his people, predicted by an old village woman
who must have been something of a seeress. She and others
rationalise the forthcoming troubles, however, by saying that
because idolatory has polluted the faith of the Frisians, Frya
has forsaken her people. Frethorik learns that another
Burgtmaagd has forsaken her vows of chastity and that
several of the male elders, or aldermen, have betrayed their
people to the Magyars. Young people were rebelling against
the long-established traditions of their parents, those still
faithful to Frya were being secretly murdered and soon the
Magy was able to seize command. The good and honest folk
turned to the upright Saxmen as worthy adherents to the true
Frisian code.

Yet there is some mystery here. Frethorik, when wanting
to learn of the 'monstrous idolatrous images' and the coming 'bad times' is told by an old man that he must first learn
to read and write. It is highly unlikely that this reference is
to reading and writing in the normal sense. He would hardly
require these abilities simply to be shown idols nor to be told
verbally of the forthcoming troubles. The implication is that
he had somehow to acquire powers which would allow him
to see the portents of disaster – by scrying, divination or
clairvoyance, perhaps.

But the Magyars are not to go unpunished for their trans-
gressions against Frya and her people. A second cataclysm,
not perhaps as devastating as the one which sank Atland,
occurs. From the harvest month of one year, to May of two
years later, the earth undergoes convulsions and volcanic upheavals. Friesland is covered in ice, only to be flooded and
ravaged further when the earth heaves again and the ice
melts. Forests are swept away, citadels are destroyed and
coastal lands are submerged permanently. This would, of
course, account for the fact that none of these citadels,
with their tall towers, has been found to date, and for the
swamped and flood-prone territories of the Netherlands.
Only the citadel at Texland remained, says Frethorik, and
even there all the lands to the north of it were irretrievably

submerged. People fled in ships to the north taking with them what they could salvage and the ones who eventually returned lived within the confines of the Texland citadel buildings, because beyond its boundaries, all was swamp and marsh.

This catastrophe, we are told, took place around 305 B.C.

After things had settled down somewhat the people chose an Eeremoeder for the first time since the murder of Frana by the Magy who himself was drowned.

The next section of the book contains a fairly self-explanatory account of the return of many of the Greek and Punjab settlers of Frisian origin. Following this, from the diary of the admiral Liudgert of Wichhirt, is a narrative which incorporates actual historical people and events verifiable from other sources, and allows us to estimate accurately the times of the events portrayed.

The history books tell us that Alexander invaded India in 327 B.C. Having defeated Porus at the River Jhelum, in what is now West Pakistan, he advanced as far as the River Sutlej to the east. But his Macedonian followers would go no further so he turned back, sailed down the Jhelum into the Indus with some of his men, while the rest marched along the banks. They reached the Indian Ocean in the summer of 326 and it was from there that Alexander sent Nearchus with his fleet along the Persian Gulf, while the king and the rest of his people marched overland.

Following the incredible feat of hauling his ships across the then-impassable strait into the Mediterranean, Alexander died of a fever in Babylon in 323 B.C.

The Frisians who had gone to the Punjab with Geert are said to have been there for 1,224 years when Alexander's expedition found them. Indeed, the historian Strabo wrote of a race of so-called Indo-Scythians – a white people of European origin, encountered by Alexander. Strabo said they spoke German and were distinct from the Brahmins in both religion and customs.

According to the account of Liudgert in the *Oera Linda Book*, Alexander had designs on re-opening the strait leading into the Mediterranean. Had he realised this project, no doubt he would be remembered not only for his other amazing achievements, but also as being the architect of the Suez Canal. However, he died before the plan was possible. Although Alexander's death at 33 is generally attributed by scholars to fever, it retains some aura of mystery. Liudgert says he 'destroyed himself by wine and rashness' and there is some evidence that Alexander's fever followed a particularly fierce drinking bout.

After Alexander and his officer Nearchus, the next historically verifiable figures to be encountered are Antigonus I, one of Alexander's generals, and the father of Demetrius Poliorcetes, whose surname means 'the Besieger'. As the account of Liudgert relates, Demetrius did indeed defeat Ptolemy in 307 B.C. with the help, we are told, of Frisian reinforcements. He also attacked Rhodes, in 305 B.C. but failed to take the city and the following year concluded a treaty. He died in captivity in Asia in 288 B.C. after a coalition of Pyrrhus, Ptolemy and Lysimachus had forced him out of Macedonia.

But he drops out of Liudgert's story long before this when Friso, determined to return to his homeland, manages to shake off Demetrius's pursuing fleet – with the aid of the powerful Frisian crossbows which we have already encountered at the Citadel of Liudgaarde.

CHAPTER SIXTEEN

SEA-KINGS, EARTHQUAKES AND PROPHECY

The following concludes the writings of Frethorik and, upon his death, the narrative is taken up by his widow, Wiljo:

THIS WRITING HAS BEEN GIVEN TO ME ABOUT
NORTHLAND AND SCHOONLAND

When our land was submerged I was in Schoonland. It was very bad there. There were great lakes which rose from the earth like bubbles, then burst asunder, and from the rents flowed a stuff like red-hot iron. The tops of high mountains fell and destroyed whole forests and villages. I myself saw one mountain torn from another and fall straight down. When I afterwards went to see the place there was a lake there. When the earth was composed there came a duke of Lindasburgt with his people, and one maiden who cried everywhere, Magy is the cause of all the misery that we have suffered. They continued their progress and their hosts increased. The Magy fled, and his corpse was found where he had killed himself. Then the Finns were driven to one place where they might live. There were some of mixed blood who were allowed to stay, but most of them went with the Finns. The duke was chosen as king. The temples which had remained whole were destroyed. Since that time the good Northmen come often to Texland for the advice of the mother; still we cannot consider them real Frisians. In Denmark it has certainly happened as with us. The sea-people, who call themselves famous sea-warriors, went on board their ships, and afterwards went back again.

Heil!

Whenever the Carrier has completed a period, then posterity shall understand that the faults and misdeeds that the Brokmannen have brought with them belonged to their forefathers; therefore I will watch, and will describe as much of their manners as I have seen. The Geert-mannen I can readily pass by. I have not had much to do with them, but as far as I have seen they have mostly retained their language and customs. I cannot say that of the others. Those who descend from the Greeks speak a bad language, and have not much to boast of in their manners. Many have brown eyes and hair. They are envious and impudent, and cowardly from superstition. When they speak, they put the words first that ought to come last. For old they say *at*; for salt, *sât*; and for man, *ma* – too many to mention. They also use abbreviations of names, which have no meaning. The Joniers speak better, but they drop the H, and put it where it ought not to be. When they make a statue of a dead person they believe that the spirit of the departed enters into it; therefore they have hidden their statues of Frya, Fasta, Medea, Thiania, Hellenia, and many others. When a child is born, all the relatives come together and pray to Frya to send her servants to bless the child. When they have prayed, they must neither move nor speak. If the child begins to cry, and continues some time, it is a bad sign, and they suspect that the mother has committed adultery. I have seen very bad things come from that. If the child sleeps, that is a good sign – Frya's servants are come. If it laughs in its sleep, the servants have promised it happiness. Moreover, they believe in bad spirits, witches, sorcerers, dwarfs, and elves, as if they descended from the Finns. Herewith, I will finish, and I think I have written more than any of my forefathers. Frethorik.

* * *

Frethorik, my husband, lived to the age of 63. Since 108 years he is the first of his race who died a peaceable death; all the others died by violence, because they all fought with their own people, and with foreigners for right and duty.

My name is Wiljo. I am the maiden who came home with him from Saxsenmarken. In the course of conversation it came out that we were both of Adela's race – thus our affection commenced, and we became man and wife. He left me with five children, two sons and three daughters. Konreed was my eldest son, Hachgana my second. My eldest daughter is called Adela, my second Frulik, and the youngest Nocht. When I went to Saxsenmarken I preserved three books – the book of songs, the book of narratives, and the Hellenia book.

I write this in order that people may not think they were by Apollonia. I have had a good deal of annoyance about this, and therefore now wish to have the honour of it. I also did more. When Gosa Makonta died, whose goodness and clearsightedness have become a proverb, I went alone to Texland to copy the writings that she had left; and when the last will of Frana was found, and the writings left by Adela or Hellenia, I did that again. These are the writings of Hellenia. I have put them first because they are the oldest.

HAIL TO ALL TRUE FRISIANS

In the olden times, the Slavonic race knew nothing of liberty. They were brought under the yoke like oxen. They were driven into the bowels of the earth to dig metals, and had to build houses of stone as dwelling-places for princes and priests. Of all that they did nothing came to themselves, everything must serve to enrich and make more powerful the priests and the princes, and to satisfy them. Under this treatment they grew gray and old before their time, and died without any enjoyment; although the earth produces abundantly for the good of all her children. But our runaways and exiles came through Twiskland to their boundaries, and our sailors came to their harbours. From them they heard of liberty, of justice, and laws, without which men cannot exist. This was all absorbed by the unhappy people like dew into an arid soil. When they fully understood this, the most courageous among them began to clank their chains, which grieved the princes. The princes are proud and warlike; there is therefore some virtue in their hearts. They consulted together and bestowed some of their superfluity; but the cowardly hypocritical priests could not suffer this. Among their false gods they had invented also wicked cruel monsters. Pestilence broke out in the country; and they said that the gods were angry with the domineering of the wicked. Then the boldest of the people were strangled in their chains. The earth drank their blood, and that blood produced corn and fruits that inspired with wisdom those who ate them.

Sixteen hundred years ago, Atland was submerged;[1]

1. 2193−1600=593 B.C., the time at which Hellenia wrote.

and at that time something happened which nobody had reckoned upon. In the heart of Findasland, upon a mountain, lies a plain called Kasamyr[2] that is 'extraordinary'. There was a child born whose mother was the daughter of a king, and whose father was a high-priest. In order to hide the shame they were obliged to renounce their own blood. Therefore it was taken out of the town to poor people. As the boy grew up, nothing was concealed from him, so he did all in his power to acquire wisdom. His intellect was so great that he understood everything that he saw or heard. The people regarded him with respect, and the priests were afraid of his questions. When he was of full age he went to his parents. They had to listen to some hard language; and to get rid of him they gave him a quantity of jewels, but they dared not openly acknowledge him. Overcome with sorrow at the false shame of his parents, he wandered about. While travelling he fell in with a Frisian sailor who was serving as a slave, and who taught him our manners and customs. He bought the freedom of the slave, and they remained friends till death. Wherever he went he taught the people not to tolerate rich men or priests, and that they must guard themselves against false shame, which everywhere did harm to love and charity. The earth, he said, bestowed her treasures on those who scratch her skin; so all are obliged to dig, and plough, and sow if they wish to reap, but no one is obliged to do anything for another unless it be out of goodwill. He taught that men should not seek in her bowels for gold, or silver, or precious stones, which occasion envy and destroy love. To embellish your wives and daughters, he said, the river offers her pure stream. No man is able to make everybody equally rich and happy, but it is the duty of all men to make each other as equally rich and as happy as possible. Men should not despise any knowledge; but justice is the greatest knowledge that time can teach, because she wards off offences and promotes love.

2. Kasamyr – Kashmir.

His first name was Jessos, but the priests, who hated him, called him Fo, that is, false; the people called him Krishna, that is, shepherd; and his Frisian friend called him Buddha (purse), because he had in his head a treasure of wisdom, and in his heart a treasure of love.

At last he was obliged to flee from the wrath of the priests; but wherever he went his teaching had preceded him, whilst his enemies followed him like his shadow. When Jessos had thus travelled for twelve years he died; but his friends preserved his teaching, and spread it wherever they found listeners.

What do you think the priests did then? That I must tell you, and you must give your best attention to it. Moreover, you must keep guard against their acts and their tricks with all the strength that Wr-alda has given you. While the doctrine of Jessos was thus spreading over the earth, the false priests went to the land of his birth to make his death known. They said they were his friends, and they pretended to show great sorrow by tearing their clothes and shaving their heads. They went to live in caves in the mountains, but in them they had hid all their treasures, and they made in them images of Jessos. They gave these statues to simple people, and at last they said that Jessos was a god, that he had declared this himself to them, and that all those who followed his doctrine should enter his kingdom hereafter, where all was joy and happiness. Because they knew that he was opposed to the rich, they announced everywhere that poverty, suffering and humility were the door by which to enter into his kingdom, and that those who had suffered the most on earth should enjoy the greatest happiness there. Although they knew that Jessos had taught that men should regulate and control their passions, they taught that men should stifle their passions, and that the perfection of humanity consisted in being as unfeeling as the cold stones. In order to make the people believe they did as they preached, they pretended to outward poverty; and that they had overcome all sensual feelings, they took no wives. But if any young girl had made a false step, it was

177

quickly forgiven; the weak, they said, were to be assisted, and to save their souls men must give largely to the Church. Acting in this way, they had wives and children without households, and were rich without working; but the people grew poorer and more miserable than they had ever been before. This doctrine, which requires the priests to possess no further knowledge than to speak deceitfully, and to pretend to be pious while acting unjustly, spreads from east to west, and will come to our land also.

But when the priests fancy that they have entirely extinguished the light of Frya and Jessos, then shall all classes of men rise up who have quietly preserved the truth among themselves, and have hidden it from the priests. They shall be of princely blood of priests, Slavonic, and Frya's blood. They will make their light visible, so that all men shall see the truth; they shall cry woe to the acts of the princes and the priests. The princes who love the truth and justice shall separate themselves from the priests; blood shall flow, but from it the people will gather new strength. Finda's folk shall contribute their industry to the common good, Linda's folk their strength, and we our wisdom. Then the false priests shall be swept away from the earth. Wr-alda's spirit shall be invoked everywhere and always; the laws that Wr-alda in the beginning instilled into our consciences shall alone be listened to. There shall be neither princes, nor masters, nor rulers, except those chosen by the general voice. Then Frya shall rejoice, and the earth will only bestow her gifts on those who work. All this shall begin 4,000 years after the submersion of Atland, and 1,000 years later there shall exist no longer either priest or oppression.

Dela, surnamed Hellenia, watch!

Thus runs Frana's last will: All noble Frisians, Heil! In the name of Wr-alda, of Frya, and of Freedom, I greet you; and pray you if I die before I have named a successor, then I recommend to you Teuntja, who is Burgtmaagd in the citadel of Medeasblik; till now she is the best.

178

This Gosa has left behind her: Hail to all men! I have named no Eeremoeder, because I know none, and because it is better for you to have no mother than to have one you cannot trust. One bad time is passed by, but there is still another coming. Irtha has not given it birth, and Wr-alda has not decreed it. It comes from the East, out of the bosom of the priests. It will breed so much mischief that Irtha will not be able to drink the blood of her slain children. It will spread darkness over the minds of men like storm-clouds over the sunlight. Everywhere craft and deception shall contend with freedom and justice. Freedom and justice shall be overcome, and we with them. But this success will work out its own loss. Our descendants shall teach their people and their slaves the meaning of three words; they are *universal law*, *freedom*, and *justice*. At first they shall shine, then struggle with darkness, until every man's head and heart has become bright and clear. Then shall oppression be driven from the earth, like the thunder-clouds by the storm-wind, and all deceit will cease to have any more power. Gosa.

Commentary

Frethorik's narrative continues with yet another eye-witness account of the second deluge that swamped Northern Europe, this time from the viewpoint of an unnamed writer in Scandinavia (Schoonland). Apart from the volcanic eruptions which made lakes boil, and the toppling of mountains which smashed whole forests and villages, we are informed also of the suicide of another of the Magyar leaders.

Following the Magy's death, a duke of Lindasburgt was elected king and, says the writer, since that time, with all the other citadels destroyed, northern sea-warriors – forerunners of the Norsemen or Vikings – sought advice at the only remaining and original citadel of Texland.

Those who escaped this second upheaval did so by taking refuge aboard their ships, returning to their lands when calm was restored.

Next, Frethorik tells of the speech-customs, appearance and, to him, distorted religious practices of the 'Brok-

179

mannen' or descendants of the Greeks. This passage, with its references to beliefs in spirits inhabiting statues, in sorcerers, witches, dwarfs and elves gives an idea of how such folklore began to insinuate itself into the mythologies of the Northern peoples.

Wiljo, who takes over the work from her dead husband, makes reference to a further Frisian book that appears to have been lost to posterity. She writes of a book of songs which, so far, has not come down to us. She has, however, preserved the narratives and the writings of Hellenia, which she gives here. Hellenia, however, is clearly not the same person as Min-erva, as the end-signature to the narrative, 'Dela, surnamed Hellenia', demonstrates. Dela may, however, in view of the similarity of her surname to Nyhellenia, have been of the same line.

What Dela has to say about the Slavonic races is particularly interesting, in view of historical evidence. The Slavs are believed to have come from Aryan stock which, the *Oera Linda Book* suggests, were the original Frisians before the sinking of Atland. Slavs were supposed to have settled in pre-historic times from the frozen north to the Black Sea and to have filtered over the whole of eastern Europe. Later, it is believed, they interbred with the Magyar races. The mixture of blood has caused historians to identify the Slavs with Hungarians, Russians, Germans, Bulgarians, Serbs, etc., when they formed independent states.

The early Slav-Thracians, already mentioned in the commentary on Chapter One, became slaves of the later Thracian kings who over-ran their territories. As Dela tells us, they were 'brought under the yoke like oxen', digging for metals and building stone houses for the tyrannical princes and priests. But something of the original Frisian spirit was revived in them when travellers by land and sea from Friesland infiltrated their lands.

The next section of the narrative of Dela contains the amazing reference to the holy man known as Jessos. My copy of the *Oera Linda Book* translation has a footnote that says: 'Jesus – not to be confused with Jesus any more than Krisen (Krishna) with Christ'.

Yet in fact, in studying the story and sayings of this wandering 'shepherd', known variously as Jessos, Krishna and Buddha, one is forced to conclude that he contains within him elements of all three figures of the Christian, Hindu and Buddhist faiths. It is possible that he is a deliberately contrived pot-pourri, designed to illustrate the principle, referred to earlier in this book, of a line of Prophets, all of whom are manifestations of God, throughout the ages, and whose teachings are designed to adapt to their own time. The story that follows – of how the priests distorted the name and teachings of Jessos to their own ends – could also be a moral tale of how false teachers can manipulate the doctrines of true prophets.

The passages which follow the story of Jessos also tend to suggest that his nature is metaphorical. Dela says that when the false priests imagine that they have totally obliterated the truth, or 'light' of Frya and Jessos, then men will rise up against them – men who have quietly preserved the original truths and beliefs. These will then enlighten the rest of mankind who will turn upon the false priests. Eventually, Dela prophesies, only the genuine essence of the eternal spirit of Wr-alda will prevail and there will be no need for masters, princes, rulers and priests, except those that the people choose. All this, she says, will occur in about 2000 A.D. – 4,000 years after the submersion of Atland. One thousand years after that, she adds, there will be no priests and no oppression.

Similarly, the Eeremoeder Gosa leaves behind a prophecy of bloodshed from the East (Byzantium, perhaps?), followed by a struggle to establish universal law, freedom and justice, after which 'oppression' shall be driven from the earth.

These predictions of European and world events over a period of some 5,000 years is, in different words, similar to that given by the Eeremoeder Frana who was murdered by the Magy.

CHAPTER SEVENTEEN

THE WRITINGS OF KONERÊD

Here, the further history of the Frisians is taken up by
Konerêd, eldest son of Frethorik and Wiljow:

My forefathers have written this book in succession. I
will do this, the more because there exists no longer in
my state any citadel on which events are inscribed as used
to be the case. My name is Konerêd. My father's name
was Frethorik, my mother's name was Wiljow. After my
father's death I was chosen as his successor. When I was
fifty years old I was chosen for chief Grevetman. My
father has written how the Lindaoorden and Liudgaarden
were destroyed. Lindahem is still lost, the Lindaoorden
partially, and the north Lindgaarden are still concealed
by the salt sea. The foaming sea washes the ramparts of
the castle. As my father has mentioned, the people, being
deprived of their harbour, went away and built houses inside the ramparts of the citadel; therefore the bastion is
called Lindwerd. The sea-people say Linwerd, but that is
nonsense. In my youth there was a portion of land lying
outside the rampart all mud and marsh; but Frya's people
were neither tired nor exhausted when they had a good
object in view. By digging ditches, and making dams of
the earth that came out of the ditches, we recovered a
good space of land outside the rampart, which had the
form of a hoof three poles eastwards, three southwards,
and three westwards. At present we are engaged in ram-
ming piles into the ground to make a harbour to protect
our rampart. When the work is finished, we shall attract
mariners. In my youth it looked very queer, but now there
stands a row of houses. Leaks and deficiencies produced
by poverty have been remedied by industry. From this
men may learn that Wr-alda, our universal father, pro-
tects all his creatures, if they preserve their courage and
help each other.

Friso, who was already powerful by his troops, was chosen chief Grevetman of the districts round Staveren. He laughed at our mode of defending our land and our sea-fights; therefore he established a school where the boys might learn to fight in the Greek manner, but I believe that he did it to attach the young people to himself. I sent my brother there ten years ago, because I thought, now that we have not got any mother, it behoves me to be doubly watchful, in order that he may not become our master.

Gosa has given us no successors. I will not give any opinion about that; but there are still old suspicious people who think that she and Friso had an understanding about it. When Gosa died, the people from all parts wished to choose another mother; but Friso, who was busy establishing a kingdom for himself, did not desire to have any advice or messenger from Texland. When the messengers of the Landsaten[1] came to him, he said that Gosa had been far-seeing and wiser than all the counts together, and yet she had been unable to see any light or way out of this affair; therefore she had not had the courage to choose a successor, and to choose a doubtful one she thought would be very bad; therefore she wrote in her last will, It is better to have no mother than to have one on whom you cannot rely. Friso had seen a great deal. He had been brought up in the wars, and he had just learned and gathered as much of the tricks and cunning ways of the Gauls and the princes as he required, to lead the other counts wherever he wished. See here how he went to work about that.

Friso had taken here another wife, a daughter of Wilfrêthe, who in his lifetime had been chief count of Staveren. By her he had two sons and two daughters. By his wish Kornelia, his youngest daughter, was married to my brother. Kornelia is not good Frisian; her name ought to be written Korn-helia. Weemoed, his eldest daughter, he

1. Landsaten – Inland-dwellers.

married to Kauch. Kauch, who went to school with him, is the son of Wichhirte, the king of the Geertmen. But Kauch is likewise not good Frisian, and ought to be Kaap. So they have learned more bad language than good manners.

Now I must return to my story.

After the great flood of which my father wrote an account, there came many Jutlanders and Letlanders out of the Baltic, or bad sea. They were driven down the Kattegat in their boats by the ice as far as the coast of Denmark, and there they remained. There was not a creature to be seen; so they took possession of the land, and named it after themselves, Jutland. Afterwards, many of the Denmarkers returned from the higher lands, but they settled more to the south; and when the mariners returned who had not been lost, they all went together to Zeeland.[2] By this arrangement the Jutlanders retained the land to which Wr-alda had conducted them. The Zeeland skippers, who were not satisfied to live upon fish, and who hated the Gauls, took to robbing the Phoenician ships. In the south-west point of Scandinavia there lies Lindasburgt, called Lindasnose, built by one Apol, as is written in the book. All the people who live on the coasts, and in the neighbouring districts, had remained true Frisians; but by their desire for vengeance upon the Gauls, and the followers of Kaltana, they joined the Zeelanders. But that connection did not hold together, because the Zeelanders had adopted many evil manners and customs of the wicked Magyars, in opposition to Frya's people. Afterwards, everybody went stealing on his own account; but when it suited them they held all together. At last the Zeelanders began to be in want of good ships. Their shipbuilders had died, and their forests as well as their land had been washed out to sea. Now there arrived unexpectedly three ships, which anchored off the ringdyk of our citadel. By the disruption of our land they had lost themselves, and had missed Flymond. The merchant who

2. Zeeland – the Danish Islands.

184

was with them wished to buy new ships from us, and for that purpose had brought all kinds of valuables, which they had stolen from the Celtic country and Phoenician ships. As we had no ships, I gave them active horses and four armed couriers to Friso; because at Stavere, along the Alberga, the best ships of war were built of hard oak which never rots. While these sea rovers remained with us, some of the Jutmen had gone to Texland, and thence to Friso. The Zeelanders had stolen many of their strongest boys to row their ships, and many of their finest daughters to have children by. The great Jutlanders could not prevent it, as they were not properly armed. When they had related all their misfortunes, and a good deal of conversation had taken place, Friso asked them at last if they had no good harbours in their country. Oh, yes, they answered; a beautiful one, created by Wr-alda. It is like a bottle, the neck narrow, but in the belly a thousand boats may lie; but we have no citadel and no defences to keep out the pirate ships. Then you shall make them, said Friso. That is very good advice, said the Jutlanders; but we have no workmen and no building materials; we are all fishermen and trawlers. The others are drowned or fled to the higher lands. While they were talking in this way, my messengers arrived at the court with the Zeeland gentlemen. Here you must observe how Friso understood deceiving everybody, to the satisfaction of both parties, and to the accomplishment of his own ends. To the Zeelanders he promised that they should have yearly fifty ships of a fixed size for a fixed price, fitted with iron chains and crossbows, and full rigging as is necessary and useful for men-of-war, but that they should leave in peace the Jutlanders and all the people of Frya's race. But he wished to do more; he wanted to engage all our sea rovers to go with him upon his fighting expedition. When the Zeelanders had gone, he loaded forty old ships with weapons for wall defences, wood, bricks, carpenters, masons, and smiths, in order to build citadels. Witto, or Witte, his son, he sent to superintend. I have never been well informed of what happened; but this much is clear to me, that on each

185

side of the harbour a strong citadel has been built, and garrisoned by people brought by Friso out of Saksenmarken. Witto courted Siuchthirte and married her. Wilhelm, her father, was chief Alderman of the Jutmen – that is, chief Grevetman or Count. Wilhelm died shortly afterwards, and Witto was chosen in his place.

WHAT FRISO DID FURTHER

Of his first wife he still had two brothers-in-law, who were very daring. Hetto – that is, heat – the youngest, he sent as messenger to Kattaburgt, which lies far in the Saxsenmarken. Friso gave him to take seven horses, besides his own, laden with precious things stolen by the sea-rovers. With each horse there were two young sea-rovers and two young horsemen, clad in rich garments, and with money in their purses. In the same way as he sent Hetto to Kattaburgt, he sent Bruno – that is, brown – the other brother-in-law, to Mannagarda oord. Mannagarda oord was written Mannagarda ford in the earlier part of this book, but that is wrong. All the riches that they took with them were given away, according to circumstances, to princes, princesses, and chosen young girls. When his young men went to the tavern to dance with the young people there, they orderded baskets of spice, gingerbread, and tuns of the best beer. After these messengers he let his young people constantly go over to the Saxsenmarken, always with money in their purses and presents to give away, and they spent money carelessly in the taverns. When the Saxsen youths looked with envy at this they smiled, and said, If you dare go and fight the common enemy you would be able to give much richer presents to your brides, and live much more princely. Both the brothers-in-law of Friso had married daughters of the chief princes, and afterwards the Saxsen youths and girls came in whole troops to the Flymeer.

The burgtmaidens and old maidens who still remembered their greatness did not hold with Friso's object, and therefore they said no good of him; but Friso, more cun-

ning than they, let them chatter, but the younger maidens
he led to his side with golden fingers. They said everywhere, For a long time we have had no mother, but that
comes from our being fit to take care of ourselves. At
present it suits us best to have a king to win back our
lands that we have lost through the imprudence of our
mothers. Further, they said, Every child of Frya has
permission to let his voice be heard before the choice of a
prince is decided; but if it comes to that, that you choose
a king, then also we will have our say. From all that we
can see, Wr-alda has appointed Friso for it, for he has
brought him here in a wonderful way. Friso knows the
tricks of the Gauls, whose language he speaks; he can
therefore watch against their craftiness. Then there is
something else to keep the eye upon. What count could
be chosen as king without the others being jealous of him?
All such nonsense the young maidens talked; but the old
maidens, though few in number, tapped their advice out
of another cask. They said always and to every one: Friso
does like the spiders. At night he spreads his webs in all
directions, and in the day he catches in them all his un-
suspecting friends. Friso says he cannot suffer any priests
or foreign princes, but we say that he cannot suffer anybody but himself; therefore he will not allow the citadel
of Stavia to be rebuilt; therefore he will not have the
mother again. To-day Friso is your counsellor, tomorrow
he will be your king, in order to have full power over you.
Among the people there now existed two parties. The old
and the poor wished to have the mother again, but the
young and the warlike wished for a father and a king. The
first called themselves mother's sons, the others father's
sons, but the mother's sons did not count for much; because there were many ships to build, there was a good
time for all kinds of workmen. Moreover, the sea-rovers
brought all sorts of treasures, with which the maidens
were pleased, the girls were pleased, and their relations
and friends.

When Friso had been nearly forty years at Staveren he
died. Owing to him many of the states had been joined

187

together again, but that we were the better off for it I am not prepared to certify. Of all the counts that preceded him there was none so renowned as Friso; for, as I said before, the young maidens spoke in his praise, while the old maidens did all in their power to make him hateful to everybody. Although the old women could not prevent his meddling, they made so much fuss that he died without becoming king.

NOW I WILL WRITE ABOUT HIS SON ADEL

Friso, who had learned our history from the book of the Adelingen,[3] had done everything in his power to win their friendship. His eldest son, whom he had by his wife Swethirte, he named Adel; and although he strove with all his might to prevent the building or restoring of any citadels, he sent Adel to the citadel of Texland in order to make himself better acquainted with our laws, language and customs. When Adel was twenty years old Friso brought him into his own school, and when he had fully educated him he sent him to travel through all the states. Adel was an amiable young man, and in his travels he made many friends, so the people called him Atharik – that is, rich in friends – which was very useful to him afterwards, for when his father died he took his place without a question of any other count being chosen.

While Adel was studying at Texland there was a lovely maiden at the citadel. She came from Saxsenmarken, from the state of Suebaland,[4] therefore she was called at Texland Suobene, although her name was Ifkja. Adel fell in love with her, and she with him, but his father wished him to wait a little. Adel did as he wished, but as soon as he was dead, sent messengers to Berthold, her father, to ask her in marriage. Berthold was a prince of high-principled feelings. He had sent his daughter to Texland in the hope

3. *The Book of Adela's Followers.*
4. Suebi was a name given by the Romans to a group of peoples inhabiting central Germany. Tacitus, however, uses the name to include all the tribes to the north, east and in the basin of the Elbe.

that she might be chosen Burgtmaagd in her country, but when he knew of their mutual affection, he bestowed his blessing upon them. Ifkja was a clever Frisian. As far as I have been able to learn, she always toiled and worked to bring the Frya's people back under the same laws and customs. To bring the people to her side, she travelled with her husband through all Saxenmarken, and also to Geertmannia – as the Geertmen had named the country which they had obtained by means of Gosa. Thence they went to Denmark, and from Denmark by sea to Texland. From Texland they went to Westflyland, and so along the coast to Walhallagara; thence they followed the Zuiderryn[5] till, with great apprehension, they arrived beyond the Rhine at the Marsaten of whom our Apollonia has written. When they had stayed there a little time, they returned to the lowlands. When they had been some time descending towards the lowlands, and had reached about the old citadel of Aken, four of their servants were suddenly murdered and stripped. They had loitered a little behind. My brother, who was always on the alert, had forbidden them to do so, but they did not listen to him. The murderers that had committed this crime were Twisklanders, who had at that time audaciously crossed the Rhine to murder and to steal. The Twisklanders are banished and fugitive children of Frya, but their wives they have stolen from the Tartars. The Tartars are a brown tribe of Finda's people, who are thus named because they make war on everybody. They are all horsemen and robbers. This is what makes the Twisklanders so bloodthirsty. The Twisklanders who had done the wicked deed called themselves Frijen or Franken. There were among them, my brother said, red, brown, and white men. The red and brown made their hair white with lime-water – but as their faces remained brown, they were only the more ugly. In the same way as Apollonia, they visited Lydasburgt and the Alderga. Afterwards they made a tour of all the neighbourhood of Stavera. They behaved with so much amia-

5. The River Waal, in the Netherlands.

bility, that everywhere the people wished to keep them. Three months later, Adel sent messengers to all the friends that he had made, requesting them to send to him their 'wise men' in the month of May . . .

(According to an annotation in my translation of the *Oera Linda Book*, here the copyist, Hiddo oera Linda, has turned over a leaf too many and has thus omitted two pages.)

. . . his wife, he said, who had been maagd of Texland, had received a copy of it. In Texland many writings are still found which are not copied in the book of Adeligen. One of these writings had been placed by Gosa with her last will, which was to be opened by the oldest maiden, Albetha, as soon as Friso was dead.

CHAPTER EIGHTEEN

FINAL FRAGMENTS

The rest of the *Oera Linda Book* consists of the advice of the Eeremoeder Gosa; further information about the Punjab and other lands, from Liudgert the Geertman; the writing of Beeden, including a letter read at a Juulfeast by Rike; and a final, unsigned, incomplete portion giving the later history of the Frisians. This section contains several lacunae, where portions of the text have been missed out or lost.

There is little to suggest in the counsel of Gosa, which comes first, the kind of collusion between herself and Friso, hinted at in the preceeding passages by Konerêd.

HERE IS THE WRITING WITH GOSA'S ADVICE

When Wr-alda gave children to the mothers of mankind, he gave one language to every tongue and to all lips. This gift Wr-alda had bestowed upon men in order that by its means they might make known to each other what must be avoided and what must be followed to find salvation, and to hold salvation to all eternity. Wr-alda is

190

wise and good, and all-foreseeing. As he knew that happiness and holiness would flee from the earth when wickedness would overcome virtue, he has attached to the language an equitable property. This property consists in this, that men can neither lie nor use deceitful words without stammering or blushing, by which means the innately bad are easily known.

As thus our language opens the way to happiness and blessedness, and thus helps to guard against evil inclinations, it is rightly named the language of the gods, and all those by whom it is held in honour derive honour from it. But what has happened? As soon as among our half brothers and sisters deceivers arose, who gave themselves out as servants of the good, it soon became otherwise. The deceitful priests and the malignant princes, who always clung together, wished to live according to their own inclinations, without regard to the laws of right. In their wickedness they went so far as to invent other languages, so that they might speak secretly in anybody's presence of their wicked and unworthy affairs without betraying themselves by stammering, and without showing a blush upon their countenances. But what has that produced? Just as the seed of good herbs which has been sown by good men in the open day springs up from the ground, so time brings to light the evil seed which has been sown by wicked men in secret and in darkness.

The wanton girls and effeminate youths who consorted with the immoral priests and princes, taught the new language to their companions, and thus spread it among the people till God's language was clean forgotten. Would you know what came of all this? How that stammering and blushing no longer betrayed their evil doings; – virtue passed away, wisdom and liberty followed; unity was lost, and quarrelling took its place; love flew away, and unchastity and envy met round their tables; and where justice previously reigned, now it is the sword. All are slaves – the subjects of their masters, envy, bad passions and covetousness. If they had only invented one language things might possibly have still gone on well; but they in-

191

vented as many languages as there are states, so that one people can no more understand another people than a cow, a dog, or a wolf a sheep. The mariners can bear witness to this. From all this it results that all the slave people look upon each other as strangers; and that as a punishment of their inconsiderateness and presumption, they must quarrel and fight till they are all destroyed.

HERE IS MY COUNSEL

If you wish that you alone should inherit the earth, you must never allow any language but God's language to pass your lips, and take care that your own language remains free from outlandish sounds. If you wish that some of Lyda's children and some of Finda's children remain, you must do the same. The language of the East Schoonlanders has been perverted by the vile Magyars, and the language of the followers of Kaltana has been spoiled by the dirty Gauls. Now, we have been weak enough to admit among us the returned followers of Hellenia, but I anxiously fear that they will reward our weakness by debasing our pure language.

Many things have happened to us, but among all the citadels that have been disturbed and destroyed in the bad time, Irtha has preserved Fryasburgt uninjured; and I may remark that Frya's or God's language has always remained here untainted.

Here in Texland, therefore, schools should be established; and from all the states that have kept to the old customs the young people should be sent here, and afterwards those whose education is complete can help those who remain at home. If foreigners come to buy ironwares from you, and want to talk and bargain, they must come back to God's language. If they learn God's language, then the words, 'to be free', and 'to have justice', will come to them, and glimmer and glitter in their brains to a perfect light, and that flame will destroy all bad princes and hypocritical dirty priests.

(Here, Gosa's counsel ends, and Konerêd continues:)

The native and foreign messengers were pleased with that writing, but no schools came from it. Then Adel established schools himself. Every year Adel and Ifkja went to inspect the schools. If they found a friendly feeling existing between the natives and foreigners, they were extremely pleased. If there were any who had sworn friendship together, they assembled the people, and with great ceremony let them inscribe their names in a book which was called the Book of Friendship, and afterwards a festival was held. All these customs were kept up in order to bring together the separate branches of Frya's race; but the maidens who were opposed to Adel and Ifkja said that they did it for no other reason than to make a name for themselves, and to bring all the other states under their subjection.

Among my father's papers I found a letter from Liudgert the Geertman. Omitting some passages which only concern my father, I proceed to relate the rest.

Punjab, that is five rivers, and by which we travel, is a river of extraordinary beauty, and is called Five Rivers, because four other streams flow into the sea by its mouth. Far away to the eastward is another large river, the Holy or Sacred Ganges. Between these two rivers is the land of the Hindoos. Both rivers run from the high mountains to the plains. The mountains in which their sources lie are so high that they reach the heavens (*laia*), and therefore these mountains are called Himmellaia. Among the Hindoos and others of these countries there are people who meet together secretly. They believe that they are pure children of Finda, and that Finda was born in the Himmellaia mountains, whence she went with her children to the lowlands. Some of them believe that she, with her children, floated down upon the foam of the Ganges, and that is the reason why the river is called the Sacred Ganges. But the priests, who came from another country, traced out these people, and had them burnt, so that they do not dare to declare openly their creed. In this country all the priests are fat and rich. In their churches there are all kinds of

193

monstrous images, many of them of gold. To the west of the Punjab are the Yren,[1] or morose (Drangianen), the Gedrosten, or runaways, and the Urgetten, or forgotten. These names are given by the priests out of spite, because they fled from their customs and religion. On their arrival our forefathers likewise established themselves to the east of the Punjab, but on account of the priests they likewise went to the west. In that way we learned to know the Yren and other people. The Yren are not savages, but good people, who neither pray to nor tolerate images; neither will they suffer priests or churches; but as we adhere to the light of Fasta, so they everywhere maintain fire in their houses. Coming still further westward, we arrive at the Gedrosten. Regarding the Gedrosten: They have been mixed with other people, and speak a variety of languages. These people are really savage murderers, who always wander about the country on horseback hunting and robbing, and hire themselves as soldiers to the surrounding princes, at whose command they destroy whatever they can reach.

The country between the Punjab and the Ganges is as flat as Friesland near the sea, and consists of forests and fields, fertile in every part, but this does not prevent the people from dying by thousands of hunger. The famines, however, must not be attributed to Wr-alda or Irtha, but to the princes and priests. The Hindoos are timid and submissive before their princes, like hinds before wolves. Therefore the Yren and others have called them Hindoos, which means hinds. But their timidity is frightfully abused. If strangers come to purchase corn, everything is turned into money, and this is not prevented by the priests, because they, being more crafty and rapacious than all the princes put together, know very well that all the money will come into their pockets. Besides what the people suffer from their princes, they suffer a great deal from poisonous and wild beasts. There are great elephants that sometimes go about in whole flocks and trample down

1. Iranians.

194

cornfields and whole villages. There are great black and white cats which are called tigers. They are as large as calves, and they devour both men and beasts. Besides other creeping animals there are snakes from the size of a worm to the size of a tree. The largest can swallow a cow, but the smallest are the most deadly. They conceal themselves among the fruits and flowers, and surprise the people who come to gather them. Any one who is bitten by them is sure to die, as Irtha has given no antidote to their poison, because the people have so given themselves up to idolatry. There are, besides, all sorts of lizards, tortoises and crocodiles. All these reptiles, like the snakes, vary from the size of a worm to the trunk of a tree. According to their size and fierceness, they have names which I cannot recollect, but the largest are called alligators, because they eat as greedily the putrid cattle that float down the stream as they do the living animals that they seize. On the west of the Punjab where we come from, and where I was born, the same fruits and crops grow as on the east side. Formerly there existed also the same crawling animals, but our forefathers burnt all the underwood, and so diligently hunted all the wild animals, that there are scarcely any left. To the extreme west of the Punjab there is found rich clay land as well as barren heaths, which seem endless, occasionally varied lovely spots on which the eye rests enchanted. Among the fruits there are many that I have not found here. Among the various kinds of corn some is as yellow as gold. There are also golden apples, of which some are as sweet as honey, and others as sour as vinegar. In our country there are nuts as large as a child's head. They contain cheese and milk. When they are old oil is made from them. Of the husks ropes are made, and of the shells cups and other household utensils are made. I have found in the woods here bramble and holly berries. In my country we have trees bearing berries, as large as your limetrees, the berries of which are much sweeter and three times as large as your gooseberries. When the days are at the longest, and the sun is in the zenith, a man's body has no shadow. If you sail very far to the south and look to the east at mid-day, the sun shines on your left side as it does in other countries on the right side. With this I will finish. It will be easy for you, by means of what I have written, to distinguish between false accounts and true descriptions. – Your Liudgert.

THE WRITING OF BEEDEN

My name is Beeden, son of Hachgana. My uncle, not having married, left no children. I was elected in his place. Adel, the third king of that name, approved of the choice, provided I should acknowledge him as master. In addition to the entire inheritance of my uncle, he gave me some land which joined my inheritance, on condition that I would settle people there who should never his people ...[2]

... therefore I will allow it a place here.

LETTER OF RIKA THE OUDMAAGD, READ
AT STAVEREN AT THE JUUL FEAST

My greeting to all of you whose forefathers came here with Friso. According to what you say, you are not guilty of idolatry. I will not speak of that now, but will at once mention a failing which is very little better. You know, or you do not know, how many titles Wr-alda has; but you all know that he is named universal provider, because that everything comes and proceeds from him for the sustenance of his creatures. It is true that Irtha is named sometimes the feeder of all, because she brings forth all the fruits and grains on which men and beasts are fed; but she would not bear any fruit or grain unless Wr-alda gave her the power. Women who nourish their children at their breasts are called nurses, but if Wr-alda did not give them milk the children would find no advantage; so that, in

2. Here, twenty or perhaps more pages are missing from the manuscript in which, according to an annotation in my copy of the translation, Beeden wrote about the King Adel the Third, called Ubbo.

short, Wr-alda really is the nourisher. That Irtha should be called the universal nourisher, and that a mother should be called a feeder, one can understand, figuratively speaking; but that a father should be called a feeder, because he is a father, goes against all reason. Now I know whence all this folly comes. Listen to me. It comes from our enemies; and if this is followed up you will become slaves, to the sorrow of Frya and to the punishment of your pride. I will tell you what happened to the slave people; from that you may take warning. The foreign kings, who follow their own will, place Wr-alda below the crown. From envy that Wr-alda is called the universal father, they wish also to be called fathers of the people. Now, everybody knows that kings do not regulate the productiveness of the earth; and that they have their sustenance by means of the people, but still they will persist in their arrogance. In order to attain their object they were not satisfied from the beginning with free gifts, but imposed a tax upon the people. With the tax thus raised they hired foreign soldiers, whom they retained about their courts. Afterwards they took as many wives as they pleased, and the smaller princes and gentry did the same. When, in consequence, quarrels and disputes arose in the households, and complaints were made about it, they said every man is the father (feeder) of his household, therefore he shall be master and judge over it. Thus arose arbitrariness, and as the men ruled over their households the kings would do over their people. When the kings had accomplished that, they should be called fathers of the people, they had statues of themselves made, and erected in the churches beside the statues of the idols, and those who would not bow down to them were either killed or put in chains. Your forefathers and the Twisklanders had intercourse with the kings, and learned these follies from them. But it is not only that some of your men have been guilty of stealing titles, I have also much to complain of against your wives. If there are men among you who wish to put themselves on a level with Wr-alda, there are also women who wish to consider themselves equals of Frya. Because

197

they have borne children, they call themselves mothers; but they forget that Frya bore children without having intercourse with a man. Yes, they not only have desired to rob Frya and the Eeremoeders of their honourable title (with whom they cannot put themselves upon an equality), but they do the same with the honourable titles of their fellow-creatures. There are women who allow themselves to be called ladies, although they know that only belongs to the wives of princes. They also let their daughters be called maagden, although they know that no young girls are so called unless they belong to a citadel. You all fancy that you are better for this name-stealing, but you forget that jealousy clings to it, and that every wrong sows the seed of its own rod. If you do not alter your course, in time it will grow so strong that you cannot see what will be the end. Your descendants will be flogged by it, and will not know whence the stripes come. But although you do not build citadels for the maidens and leave them to their fate, there will still remain some who will come out of woods and caves, and will prove to your descendants that you have by your disorderliness been the cause of it. Then you will be damned. Your ghosts will rise frightened out of their graves. They will call upon Wr-alda, Frya, and her maidens, but they shall receive no succour before the Juul shall enter upon a new circuit, and that will only be three thousand years after this century.

•

THE END OF RIKA'S LETTER

(Here, the writing of Beeden ends. According to the paging of the manuscript, two successive pages are missing, but it is possible that even more are wanting. The abrupt opening of the succeeding passage shows that the beginning – and name of the author – have been lost. However, a footnote in my copy of the translation says that the writer may have been a son or grandson of Beeden.)

... therefore I will first write about black Adel. Black Adel was the fourth king after Friso. In his youth he studied first at Texland, and then at Staveren, and afterwards travelled through all the states. When he was twenty-four years old his father had him elected Asega-Asker. As soon as he became Asker he always took the part of the poor. The rich, he said, do enough of wrong by means of their wealth, therefore we ought to take care that the poor look up to us. By arguments of this kind he became the friend of the poor and the terror of the rich. It was carried so far that his father looked up to him. When his father died he succeeded, and then he wished to retain his office as well, as the kings of the East used to do. The rich would not suffer this, so all the people rose up, and the rich were glad to get out of the assembly with whole skins. From that time there was no more talk of equality. He oppressed the rich and flattered the poor, by whose assistance he succeeded in all his wishes. King Askar, as he was always called, was seven feet high, and his strength was as remarkable as his height. He had a clear intellect, so that he understood all that was talked about, but in his actions he did not display much wisdom. He had a handsome countenance and a smooth tongue, but his soul was blacker than his hair. When he had been king for a year, he obliged all the young men in the state to come once a year to the camp to have a sham fight. At first he had some trouble with it, but at last it became such a habit that old and young came from all sides to ask if they might take part in it. When he had brought it to this point, he established military schools. The rich complained that their children no longer learned to read and write. Askar paid no attention to it; but shortly afterwards when a sham fight was held, he mounted a throne and spoke aloud: The rich have come to complain to me that their boys do not learn to read and write. I answered nothing; but I will now declare my opinion, and let the general assembly decide. While they all regarded him with curiosity, he said further: According to my idea, we ought to leave reading and writing at present to the maagden and wise people. I do not wish to speak ill of our forefathers; I will only say that in the times so vaunted by

199

some, the Burgtmaagden introduced disputes into our country, which the mothers were unable, either first or last, to put an end to. Worse still, while they talked and chattered about useless customs the Gauls came and seized all our beautiful southern country. Even at this very time our degenerate brothers and their soldiers have already come over the Scheldt. It therefore remains for us to choose whether we will carry a yoke or a sword. If we wish to be and to remain free, it behoves our young men to leave reading and writing alone for a time; and instead of playing games of swinging and wrestling, they must learn to play with sword and spear. When we are completely prepared, and the boys are big enough to carry helmet and shield and to use their weapons, then, with your help, I will attack the enemy. The Gauls may then record the defeat of their helpers and soldiers upon our fields with the blood that flows from their wounds. When we have once expelled the enemy, then we must follow it up till there are no more Gauls, Slaves or Tartars to be driven out of Frya's inheritance. That is right, the majority shouted, and the rich did not dare to open their mouths. He must certainly have thought over this address and had it written out, for on the evening of the same day there were copies in at least twenty different hands, and they all sounded the same. Afterwards he ordered the ship people to make double prows, upon which steel crossbows could be fixed. Those who were backward in doing this were fined, and if they swore that they had no means, the rich men of the village were obliged to pay. Now we shall see what resulted from all this bustle. In the north part of Britain there exists a Scotch people – the most of them spring from Frya's blood – some of them are descended from the followers of Keltana, and, for the rest, from Britons and fugitives who gradually, in the course of time, took refuge there from the tin mines. Those who come from the tin mines have wives, either altogether foreign or of foreign descent. They are all under the dominion of the Gauls. Their arms are wooden bows and arrows pointed with stag's horn or flint. Their houses are of turf and straw, and some of them live in caves in the mountains. Sheep that they have stolen form their only wealth. Some of the descendants of Keltana's followers still have iron weapons, which they have inherited from their forefathers. In order to make myself well understood, I must let alone for a while my account of the Scotch people, and write something about the near Krekalanders.[3] The Krekalanders formerly belonged to us only, but from time immemorial descendants of Lyda and Finda have established themselves there. Of these last there came in the end a whole troop from Troy. Troy is the name of a town that the far Krekalanders[3] had taken and destroyed. When the Trojans had nestled themselves among the near Krekalanders, with time and industry they built a strong town with walls and citadels named Rome, that is, Spacious. When this was done, the people by craft and force made themselves masters of the whole land. The people who live on the south side of the Mediterranean Sea, come for the most part from Phoenicia. The Phoenicians (Puniers or Carthaginians) are a bastard race of the blood of Frya, Finda, and Lyda. The Lyda people were there as slaves, but by the unchastity of the women these black people have degenerated the other people and dyed them brown. These people and the Romans are constantly struggling for the supremacy over the Mediterranean Sea. The Romans, moreover, live at enmity with the Phoenicians; and their priests, who wish to assume the sole government of the world, cannot bear the sight of the Gauls. First they took from the Phoenicians Marseilles – then all the countries lying to the south, the west, and the north, as well as the southern part of Britain – and they have always driven away the Phoenician priests, that is the Gauls, of whom thousands have sought refuge in North Britain. A short time ago the chief of the Gauls was established in the citadel, which is called Kerenac,[4] that is the corner, whence he issued his commands to the Gauls. All their gold was like-

3. In this context, 'near Krekalanders' would appear to denote Italians, while 'far Krekalanders' refers to the Greeks.
4. Kerenac – Carnac, in Brittany.

wise collected there. Keeren Herne (chosen corner), or Kerenac, is a stone citadel which did belong to Kalta. Therefore the maidens of the descendants of Kaltana's followers wished to have the citadel again. Thus through the enmity of the maidens and the Gauls, hatred and quarrelling spread over the mountain country with fire and sword. Our sea people often came there to get wool, which they paid for with prepared hides and linen. Askar had often gone with them, and had secretly made friendship with the maidens and some princes, and bound himself to drive the Gauls out of Kerenac. When he came back there again he gave to the princes and the fighting men iron helmets and steel bows. War had come with him, and soon blood was streaming down the slopes of the mountains. When Askar thought a favourable opportunity occurred, he went with forty ships and took Kerenac and the chief of the Gauls, with all his gold. The people with whom he fought against the soldiers of the Gauls, he had enticed out of the Saxenmarken by promises of much booty and plunder. Thus nothing was left to the Gauls. After that he took two islands for stations for his ships, from which he used later to sally forth and plunder all the Phoenician ships and towns that he could reach. When he returned he brought nearly six hundred of the finest youths of the Scotch mountaineers with him. He said that they had been given him as hostages, that he might be sure that the parents would remain faithful to him; but this was untrue. He kept them as a bodyguard at his court, where they had daily lessons in riding and in the use of all kinds of arms. The Denmarkers, who proudly considered themselves sea-warriors above all the other sea-people, no sooner heard of the glorious deeds of Askar, than they became jealous of him to such a degree, that they would bring war over the sea and over his lands. See here, then, how he was able to avoid a war. Among the ruins of the destroyed citadel of Stavia there was still established a clever Burgtmaagd, with a few maidens. Her name was Reintja, and she was famed for her wisdom. This maid offered her assistance to Askar, on condition that he should afterwards rebuild the citadel of Stavia. When he had bound himself to do this, Reintja went with three maidens to Hals.[5] She travelled by night, and by day she made speeches in all the markets and in all the assemblies. Wralda, she said, had told her by his thunder that all the Frya's people must become friends, and united as brothers and sisters, otherwise Finda's people would come and sweep them off the face of the earth. After the thunder Frya's seven watch-maidens appeared to her in a dream seven nights in succession. They had said, Disaster hovers over Frya's land with yoke and chains; therefore all the people who have sprung from Frya's blood must do away with their surnames, and only call themselves Frya's children, or Frya's people. They must all rise up and drive Finda's people out of Frya's inheritance. If you will not do that, you will bring the slave-chains around your necks, and the foreign chiefs will ill-treat your children and flog them till the blood streams into your graves. Then shall the spirits of your forefathers appear to you, and reproach your cowardice and thoughtlessness. The stupid people who, by the acts of the Magyars, were already so much accustomed to folly, believed all that she said, and the mothers clasped their children to their bosoms. When Reintja had brought the king of Hals and the others to an agreement, she sent messengers to Askar, and went herself along the Baltic Sea. From there she went to the Lithauers,[6] so-called because they always strike at their enemy's face. The Lithauers are fugitives and banished people of our own race, who wander about in the Twisklanden. Their wives have been mostly stolen from the Tartars. The Tartars are a branch of Finda's race, and are thus named by the Twisklanders because they will never be at peace, but provoke people to fight. She proceeded on beyond the Saxsenmarken, crossing through the other Twisklanders in order always to repeat the same thing. After two years had passed, she came along the Rhine home. Among the Twisklanders she gave herself

5. Hals – Holstein.
6. Lithauers – Face-hewers.

203

out for a mother, and said that they might return as free and true people; but then they must go over the Rhine and drive the Gauls out of Frya's south lands. If they did that, then her King Askar would go over the Scheldt and win back the land. Among the Twisklanders many bad customs of the Tartars and Magyars have crept in, but likewise many of our laws have remained. Therefore they still have Maagden, who teach the children and advise the old. In the beginning they were opposed to Reintja, but at last she was followed, obeyed, and praised by them where it was useful or necessary.

As soon as Askar heard from Reintja's messengers how the Jutlanders were disposed, he immediately, on his side, sent messengers to the King of Hals. The ship in which the messengers went was laden with women's ornaments, and took also a golden shield on which Askar's portrait was artistically represented. These messengers were to ask the King's daughter, Frethogunsta, in marriage for Askar. Frethogunsta came a year after that to Staveren. Among her followers was a Magy, for the Jutlanders had been long ago corrupted. Soon after Askar had married Frethogunsta, a church was built at Staveren. In the church were placed monstrous images bedecked with gold-woven dresses. It is also said that Askar, by night, and at unseasonable times, kneeled to them with Frethogunsta; but one thing is certain, the citadel of Stavia was never rebuilt. Reintja was already come back, and went angrily to Prontlik the mother, at Texland, to complain. Prontlik sent out messengers in all directions, who proclaimed that Askar is gone over to Idolatry. Askar took no notice of this, but unexpectedly a fleet arrived from Hals. In the night the maidens were driven out of the citadel, and in the morning there was nothing to be seen of the citadel but a glowing heap of rubbish. Prontlik and Reintja came to me for shelter. When I reflected upon it, I thought that it might prove bad for my state. Therefore, we hit upon a plan which might serve us all. This is the way we went to work. In the middle of the Krijlwood, to the east of Liudwerd, lies our place of refuge, which can only be reached

204

by a concealed path. A long time ago I had established a garrison of men who all hated Askar, and kept away all other people. Now it was come to such a pitch among us, that many women, and even men, talked about ghosts, white women and gnomes, just like the Denmarkers. Askar had made use of all these follies for his own advantage, and we wished to do the same. One dark night I brought the Maagden to the citadel, and afterwards they went with their serving-maids dressed in white along the path, so that nobody dare go there any more. When Askar thought he had his hands free, he let the Magyars travel through his states under all kinds of names, and, except in my state, they were not turned away anywhere. After that Askar had become so connected with the Jutlanders and the Denmarkers, they all went roving together; but it produced no real good to them. They brought all sorts of foreign treasures home, and just for that reason the young men would learn no trades, nor work in the fields; so at last he was obliged to take slaves; but that was altogether contrary to Wr-alda's wish and to Frya's counsel. Therefore the punishment was sure to follow it. This is the way in which the punishment came. They had all together taken a whole fleet that came out of the Mediterranean Sea. This fleet was laden with purple cloths and other valuables that came from Phoenicia. The weak people of the fleet were put ashore south of the Seine, but the strong people were kept to serve as slaves. The handsomest were retained ashore, and the ugly and black were kept on board ship as rowers. In the Fly the plunder was divided, but, without their knowing it, they divided the punishment too. Of those who were placed in the foreign ships six died of colic. It was thought that the food and drink were poisoned, so it was all thrown overboard, but the colic remained all the same. Wherever the slaves or the goods came, there it came too. The Saxsen-men took it over to their marches. The Jutlanders brought it to Schoonland and along the coasts of the Baltic Sea, and with Askar's mariners it was taken to Britain. We and the people of Grenega did not allow either the people or the goods to come over our boundaries, and therefore we remained free from it. How many people were carried off by this disease I cannot tell; but Prontlik, who heard it afterwards from the maidens, told me that Askar had helped out of his states a thousand times more free-men than he had brought dirty slaves in. When the pest had ceased, the Twisklanders who had become free came to the Rhine, but Askar would not put himself on an equality with the princes of that vile degenerate race. He would not suffer them to call themselves Frya's children, as Reintja had offered them, but he forgot then that he himself had black hair. Among the Twisklanders there were two tribes who did not call themselves Twisklanders. One came from the far south-east, and called themselves Allemannen. They had given themselves this name when they had no women among them, and were wandering as exiles in the forests. Later on they stole women from the slave people like the Lithauers, but they kept their name. The other tribe, that wandered about in the neighbourhood, called themselves Franks, not because they were free, but the name of their first king was Frank, who, by the help of the degenerate maidens, had had himself made hereditary king over his people. The people nearest to him called themselves Thioth – his sons, that is, sons of the people. They had remained free, because they never would acknowledge any king, or prince, or master except those chosen by general consent in a general assembly. Askar had already learned from Reintja that the Twisklander princes were almost always at war with each other. He proposed to them that they should choose a duke from his people, because, as he said, he was afraid that they would quarrel among themselves for the supremacy. He said also that his princes could speak with the Gauls. This, he said, was also the opinion of the mother. Then the princes of the Twisklanders came together, and after twenty-one days they chose Alrik as duke. Alrik was Askar's nephew. He gave him two hundred Scotch and one hundred of the greatest Saksmannen to go with him as a bodyguard. The princes were to send twenty-one of their sons as hostages for their fidelity. Thus far all had gone according to his wishes; but when they were to go over the Rhine, the king of the Franks would not be under Alrik's command. Thereupon all was confusion. Askar, who thought that all was going on well, landed with his ships on the other side of the Scheldt; but there they were already aware of his coming, and were on their guard. He had to flee as quickly as he had come, and was himself taken prisoner. The Gauls did not know whom they had taken, so he was afterwards exchanged for a noble Gaul whom Askar's people had taken with them. While all this was going on, the Magyars went about audaciously over the lands of our neighbours. Near Egmuda,' where formerly the citadel Forana had stood, they built a church larger and richer than that which Askar had built at Staveren. They said afterwards that Askar had lost the battle against the Gauls, because the people did not believe that Wodin could help them, and therefore they would not pray to him. They went about stealing young children, whom they kept and brought up in the mysteries of their abominable doctrines. Were there people who....

(Here the manuscript simply ends abruptly).

Commentary

Once again, this time in the counsel of the Eeremoeder Gosa, emerges the somewhat understandable, near-obsession with keeping the race of Frya's children pure and free from outside influence. But in Gosa's case, the emphasis is upon preserving the Frisian tongue.

According to Gosa, however, it is not simply a matter of nationalism. The language, she claims, was given by Wr-alda, the eternal spirit, and is the 'language of the gods' which no one can use deceitfully or falsely without faltering, stammering or blushing. Her account of evil priests and princes inventing their own languages for secret purposes and its result has some affinity with the Biblical story of Babel, when initially men spoke all one language. But then, as they became over-ambitious and sought to be godlike themselves and built themselves a tower in an attempt to reach heaven, their tower was destroyed, they were scattered and spoke different tongues so that none could understand each other's 'babble'.

In the Frisian case, the distortion and changing of the language, with its built-in 'lie detector' qualities, allowed men to become corrupt without giving away their dishonesty and deceit.

To combat this problem, Gosa advised setting up schools at Texland, the only remaining place whose citadel was intact. She also suggested that foreign trade deals should be negotiated only in 'God's language' thus promoting its use and spread.

Konered says, however, that while both Frisians and foreigners were pleased with Gosa's advice, no schools were established as a direct result of it. It was left to Adel and Ifka to promote learning and goodwill and to try to cement relations between the branches of Frya's people. Even then they were suspected by some of the burgtmaagden of seeking only fame for themselves.

The letter of Liudgert the Geertman sheds more, interesting light on the life of the Frisians who settled in the Punjab. He explains the meaning of the name given to the Himalayas (Himmellaia) which, he says, was believed to have been the birthplace of Finda and her people; the yellow races.

The reference to the Yren (Iranians), with their fire-cult is particularly interesting, since it was to the western parts of India that the Parsees, a sect of the Persian Zoroastrian religion fled to avoid forceable conversion to Islam around the fourth or fifth century A.D. At each of their colonies they established fire temples, Liudgert must have encountered their very early predecessors.

The Punjab-born Frisian writer says that the Hindoos (Hindus) became so-called because of their submissive attitudes towards their tyrannical princes – 'like hinds before wolves'. It is perhaps significant that the word 'hind' also became a term for a rustic farm servant in northern England and Scotland. Liudgert notes that, as is the case today, these regions were prone to famine, despite the fertility of the lands in his time.

He describes the flora and fauna – including tigers: 'great black and white cats' – and his account of 'golden apples, of which some are as sweet as honey [oranges] and others as sour as vinegar [lemons]' and of the uses to which coconuts may be put, is particularly vivid.

The writings of Beeden, because of a large amount of missing material – twenty pages or possibly even more – are brief, and consist, apart from his brief introduction, of the letter of Rika. Her title, 'Oudmaagd', is not explained, but it would seem to denote a female elder, possibly a veteran burgtmaagd.

The underlying principles behind Rika's words are, in my opinion, based on sound sense and practical values. They stem from one of the fundamental doctrines of the Frisian faith: that the earth belongs only to God and therefore cannot belong to any man; that the fruits of the earth are likewise of God and, through Him, belong to all men who labour in their growth and harvest. It is a simple faith, yet one based on common sense and one which provides the only practical guide lines for a peaceful, just and happy world.

These writings have much to say on the subjects of freedom and justice and, as they so often reiterate, the meaning of these two words will never be fully appreciated until the oppressed realise that everyone has the God-given right to share, without let or hindrance, in the fruits of the earth through human labour. This was the Frisian conception of freedom and justice. Since labour was necessary to obtain the fruits of the earth which all had the right to enjoy, the actual work to bring this bounty forth, was a virtue, similar in concept to that of the Incas and of the modern Chinese.

Since the Frisian faith precluded any person – king or commoner – possessing land permanently as his private property, it was only natural that it was opposed by all the princes and priests of Europe. One of the suppositions of those to whom the Frisian way was anathema was that the priest or king held the land under God for the people. They then assumed the right to assign land as a personal possession to those they favoured. Gradually, the common right to own land sufficient to produce the necessities of life and upon which to build a house was taken from the people – as, for instance, in the English Enclosure Acts of the 17th, 18th and 19th centuries. Nowadays, people find that their homes, farms, factories and the very ground beneath their feet, and the wealth of goods and services they produce by their joint efforts, along with the government which claims to rule their country, are mortgaged to those who manipulate the monetary system. This adds up to a colossal national debt which denies all the right to live freely and to enjoy to the full their natural rights to the necessities and amenities of their corporate labours.

The authorship of the final segment of the *Oera Linda Book* is unknown and, unfortunately, its beginning and ending have been lost. The anonymous writer describes the militarist policies of Black Adel or Askar, against the Gauls, his degeneration into idolatry, and how the Gauls fled from their former headquarters at Carnac, in Brittany, to northern Europe. He allowed Magyars to roam freely about Frisian territory, formed an allegiance with the Jutlanders and Danes and eventually resorted to slavery.

A plague of colic which swept the land was attributed to the punishment of Wr-alda for this lapse. Askar finally loses his battle against the Gauls, and, say the Magyars, it is because the people would not pray to Wodin. The manuscript ends suddenly, after telling us that the Magyars went about stealing children and initiating them in 'the mysteries of their abominable doctrines'.

So ends the story, faithfully preserved in inscriptions on stone and manuscript, for more than 2,500 years, of a happy land and a people lost to history; of a race which valued freedom and justice above all else on earth; of a religion which must have endured for at least 3,000 years without need of temples, priests or images, because the worship of God was in personal nobility, honesty in word and deed and in following the customs and laws ordained by the founding mother. It was a way of life taught to friends and enemies and carried to the ends of the earth. That the deceptions and violence of others destroyed the Frisian people and their religion was a loss to the world.

Official history has little to say about the Frisians, except that for many years they refused conversion to the Christian faith and resisted subjection by power-hungry princes and kings; that they eventually lost all their lands in Europe except the Netherlands, and even this oasis of independence became as lost when William IV in 1748 was made stadholder of all the provinces and his grandson in 1815 took the title of King of the Netherlands.

From The Saturday Review, July 1, 1876

THE OERA LINDA BOOK

The title of this book will prepare the reader for some narrative of a character as exceptional as itself, and that first impression concerning it will be fully verified on the perusal of its pages. It has been everywhere supposed that the works of Greek and Latin writers which have come down to us, supplemented by others of Eastern origin and by the monuments of antiquity which have survived the ravages of time, have told us everything that is to be learned now concerning the early history of the world and of its inhabitants, and that the careful and laborious comparison of these records of the past have presented the story to us with the utmost attainable completeness and accuracy. This idea, however, will have to undergo considerable modification if any reliance whatever is to be placed in the remarkable work entitled *The Oera Linda Book*; and the arguments in favour of its authenticity and genuineness are numerous and apparently conclusive. From a quarter and at a period the most unexpected a flood of light has thus been thrown on several great events of ancient history, and on various matters of deep scientific interest which, if it be not altogether spurious and deceptive, startles us by the suddenness, the extent, and the importance of its revelations. Whether this virgin mine be charged with untold treasure for the more perfect compilation of the history of our race, or whether the ground has merely been 'salted' by clever but designing hands for the delusion of the unwary; whether, in fact, these revelations are nothing but a learned hoax, is a question which has been for some years occupying the attention of many continental scholars and which as yet has not been entirely closed. In the account of the book which we now proceed to give the consideration tending to favour the conclusion that it is what it purports to be will be carefully pointed out; and though it would certainly have been satisfactory if equal prominence could be given to the arguments adduced in support of a contrary view, it will be seen that a very high antiquity has been already established for the book, and that the reasons for suspecting it rest mainly on the novelty of the assertions found in it, and the extreme degree in which they conflict with long-cherished convictions.

The manuscript set forth in the book has been from time immemorial preserved in the family of C. Over de Linden, chief superintendent[1] of the royal dockyard at the Helder, Holland. No one could give any account of it, nor could understand the language in which it was written. It was only known that it had been handed down from generation to generation in this family, and that a tradition which was embodied in it enjoined its careful preservation. The present possessor being a child at the death of his father, it was taken care of for him by an aunt, and so came into his actual possession only in the year 1848. Dr. E. Verwijs heard of it some time afterwards, and having requested permission to examine it, recognised the language in which it was written as being very ancient Frisian. A copy of it was subsequently made, and a paper on the subject read before the Frisian Society in 1871. The manuscript is not complete, and several writers, at least eight in number, originally worked upon it. Their labours extended over a considerable interval of time, and the first and second portions of it are ascertained to be separated by a period of two centuries. In the volume which now gives it to the British public the Frisian text is printed in Roman characters on the left-hand pages, and the English version on the right hand. The original character of the manuscript bears a rough resemblance to Greek, and this circumstance suggested to the author of the paper referred to – Dr. Verwijs we presume – a strong argument in favour of its *bona fides* because, as he points out, Caesar, in speaking of the Gauls and the Helvetians in his 'Commentaries',

1. A more accurate translation of *rijkshelling-baas*, would be 'master shipwright'.

213

expressly states that they use Greek characters. The particular kind of Greek character here met with is that which is found on old monuments and in old manuscripts which is known as 'lapidary'. How this Frisian people, who at one period of their history took part in the Saxon invasion of England, became acquainted with the Greek character and employed, apparently, for all important public purposes, is explained in this way: The Frisians were enterprising and daring mariners, who were in the habit of trading largely to the Mediterranean. It is argued, and fairly enough, that this fact, which is exhibited most circumstantially and minutely in the narratives of some of their voyages related in the book, is in itself not more improbable than that the Phoenicians at the same period should trade in England for tin, and to the Baltic for amber. It is related in *The Book of Adela's Followers*, in the first part of the manuscript, that many centuries before our era the Phoenicians traded largely also with the Frisians; so that it is certain that the maritime enterprise of the latter would naturally tempt them to visit the shores of the Mediterranean. We read in histories of Greece that the Greeks derived their alphabet from the Phoenicians; but it seems clear that Cadmus can have introduced only the names of the Greek characters attributed to him, their farms differing widely from those used in Phoenician and Hebrew writing. From what source, then, did the Greeks obtain the forms of their characters? The reply which is given here to this question will, doubtless, startle many a reader, and amuse all; but the answer made to it by this manuscript is that, finding the Phoenician characters troublesome and difficult, they, and even the Tyrians, learned the 'writing of Frya', in other words, ancient Fries. The remark made by Caesar is certainly very curious and interesting in its bearing on this subject, and gives a powerful support to the argument in favour of the genuineness of the manuscript. Another point, in which our common belief in reference to the origin of an important portion of our modern characters is corrected, is that in reference to the source whence the numerals in common use are derived. It is here denied that they were introduced into Europe by the Arabs, as is generally supposed.

The Arabs, it is observed, like other Semitic nations, used their whole alphabet in writing numbers; and it is contended that the Fries cyphers were their true originals. This conclusion, which seems sufficiently admissible from the precise manner in which they are stated here to have been originated, is rendered still more probable from the fact that in remote times the Frisians, so-called, had a much wider geographical distribution than the limited tract between the Scheldt and the Vlie in which the Fries dialect is understood to have been spoken. Frisians, for example, are stated by Procopius to have been in his time, together with the Angles and the Britons, an inhabiting race of Britain. The term 'Frisian' is thus evidently used as an equivalent for 'Saxon'; and, further, it is expressly affirmed in old German poetry that the Frisians were formerly called Saxons.

Perhaps the most remarkable and most powerful argument upon which it is asserted that the manuscript is genuine, and one that cannot be controverted, is to be found in the fact that it contains a substantial account of the lake-dwellers of Switzerland – their habitations, mode of life, manners and customs; and it is only during the last twenty years that the remains of these dwellings on piles were first observed, having been concealed from view for twenty centuries until, in the year 1853, their existence was revealed by an exceptionally low state of the waters. They have since been found in other parts of Europe, but the information collected concerning them has been of the scantiest. All that we learn of them is the little that is mentioned of them by Herodotus, who describes some of the lake-dwellers of Thrace; and in one of the panels of Trajan's Pillar there is represented the destruction of a pile-village in Dacia, commemorative of his conquest of that country. The account here given of the Swiss lake-dwellers dates from the sixth century before our era, and is given by Apollonia, the 'Burgtmaagd', or chief of the Virgins, who travelled up the Rhine, and in Switzerland became acquainted with these lacustrine communities. She states that they lived by fishing and hunting, and that they prepared the skins of animals with the bark of the birch tree to sell the furs to the Rhine boatmen, by whom they were brought into commerce. On the discovery of these dwellings, fragments of arms, tools and household articles were also found; but until now these memorials of an extinct race have remained without explanation.

The manuscript circumstantially records, also, the laws which governed the ancient Frisians, and the manner in which they were enforced. It appears that in those remote times the ladies held the place of honour as rulers and law-givers. Each town had its Burgtmaagd, who was selected for her prudence and other good qualities, and was at the head of a council of virgins, while the chief of the Burgtmaagden was the Eeremoeder of Texland. These institutions were partly religious and partly municipal in their character. In their religious aspect they closely resemble the Vestal Virgins of Rome, as it was one of the duties of these priestesses to keep a lamp perpetually burning, and in this consisted the worship of Frya. The 'text', or first law, promulgated in the name of Frya, is set out in several sections. Its provisions are characterised by a spirit of equity, every member of the community enjoying the same rights and being subject to the same restraints as the other members; and they have, moreover, a strong moral tendency, and inculcate an enlightened patriotism. But they are evidently adapted to an almost elementary state of society, and would be altogether insufficient for the complex relations which in our days exist amongst individuals. What surprises us most of all, however, in connection with this matter is to find it here related that the divine Minerva – that Athena Parthenos, in whose honour the magnificent temple which crowns the Athenian Acropolis was erected, and upon whose form Phidias lavished all the resources of the highest Greek art – was originally only a Frisian Burgtmaagd, having been a princess of Frya at Walhallaraga, better known to readers of English history as Walcheren. The history of the landing of a Frisian colony in Greece (about 1600 years before Christ) – Krekaland the Frisians termed it – is related here, and it is observed that while the word Athena has no meaning in Greek, it has a relevant one in Fries, and implied that the colonists

216

entered the country as friends. If this story is deemed improbable, it is certainly not more so than the miraculous origin which the Greek mythology ascribes to Minerva. There is some support of it, moreover, in the fact that in later times the figure of Minerva is found on the Roman votive stones in Walcheren. There are some other mythological curiosities to be met with in the manuscript which will interest those who are fond of this description of research. In none of these relations, however strange and incredible they may appear, is there any statement which absolutely conflicts with the records transmitted to us by classical writers; and it is remarked in the paper we refer to that the name 'Batavians' nowhere appears in the manuscript. The Romans designated as Batavi the inhabitants of the banks of the Waal, which river appears to have been by them called the Patabus; but the word Batavi does not appear earlier than Tacitus and Pliny. Among other minor evidences in support of the genuineness of the manuscript are the following: The manuscript of 1256 is not original, but is a copy, as is proved by numerous faults in the writing and by the explanations given by the copyist of words which even in his time had become obsolete. In one place, also, one or more consecutive pages are lost between pages 157 and 158, which are written on the front and back of the same leaf, the omission evidently being due to the copyists having turned over two pages of the original instead of one, and thus made a complete interruption of the narrative. Another argument tending to the same conclusions is founded upon the paper upon which the manuscript is written, which is cotton-paper of a large quarto size, not very thick, without water-mark or masker's mark, made upon a frame or wire-web, with not very broad perpendicular lines. The colour of the ink used shows that it does not contain iron, and, like other carefully written manuscripts of great antiquity, the regularity of the lines proves that they must have been written within carefully-ruled lines; for which purpose writers in remote times used a thin piece of lead, a ruler and a pair of compasses to mark out the equal spaces. By these indicia the manuscript may be recognised as belonging to the 13th century. As regards the style, it is represented as being simple, concise, and unembarrassed, not presenting any difficulties of spelling, and yet displaying differences between the several writers who have worked at it, and which are due to changes occurring during the long interval of five centuries over which the whole record extends.

Of the very many subjects of deep historic interest with which *The Oera Linda Book* deals we may here advert to one or two. It would hardly be supposed that any records preserved amid the sands and marshes of ancient Holland would ever throw light on any of the great events of the world's history; yet this most remarkable document does this, and, in particular, on some of the facts connected with the Indian expedition of Alexander the Great. Of this we hear in the history of Friso, one of the known kings of Friesland. Our own chroniclers have given us information concerning this prince, but what is here related of him is altogether new, or at least is presented in a different light. This book tells that he came from India in the fleet of Nearchus, one of the officers of Alexander, that he was of Frisian origin, and, in fact, belonged to a Frisian colony which settled in the Punjab 13 centuries and a half before Christ. This fact receives confirmation from Strabo, and in ancient maps of the country names appear which are identically Frisian. The known philological affinities between the German language and those of Persia and certain parts of Northern India also favour the statement. Of the 12,000 Persian primitive words more than 4,000 are pure German. It is also known from history that large migrations of nations took place in ancient times to distant countries, so that at least there is no *a priori* improbability in this portion of the narrative. The coast of Gedrosia, up the Persian Gulf, and thence by the Red Sea to Suez, is described here with some minuteness, and one remarkable fact is mentioned of which we are not made aware from other sources. This is, that the Frisian mariners sailed through the narrow strait which in those days still ran into the Red Sea, and which is actually mentioned by Moses. Why Nearchus should be ordered by Alexander to sail up the Red Sea with all the ships is not clear from the other history. It could have been for the purposes of geographical discovery, as one or two ships would have sufficed for that, and *The Oera Linda Book* clears the matter up. Alexander wanted the ships built for him on the Indus by the Frisian colonists for subsequent service in the Mediterranean. Nearchus took them to the head-waters of the Bitter Lakes, and thence, after three months' labour, drew them overland with the aid of an immense number of elephants and men, finally launching them successfully in the Mediterranean. That the fleet did actually enter the Mediterranean is mentioned by Plutarch in his life of Alexander; but he makes Nearchus take it round Africa and through the Pillars of Hercules. Friso returned to Friesland in consequence of ill treatment from Demetrius, under whose command he was. The reader of *The Oera Linda Book* will be further surprised to hear that not only Minerva, but Calypso, was a Frisian. The wanderings of Ulysses and the story of his sojourn with the goddess were well known in the country, and the student is reminded that Tacitus mentions in his *Germanica* that he found the story current among the people of Lower Germany. Not less remarkable are the contributions which these writings make to geological science. Their explanations with reference to the formation of the Isthmus of Suez have already been referred to and it may now be further mentioned that they contain details relative to the great submersion of the land known to geologists under the name of the Cimbrian Deluge. There is a mythology also among these writings, but, unlike that of the Greeks and Romans, it is free from the confusion and the contradictions in which these abound.

In taking leave of this book we can commend it to careful study by one and all.

The Oera Linda Book. From a manuscript of the 13th century. The original Frisian text, accompanied by an English version of Dr. Ottema's Dutch translation. By W. R. Sandbach. Trubner & Co.

APPENDIX B

A paper read at a meeting of the Frisian Society, February, 1871

C. Over de Linden, Chief Superintendent of the Royal Dockyard at the Helder, possesses a very ancient manuscript which has been inherited and preserved in his family from time immemorial, without any one knowing whence it came or what it contained, owing to both the language and the writing being unknown.

All that was known was that a tradition contained in it had from generation to generation been recommended to careful preservation. It appeared that the tradition rests upon the contents of two letters, with which the manuscript begins, from Hiddo oera Linda, anno 1256, and from Liko Oera Linda, anno 803. It came to C. over de Linden by the directions of his grandfather, Den Heer Andries over de Linden, who lived at Enkhuizen, and died there on the 15th of April 1820, aged sixty-one. As the grandson was at that time barely ten years old, the manuscript was taken care of for him by his aunt, Aafje Meylhoff, born Over de Linden, living at Enkhuizen, who in August 1848 delivered it to the present possessor.

Dr. E. Verwijs having heard of this, requested permission to examine the manuscript, and immediately recognised it as very ancient Fries. He obtained at the same time permission to make a copy of it for the benefit of the Friesland Society, and was of opinion that it might be of great importance, provided it was not suppositious, and invented for some deceptive object, which he feared. The manuscript being placed in my hands, I also felt very doubtful, though I could not understand what object any one could have in inventing a false composition only to keep it a secret. This doubt remained until I had examined carefully-executed facsimiles of two fragments, and afterwards of the whole manuscript

– the first sight of which convinced me of the great age of the document.

Immediately occurred to me Caesar's remark upon the writing of the Gauls and the Helvetians in his 'Bello Gallico' (i. 29, and vi. 14), 'Graecis utuntur literis', though it appears in v. 48 that they were not entirely Greek letters. Caesar thus points out not only a resemblance – and a very true one – as the writing, which does not altogether correspond with any known form of letters, resembles the most, on a cursory view, the Greek writing, such as is found on monuments and the oldest manuscripts, and belongs to the form which is called lapidary. Besides, I formed the opinion afterwards that the writer of the latter part of the book had been a contemporary of Caesar.

The form and the origin of the writing is so minutely and fully described in the first part of the book, as it could not be in any other language. It is very complete, and consists of thirty-four letters, among which are three separate forms of *a* and *u*, and two of *e, i, y*, and *o*, besides four pairs of double consonants – *ng, th, ks*, and *gs*. The *ng*, which as a nasal sound has no particular mark in any other Western language, is an indivisible conjunction; the *th* is soft, as in English, and is sometimes replaced by *d*; the *gs* is seldom met with – I believe only in the word *segse*, to say, in modern Fries *sidse*, pronounced *sisze*.

The paper, of large quarto size, is made of cotton, not very thick, without water-mark or maker's mark, made upon a frame or wire-web, with not very broad perpendicular lines.

An introductory letter gives the year 1256 as that in which this manuscript was written by Hiddo overa Linda on foreign paper. Consequently it must have come from Spain, where the Arabs brought into the market paper manufactured from cotton.

On this subject, W. Wattenbach writes in his 'Das Schriftwesen im Mittelalter' (Leipzig, 1871), s. 93:

'The manufacture of paper from cotton must have been in use among the Chinese from very remote times, and must have become known to the Arabs by the conquest of Samarcand about the year 704. In Damascus this manufacture was

221

an important branch of industry, for which reason it was called *Charta Damascena*. By the Arabians this art was brought to the Greeks. It is asserted that Greek manuscripts of the tenth century written upon cotton paper exist, and that in the thirteenth century it was much more used than parchment. To distinguish it from Egyptian paper it was called *Charta bombicina, gossypina, cuttunea, xylina*. A distinction from linen paper was not yet necessary. In the manufacture of the cotton paper raw cotton was originally used. We first find paper from rags mentioned by Petrus Clusiacensis (1122–50).

'The Spaniards and the Italians learned the manufacture of this paper from the Arabians. The most celebrated factories were at Jativa, Valencia, Toledo, besides Fabriano in the March of Ancona'.[1]

In Germany the use of this material did not become very extended, whether it came from Italy or Spain. Therefore the further this preparation spread from the East and the adjoining countries, the more necessity there was that linen should take the place of cotton. A document of Kaubeuren on linen paper of the year 1318 is of very doubtful genuineness. Bodman considers the oldest pure linen paper to be of the year 1324, but up to 1350 much mixed paper was used. All carefully-written manuscripts of great antiquity show by the regularity of their lines that they must have been ruled, even though no traces of the ruled lines can be distinguished. To make the lines they used a thin piece of lead, a ruler, and a pair of compasses to mark the distances.

In old writings the ink is very black or brown; but while there has been more writing since the thirteenth century, the colour of the ink is often grey or yellowish, and sometimes quite pale, showing that it contains iron. All this affords convincing proof that the manuscript before us belongs to the middle of the thirteenth century, written with clear black letters between fine lines carefully traced with lead. The colour of the ink shows decidedly that it does not contain

1. Compare G. Meerman, *Admonitio de Chartae nostralis* origine. Vad. Letteroef, 1762. P. 630. J. H. de Stoppelaar, *Paper in the Netherlands*. Middelburg, 1869, P. 4.

iron. By these evidences the date given, 1256, is satisfactorily proved, and it is impossible to assign any later date. Therefore all suspicion of modern deception vanishes.

The language is very old Fries, still older and purer than the Fries Rjuchtboek or old Fries laws, differing from that both in form and spelling, so that it appears to be an entirely distinct dialect, and shows that the locality of the language must have been (as it was spoken) between the Vlie and the Scheldt.

The style is extremely simple, concise, and unembarrassed, resembling that of ordinary conversation, and free in the choice of the words. The spelling is also simple and easy, so that the reading of it does not involve the least difficulty, and yet with all its regularity, so unrestricted, that each of the separate writers who have worked at the book has his own peculiarities, arising from the changes in pronunciation in a long course of years, which naturally must have happened, as the last part of the work is written five centuries after the first.

As a specimen of antiquity in language and writing, I believe I may venture to say that this book is unique of its kind.

The writing suggests an observation which may be of great importance.

The Greeks know and acknowledge that their writing was not their own invention. They attribute the introduction of it to Kadmus, a Phenician. The names of the oldest letters, from Alpha to Tau, agree so exactly with the names of the letters in the Hebrew alphabet, with which the Phenician will have been nearly connected, that we cannot doubt that the Hebrew was the origin of the Phenician. But the form of their letters differs so entirely from that of the Phenician and Hebrew writing, that in that particular no connection can be thought of between them. Whence, then, have the Greeks derived the form of their letters?

From 'thet bok thêra Adela folstar' ('The Book of Adela's Followers') we learn that in the time when Kadmus is said to have lived, about sixteen centuries before Christ, a brisk trade existed between the Frisians and the Phenicans, whom

223

they named Kadhemar, or dwellers on the coast.

The name Kadmus comes too near the word Kadhemar for us not to believe that Kadmus simply meant a Phenician.

Further on we learn that about the same time a priestess of the castle in the island of Walcheren, Min-erva, also called Nyhellenia, had settled in Attica at the head of a Frisian colony, and had founded a castle at Athens. Also, from the accounts written on the walls of Waraburch, that the Finns likewise had a writing of their own – a very troublesome and difficult one to read – and that, therefore, the Tyrians and the Greeks had learned the writing of Frya. By this representation the whole thing explains itself, and it becomes clear whence comes the exterior resemblance between the Greek and the old Fries writing, which Caesar also remarked among the Gauls; as likewise in what manner the Greeks acquired and retained the names of the Finn and the forms of the Fries writing.

Equally remarkable are the forms of their figures. We usually call our figures Arabian, although they have not the least resemblance to those used by the Arabs. The Arabians did not bring their ciphers from the East, because the Semitic nations used the whole alphabet in writing numbers. The manner of expressing all numbers by ten signs the Arabs learned in the West, though the form was in some measure corresponding with their writing, and was written from left to right, after the Western fashion. Our ciphers seem here to have sprung from the Fries ciphers (*siffar*), which form had the same origin as the handwriting and is derived from the lines of the Juul?

The book as it lies before us consists of two parts, differing widely from each other, and of dates very far apart. The writer of the first part calls herself Adela, wife of Apol, chief man of the Linda country. This is continued by her son Adelbrost, and her daughter, Apollonia. The first book, running from page 1 to 88, is written by Adela. The following part, from 88 to 94, is begun by Adelbrost and continued by Apollonia. The second book, running from page 94 to 114, is written by Apollonia. Much later, perhaps two hundred and fifty years, a third book is written, from page 114 to 134, by Frethorik; then follows from page 134 to 143, written by his widow, Wiljow; after that from page 144 to 169 by their son, Konereed; and then from page 169 to 192 by their grandson, Beeden. Pages 193 and 194, with which the last part must have begun, are wanting, therefore the writer is unknown. He may probably have been a son of Beeden.

On page 134, Wiljow makes mention of another writing of Adela. These she names 'thet bok thêra sanga (theta boek), thêra tellinga', and 'thet Hellênia bok'; and afterwards 'tha skrifta fon Adela jeftha Hellênia'.

To fix the date we must start from the year 1256 of our era, when Hiddo overa Linda made the copy, in which he says that it was 3449 years after Atland was sunk. This disappearance of the old land (âldland, âtland) was known by the Greeks, for Plato mentions in his 'Timaeus', 24, the disappearance of Atlantis, the position of which was only known as somewhere far beyond the Pillars of Hercules. From this writing it appears that it was land stretching far out to the west of Jutland, of which Heligoland and the islands of North Friesland are the last barren remnants. This event, which occasioned a great dispersion of the Frisian race, became the commencement of a chronological reckoning corresponding with 2193 before Christ, and is known by geologists as the Cimbrian flood.

On page 80 begins an account in the year 1602, after the disappearance of Atland, and thus in the year 591 before Christ; and on page 82 is the account of the murder of Frana, 'Eeremoeder', of Texland, two years later – that is, in 589. When, therefore, Adela commences her writing with her own coming forward in an assembly of the people thirty years after the murder of the Eeremoeder, that must have been in the year 559 before Christ. In the part written by her daughter Apollonia, we find that fifteen months after the assembly Adela was killed by the Finns in an attack by surprise of Texland. This must accordingly have happened 557 years before Christ. Hence it follows that the first book, written by Adela, was of the year 558 before Christ. The second book, by Apollonia, we may assign to about the year

530 before Christ. The latter part contains the history of the known kings of Friesland, Friso, Adel (Ubbo), and Asega Askar, called Black Adel. Of the third king, Ubbo, nothing is said, or rather that part is lost, as the pages 169 to 188 are missing. Frethorik, the first writer, who appears now, was a contemporary of the occurrences which he relates, namely, the arrival of Friso. He was a friend of Liudgert den Geertman, who, as rear-admiral of the fleet of Wichhirte, the sea-king, had come with Friso in the year 303 before Christ, 1,890 years after the disappearance of Atland. He has borrowed most of his information from the log-book of Liudgert.

The last writer gives himself out most clearly as a contemporary of Black Adel or Askar, about the middle of his reign, which Furmerius states to have been from 70 before Christ to 11 after the birth of Christ, the same period as Julius Caesar and Augustus. He therefore wrote in the middle of the last century before Christ, and knew of the conquest of Gaul by the Romans. It is thus evident that there elapsed fully two centuries between the two parts of the work.

Of the Gauls we read on page 84 that they were called the 'Missionaries of Sydon'. And on page 124 'that the Gauls are druids'. The Gauls, then, were Druids, and the name Galli, used for the whole nation, was really only the name of an order of priesthood brought from the East, just as among the Romans the Galli were priests of Cybele.

The whole contents of the book are in all respects new. That is to say, there is nothing in it that we were acquainted with before. What we here read of Friso, Adel, and Askar, differs entirely from what is related by our own chroniclers, or rather presents it in quite another light. For instance, they all relate that Friso came from India, and that thus the Frisians were of Indian descent; and yet they add that Friso was a German, and belonged to a Persian race which Herodotus called Germans, (Γερμάνιοι). According to the statement in this book, Friso did come from India, and with the fleet of Nearchus; but he is not therefore an Indian. He is of

Frisian origin, of Frya's people. He belongs, in fact, to a Frisian colony which after the death of Nijhellenia, fifteen and a half centuries before Christ, under the guidance of a priestess Geert, settled in the Punjab, and took the name of Geertmen. The Geertmen were known by only one of the Greek writers, Strabo, who mentions them as Γερμάνεσ, differing totally and entirely from the Βραχμᾶνεσ in manners, language and religion.

The historians of Alexander's expeditions do not speak of Frisians or Geertmen, though they mention Indo-scythians, thereby describing a people who live in India, but whose origin is in the distant, unknown North.

In the accounts of Liudgert no names are given of places where the Frieslanders lived in India. We only know that they first established themselves to the east of the Punjab, and afterwards moved to the west of those rivers. It is mentioned, moreover, as a striking fact, that in the summer the sun at midday was straight above their heads. They therefore lived within the tropics. We find in Ptolemy (see the map of Kiepert), exactly 24°N. on the west side of the Indus, the name Minnagara; and about six degrees east of that, in 22°N., another Minnagara. This name is pure Fries, the same as Walhallagara, Folsgara, and comes from Minna, the name of an Eeremoeder, in whose time the voyages of Teunis and his nephew Inca took place.

The coincidence is too remarkable to be accidental, and not to prove that Minnagara was the headquarters of the Frisian colony. The establishment of the colonists in the Punjab in 1551 before Christ, and their journey thither, we find fully described in Adela's book; and with the mention of one most remarkable circumstance, namely, that the Frisian mariners sailed through the strait in whose times still ran into the Red Sea.

In Strabo, book i. pages 38 and 50, it appears that Eratosthenes was acquainted with the existence of the strait, of which the later geographers make no mention. It existed still in the time of Moses (Exodus xiv. 2) for he encamped at Pi-ha-chiroht, the 'mouth of the strait'. Moreover, Stabo mentions that Sesostris made an attempt to cut through the isthmus, but that he was not able to accomplish it. That in very remote times the sea really did flow through is proved by the result of the geological investigations on the isthmus made by the Suez Canal Commission, of which Mr. Renaud presented a report to the Academy of Sciences on the 19th June 1856. In that report, among other things, appears the following: 'Une question fort controversée est celle de savoir, si à L'époque où les Hebreux fuyaient de l'Egypte sous la conduite de Moïse, les lacs amers faisaient encore partie de la mer rouge. Cette dernière hypothèses'accorderait mieux qu l'hypothèse contraire avec le texte des livres sacrés, mais alors il faudrait admettre que depuis l'époque de Moïse le seuil de Suez serait sorti des eaux'.

With regard to this question, it is certainly of importance to fall in with an account in this Frisian manuscript, from which it seems that in the sixteenth century before Christ the connection between the Bitter Lakes and the Red Sea still existed, and that the strait was still navigable. The manuscript further states that soon after the passage of the Geert-men there was an earthquake; that the land rose so high that all the water ran out, and all the shallows and alluvial lands rose up like a wall. This must have happened after the time of Moses, so that at the date of the Exodus (1564 B.C.) the track between Suez and the Bitter Lakes was still navigable, but could be forded dry-foot at low water.

This point, then, is the commencement of the isthmus, after the forming of which, the northern inlet was certainly soon filled up as far as the Gulf of Pelusium.

The map by Louis Figuier, in the 'Année scientifique et industrielle' (première année), Paris, Hachette, 1857, gives a distinct illustration of the formation of this land.

Another statement, which occurs only in Strabo, finds also here a confirmation. Strabo alone of all the Greek writers relates that Nearchus, after he had landed his troops in the Persian Gulf, at the mouth of the Pasitigris, sailed out of the Persian Gulf, by Alexander's command, and steered round Arabia through the Arabian Gulf. As the account stands, it is not clear what Nearchus had to do there, and what the object of the further voyage was. If, as Strabo seems to think, it was only for geographical discovery, he need not have taken the whole fleet. One or two ships would have sufficed. We do not read that he returned. Where, then, did he remain with the fleet?

The answer to this question is to be found in the Frisian version of the story. Alexander had bought the ships on the Indus, or had had them built by the descendants of the Frisians who settled there – the Geertmen – and had taken into his service sailors from among them, and at the head of them was Friso. Alexander having accomplished his voyage and the transport of his troops, had no further use for the ships in the Persian Gulf, but wished to employ them in the Mediterranean. He had taken that idea into his head, and it must be carried into effect. He wished to do what no one had done before him. For this purpose Nearchus was to sail up the Red Sea, and on his arrival at Suez was to find 200 elephants, 1,000 camels, workmen and materials, timber and ropes &c., in order to haul the ships by land over the isthmus. This work was carried on and accomplished with so much zeal and energy that after three months' labour the fleet was launched in the Mediterranean. That the fleet really came to the Mediterranean appears in Plutarch's *Life of Alexander*; but he makes Nearchus bring the fleet round Africa, and sail through the Pillars of Hercules.

After the defeat at Actium, Cleopatra, in imitation of this example, tried to take her fleet over the isthmus in order to escape to India, but was prevented by the inhabitants of Arabia Petraea, who burnt her ships. (See Plutarch's *Life of Antony*.) When Alexander shortly afterwards died, Friso remained in the service of Antigonus and Demetrius, until, having been grievously insulted by the latter, he resolved to seek out with his sailors their fatherland, Friesland. To India he could not, indeed, return.

Thus these accounts chime in with and clear up each other, and in that way afford a mutual confirmation of the events.

Such simple narratives and surprising results led me to conclude that we had to do here with more than mere Saga and Legends.

Since the last twenty years attention has been directed to the remains of the dwellings on piles, first observed in the Swiss lakes, and afterwards in other parts of Europe. (See Dr. E. Rückert, *Die Pfahlbauten*; Wurzburg, 1869. Dr. T. C. Winkler, in the 'Volksalmanak', t.N. v. A. 1867). When they were found, endeavours were made to discover, by the existing fragments of arms, tools, and household articles, by whom and when these dwellings had been inhabited. There are no accounts of them in historical writers, beyond what Herodotus writes in book v. chapter 16, of the 'Paeonen'. The only trace that has been found is in one of the panels of Trajan's Pillar, in which the destruction of a pile village in Dacia is represented.

Doubly important, therefore, is it to learn from the writing of Apollonia that she, as 'Burgtmaagd' (chief of the virgins), about 540 years before Christ, made a journey up the Rhine to Switzerland, and there became acquainted with the Lake Dwellers (Marsaten). She describes their dwellings built upon piles – the people themselves – their manners and customs. She relates that they lived by fishing and hunting, and that they prepared the skins of the animals with the bark of the birch-tree in order to sell the furs to the Rhine boatmen, who brought them into commerce. This account of the pile dwellings in the Swiss lakes can only have been written in the time when these dwellings still existed and were lived in. In the second part of the writing, Konered oera Linda relates that Adel, the son of Friso (±250 years before Christ), visited the pile dwellings in Switzerland with his wife Ifka.

Later than this account there is no mention by any writer whatever of the pile dwellings, and the subject has remained for twenty centuries utterly unknown until 1853, when an extraordinary low state of the water led to the discovery of these dwellings. Therefore no one could have invented this account in the intervening period. Although a great portion of the first part of the work – the book of Adela – belongs to the mythological period before the Trojan war, there is a striking difference between it and the Greek myths. The Myths have no dates, much less any chronology, nor any internal coherence of successive events. The untrammelled

230

fancy develops itself in every poem separately and independently. The mythological stories contradict each other on every point. 'Les Mythes ne se tiennent pas', is the only key to the Greek Mythology.

Here, on the contrary, we meet with a regular succession of dates starting from a fixed period – the destruction of Atland, 2193 before Christ. The accounts are natural and simple, often naive, never contradict each other, and are always consistent with each other in time and place. As, for instance, the arrival and sojourn of Ulysses with the Burgtmaagd Kalip at Walhallagara (Walcheren), which is the most mythical portion of all, is here said to be 1,005 years after the disappearance of Atland, which coincides with 1188 years before Christ, and thus agrees very nearly with the time at which the Greeks say the Trojan war took place. The story of Ulysses was not brought here for the first time by the Romans. Tacitus found it already in Lower Germany (see 'Germania', Chap. 3), and says that at Asciburgium there was an altar on which the names of Ulysses and his father Laërtes were inscribed.

Another remarkable difference consists in this, that the Myths knew no origin, do not name either writers or relaters of their stories, and therefore never can bring forward any authority. Whereas in Adela's book, for every statement is given a notice where it was found or whence it was taken. For instance, 'This comes from Minno's writings – this is written on the walls of Waraburch – this in the town of Frya – this at Stavia – this at Walhallagara'.

There is also this further. Laws, regular legislative enactments, such as are found in great numbers in Adela's book, are utterly unknown in Mythology, and indeed are irreconcilable with its existence. Even when the Myth attributes to Minos the introduction of lawgiving in Crete, it does not give the least account of what the legislation consisted in. Also among the Gods of Mythology there existed no system of laws. The only law was unchangable Destiny and the will of the supreme Zeus.

With regard to Mythology, this writing, which bears no mythical character, is not less remarkable than with regard

to history. Notwithstanding the frequent and various relations with Denmark, Sweden, and Norway, we do not find
any traces of acquaintance with the Northern or Scandinavian Mythology. Only Wodin appears in the person of
Wodan, a chief of the Frisians, who became the son-in-law
of one Magy, King of the Finns, and after his death was
deified.

The Frisian religion is extremely simple, and pure Mono-
theism. Wr-alda or Wr-alda's spirit is the only eternal, unchangeable, perfect and almighty being. Wr-alda has created
everything. Out of him proceeds everything – first the beginning, then time, and afterwards Irtha, the Earth. Irtha bore
three daughters – Lyda, Finda and Frya – the mothers of the
three distinct races, black, yellow and white – Africa, Asia
and Europe. As such, Frya is the mother of Frya's people,
the Frieslanders. She is the representative of Wr-alda, and
is reverenced accordingly. Frya has established her 'Tex',
the first law, and has established the religion of the eternal
light. The worship consists in the maintenance of a
perpetually-burning lamp, *foddik*, by priestesses, virgins. At
the head of the virgins in every town was a Burgtmaagd,
and the chief of the Burgtmaagden was the Eeremoeder of
the Fryasburgt of Texland. The Eeremoeder governs the
whole country. The kings can do nothing, nor can anything
happen without her advice and approval. The first Eeremoeder was appointed by Frya herself, and was called Fasta.
In fact, we find here the prototype of the Roman Vestal
Virgins.

We are reminded here of Velleda (Welda) and Aurinia in
Tacitus ('Germania', 8. Hist., iv. 61, 65; v. 22, 24. 'Annals' i.
54), and of Gauna, the successor of Velleda, in Dio Cassius
(Fragments, 49). Tacitus speaks of the town of Velleda as
'edita turris', page 146. It was the town Mannagarda forda
(Munster).

In the country of the Marsians he speaks of the temple
Tanfane (Tanfanc), so called from the sign of the Juul.

The last of these towns was Fastaburgt in Ameland,
temple Foste, destroyed, according to Occa Scarlensis, in
806.

If we find among the Frisians a belief in a Godhead and ideas of religion entirely different from the Mythology of other nations, we are the more surprised to find in some points the closest connection with the Greek and Roman Mythology, and even with the origin of two deities of the highest rank, Min-erva and Neptune. Min-erva (Athene) was originally a Burgtmaagd, priestess of Frya, at the town Walhallagâra, Middelburg, or Domburg, in Walcheren. And this Min-erva is at the same time the mysterious enigmatical goddess of whose worship scarcely any traces remain beyond the votive stones at Domburg, in Walcheren, Nehallenia, of whom no mythology knows anything more than the name, which etymology has used for all sorts of fantastical derivations.

The other, Neptune, called by the Etrurians Nethunus, the God of the Mediterranean Sea, appears here to have been, when living, a Friesland Viking, or sea-king, whose home was Alderga (Ouddorp, not far from Alkmaar). His name was Teunis, called familiarly by his followers Neef Teunis, or Cousin Teunis, who had chosen the Mediterranean as the destination of his expeditions, and must have been deified by the Tyrians at the time when the Phenician navigators began to extend their voyages so remarkably, sailing to Friesland in order to obtain British tin, northern iron, and amber from the Baltic, about 2,000 years before Christ.

Besides these two we meet with a third mythological person – Minos, the lawgiver of Crete, who likewise appears to have been a Friesland sea-king, Minno, born at Lindaoord, between Wieringen and Kreyl, who imparted to the Cretans an 'Asagaboek'. He is that Minos who, with his brother Rhadamanthus and Aeacus, presided as judges over the fates of the ghosts in Hades, and must not be confounded with the late Minos, the contemporary of Aegeus and Theseus, who appears in the Athenian Fables.

The reader may perhaps by inclined to laugh at these statements, and apply to me the words that I myself lately used, fantastic and improbable. Indeed at first I could not believe my own eyes, and yet after further consideration I arrived at the discovery of extraordinary conformities which render the case much less improbable than the birth of Minerva from the head of Jupiter by a blow from the axe of Hephaestus, for instance.

In the Greek Mythology all the gods and goddesses have a youthful period. Pallas alone has no youth. She is no otherwise known than adult. Min-erva appears in Attica as high priestess from a foreign country, a country unknown to the Greeks. Pallas is a virgin goddess, Min-erva is a Burgtmaagd. The fair, blue-eyed Pallas, differing thus in type from the rest of the gods and goddesses, evidently belonged to Frya's people. The character for wisdom and the emblematical attributes, especially the owl, are the same for both. Pallas gives to the new town her own name, Athenai, which has no meaning in Greek. Min-erva gives to the town built by her the name Athene, which has an important meaning in Fries, namely, that they came there as friends – 'Athen'.

Min-erva came to Attica about 1600 years before Christ, the period at which the Grecian Mythology was beginning to be formed. Min-erva landed with the fleet of Jon at the head of a colony in Attica. In later times we find her on the Roman votive stones in Walcheren, under the name of Nehallenia, worshipped as a goddess of navigation; and Pallas is worshipped by the Athenians as the protecting goddess of shipbuilding and navigation.

Time is the carrier who must eternally turn the 'Jol' (wheel) and carry the sun along his course through the firmament from winter to winter, thus forming the year, every turn of the wheel being a day. In midwinter the 'Jolfeest' is celebrated on Frya's Day. Then cakes are baked in the form of the sun's wheel, because with the Jol Frya formed the letters when she wrote her 'Tex'. The Jolfeest is therefore also in honour of Frya as inventor of writing.

Just as this Jolfeest has been changed by Christianity into Christmas throughout Denmark and Germany, and into St, Nicholas' Day in Holland; so, certainly, our St. Nicholas' dolls – the lover and his sweetheart – are a memorial of

234

Frya, and the St. Nicholas letters a memorial of Frya's invention of letters formed from the wheel.

I cannot analyse the whole contents of this writing, and must content myself with the remarks that I have made. They will give an idea of the richness and importance of the contents. If some of it is fabulous, it must have an interest for us, since so little of the traditions of our forefathers remain to us.

An internal evidence of the antiquity of these writings may be found in the fact that the name Batavians had not yet been used. The inhabitants of the whole country as far as the Scheldt are Frya's people – Frieslanders. The Batavians are not a separate people. The name Batavi is of Roman origin. The Romans gave it to the inhabitants of the banks of the Waal, which river bears the name Patabus in the 'Tabula Pentingeriana'. The name Batavi does not appear earlier than Tacitus and Pliny, and is interpolated in Caesar's 'Bello Gallico', iv. 10. (See my treatise on the course of the rivers through the countries of the Frisians and Batavians, p. 49, in 'De Vrije Fries', 4th vol. 1st part, 1845.)

I will conclude with one more remark regarding the language. Those who have been able to take only a superficial view of the manuscripts have been struck by the polish of the language, and its conformity with the present Friesland language and Dutch. In this they seem to find grounds for doubting the antiquity of the manuscript.

But, I ask, is, then, the language of Homer much less polished than that of Plato or Demosthenes? And does not the greatest portion of Homer's vocabulary exist in the Greek of our day?

It is true that language alters with time, and is continually subject to slight variations, owing to which language is found to be different at different epochs. This change in the language in this manuscript accordingly gives ground for important observations to philologists. It is not only that of the eight writers who have successively worked at the book, each is recognisable by slight peculiarities in style, language and spelling; but more particularly between the two parts of the book, between which an interval of more than two centuries occurs, a striking difference of the language is visible, which shows what a slowly progressive regulation it has undergone in that period of time. As the result of these considerations, I arrive at the conclusion that I cannot find any reason to doubt the authenticity of these writings. They cannot be forgeries. In the first place, the copy of 1256 cannot be. Who could at that time have forged anything of that kind? Certainly no one. Still less any one at an earlier date. At a later date a forgery is equally impossible, for the simple reason that no one was acquainted with the language. Except Grimm, Richthofen and Hettema, no one can be named sufficiently versed in that branch of philology, or who had studied the language so as to be able to write in it. And if any one could have done so, there would have been no more extensive vocabulary at his service than that which the East Frisian laws afford. Therefore, in the centuries lately elapsed, the preparation of this writing was quite impossible. Whoever doubts this let him begin by showing where, when, by whom, and with what object such a forgery could be committed, and let him show in modern times the fellow of this paper, this writing, and this language.

Moreover, that the manuscript of 1256 is not original, but is a copy, is proved by the numerous faults in the writing, as well as by some explanations of words which already in the time of the copyist had become obsolete and little known, as, for instance, in page 82 (114), 'to thera flete jefta bedrum'; page 151 (204), 'bargum jefta tonnum fon tha besta bjar'.

A still stronger proof is that between pages 157 and 158 one or more pages are missing, which cannot have been lost out of the manuscript, because the pages 157 and 158 are on the front and the back of the same leaf.

Page 157 finishes thus: 'Three months afterwards Adel sent messengers to all the friends that he had gained, and requested them to send him intelligent people in the month of May'. When we turn over the leaf, the other side begins, 'his wife, he said, who had been Maid of Texland', had got a copy of it.

There is no connection between these two. There is wanting, at least, the arrival of the invited, and an account of what passed at their meeting. It is clear, therefore, that the copyist must have turned over two pages of the original instead of one. There certainly existed then an earlier manuscript, and that was doubtless written by Liko oera Linda in the year 803.

We may thus accept that we possess in this manuscript, of which the first part was composed in the sixth century before our era, the oldest production, after Homer and Hesiod, of European literature. And here we find in our fatherland a very ancient people in possession of development, civilisation, industry, navigation, commerce, literature, and pure elevated ideas of religion, whose existence we had never conjectured. Hitherto we have believed that the historical records of our people reach no farther back than the arrival of Friso the presumptive founder of the Frisians, whereas here we become aware that these records mount up to more than 2,000 years before Christ, surpassing the antiquity of Hellas and equalling that of Israel.

APPENDIX C

Maps of the Ancient Sea Kings

Scholars have for many years claimed that a world civilisation existed thousands of years ago, long before Egypt and perhaps even Sumerian civilisation. In his *Maps of the Ancient Sea Kings*[1] Professor Charles H. Hapgood has produced concrete evidence of such a civilisation. His most important evidence is the 'Oronteus Finaeus' World Map, drawn in 1531. When he made this map the Antarctic continent was hidden beneath a thick sheet of ice which reached out into the ocean. In places it was, and still is, two miles thick. There was no possible way the cartographer could have known the shape of the continent, or even that it existed under the ice cap. Very little was known about the Antarctic in his day. Yet he produced a map giving the correct shape of the hidden continent, correctly indicating its hidden bays and estuaries, rivers and other details of the coastline. Modern scientific investigation has shown the map to be correct, more accurate than some maps of today. Since Oronteus Finaeus had no knowledge of the Antarctic, and other parts of the world shown on the map, he must have copied it from an earlier map, or maps.

The original map must have been drawn thousands of years before his time, when the southern and northern hemispheres were warm and free of ice. There are other maps, those of Mercator and Pir Re'is, which must have been copied from an earlier map, since they also show the Antarctic continent without ice.

As yet we cannot say with certainty that the Atlanders or Frisians mapped the whole world, but we can show that it is more than likely. The *Oera Linda Book* is the only ancient written record which says that there was a warm and genial

1. Published by Turnstone Books, London 1977.

climate in the far north. It says that the earth rocked and shook and the sun sank to the horizon, bringing disaster, cold and ice to warm and sunny lands. As I have said in my comments, abundant evidence has been brought to light which demonstrates that the northern and southern frozen lands were once warm, as when the seamen of Atland were roaming the seas and oceans of the world. I have given many factual reasons for my suggestions that the axis of the earth tipped and intense cold descended upon the far north and south. I now give my reasons for suggesting that Atlander and Frisian navigators drew maps of all the distant lands they visited before and after Atland was submerged. Frisians in Europe and other parts of the world would certainly have used the earlier maps and made new ones, since sea-going and adventures in distant lands were their most honoured exploits. The following maps show clearly that the geological history given in the *Oera Linda Book* is a true account, and give strong reasons for accepting that a great forgotten civilisation existed more than 5,000 years ago and that the Atlanders and Frisians were the authors of these maps.

The terrible fires which erupted from the vitals of Mother Earth to sink the mountains and valleys of Atland beneath the sea, which destroyed many other northern lands, formed as we now know it, the Baltic Sea, changed the shape of the British Isles and many islands, is fully indicated in these maps.

They also show the glaciers which covered much of the northern lands when the great freeze followed the geological upheaval.

The Ibn Ben Zara Map shows the remains of glaciers and great lakes in parts of the British Isles and which seem to cover some of the northern parts of Europe now clear of ice and water. Note the islands north of Iceland, now vanished, the different coastline of Britain, and also the ice which covers the land which was once adjacent to Atland.

This map contains much important and interesting information, much of which bears witness to the geological changes recorded in the *Oera Linda Book*. For an example, The Spanish sector shows a large bay at the mouth of the

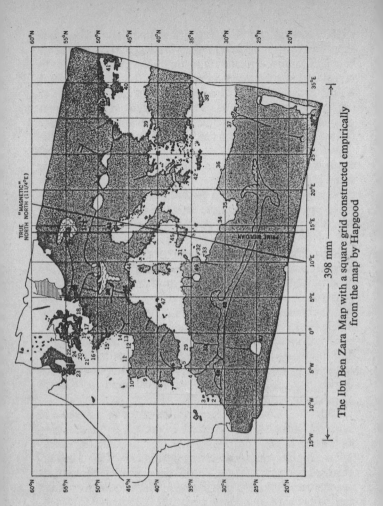

The Ibn Ben Zara Map with a square grid constructed empirically from the map by Hapgood

240

Guadalquivir River. Hapgood draws attention to the mouth of this river. A modern map shows a large delta of swamps thirty miles wide and fifty miles long. The Ibn Ben Zara Map represents the coastline before the delta was formed. It would have taken the Guadalquivir thousands of years to collect and carry sufficient sediment to its mouth to form the great swampy delta which is now the home of many rare wild fowl. It is questionable whether the river could have deposited the tremendous amount of materials required to form the delta, even over a long period of time because storms raging in the bay would have swept the small amounts of sediments out to sea. Some other factor must have caused the formation of the delta, and that factor is given clearly and dramatically in the *Oera Linda Book*. It tells of several series of earthquakes, great floods, intense cold and the formation of great sheets of ice which destroyed Frisian cities and lands all along the northern coasts of Europe in the year 305 B.C. Mountains erupted and were torn asunder. Coastal lands sank, says the history. Great waves tore inland and on returning to the sea carried away much soil which formed new islands at the mouths of rivers. Here we have a written historical account of an eye witness (see the writings of Frethorik and Wiljow) of turbulence of land, sea and climate which undoubtedly caused the formation of the great swamps and which now form the delta of the Guadalquivir.

The *Oera Linda Book* says this second great upheaval of land and turbulent seas swept away the soil of Greece, leaving behind a stony land where many crops could not thrive. We may safely assume that many islands in the Mediterranean seas sank beneath the sea and new ones formed during the two geological disturbances. The map bears witness that this is what actually happened.

Commenting on the map Hapgood says: 'There are many fewer Islands on a modern map, and many of them are smaller than shown on the old map'.

He asks: 'If the map-maker was so conscientious in drawing the smallest islands, and showing all the features of the coast with the greatest accuracy possible, why in the Aegean

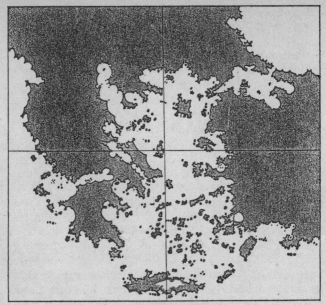

The Ibn Zara map. Aegean section (after Hapgood).

should he suddenly take leave of his senses, and fill the sea
with imaginary islands, whilst still showing the real islands
in their correct positions'?

Fifteen centuries before Christ on the island of Santorini
(Thira) the Minoans were content and happy, tending their
vines under a hot sun, or following skilled and beautiful arts
and crafts in and around their great merchant palaces, plying the seas in their merchant ships and exchanging their
goods with the Minoans of Crete and with distant Egypt,
when, suddenly, the earth beneath their feet began to shake
and heave. The walls of country villas and city buildings
began to crumble. Then, with a terrible blast of sound and
fire, the whole island exploded. Mighty waves reaching high
into the air raced across the sea, followed by thick dark
clouds of pumice dust which were carried as far as Egypt.
As for Santorini, the sea rushed into a huge crater, the site
of a once flourishing island. Only the great torn cliffs of the

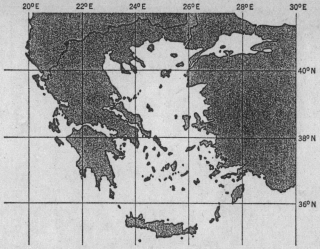

Modern map of the Aegean (after Hapgood).

little island of Thira, and other small islands on the rim of
the crater are buried deep in pumice dust. The convulsion
tore through the rock foundations of the Aegean Sea, causing many islands to sink beneath the sea. Even the large
island of distant Crete did not escape the disaster. The north
coast sank, making the island more narrow than it was
originally. Nearby islands shown on the map also sank. The
great Minoan palaces were felled to the ground; earthquake,
fire and volcanic dust destroyed Santorini's sister Minoan
civilisation.

Again the Ibn Ben Zara Map gives silent witness to those
days of terror, death and the loss of what was one of the
most peaceful cultures the world has known. The old map
shows many islands in the Aegean which were lost. It clearly
shows that the pitiful rock of Thira was once the much larger
island of Santorini which excavations are now revealing had
enjoyed an advanced civilisation. The old map shows a
broader Crete with a different coastline. I have explored the
ancient ports and quays which now disappear into the sea;
I have admired snow-capped Mount Idi reflecting redly the
sinking sun, a great mountain of many legends which the

243

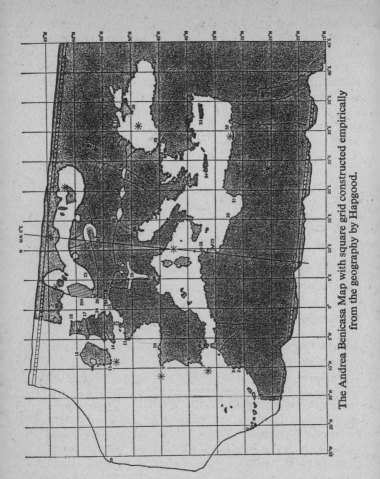

The Andrea Benicasa Map with square grid constructed empirically from the geography by Hapgood.

old map shows was surrounded by a great glacier, a feature which adds to the accumulation of evidence that the map is a copy of one drawn thousands of years ago.

Returning to Ireland with its glaciers. A carefully drawn cluster of islands is shown off the north coast. The greater number of these islands may have been submerged when the sea bed tilted, sinking north of Ireland and rising near the then south coast of Scotland to form or extend the islands of Islay, Jura, etc.

The Ibn Ben Zera Map contains another very interesting feature. There is a tiny face in a medallion in the north east corner, another at the south east corner and three more in the western seas. Map makers of the Renaissance used faces with puffed cheeks to symbolise the blowing of the wind. Portolano charts made no use of such faces. On this map there are five without puffed cheeks and quite unlike the faces sometimes shown on the later maps. The long pointed noses and firm pointed chins of the calm, intellectual, aristocratic faces resemble the Minoan and Coptic, but the clothing is not indicative of any of these people. We would like to think that these proud heads, held high with upturned faces, are those of Atlander sea-kings. In any case, there is a close similarity of features and poise with that of the Great Mother (page 76).

I will comment on one more map from Hapgood's excellent book.

Commenting on the strange features of this map (also shown on other ancient maps) Hapgood writes: 'we note details which differ considerably from other representatives of bodies of water on maps of the 15th and 16th centuries. Is this large feature really the Baltic – or is it a mass of ice? Are these blobs along the southern edge supposed to be harbours along the Baltic coast of Germany, or are they run-off lakes from melting glacier? Are these apparent islands really islands, or are they deglaciated tracks in the middle of the retreating ice caps'?

'In order to evaluate this map's most remarkable feature it is necessary to lay emphasis upon the fact that it is one of the most accurate of the portolanos in its delineation of the details of the coasts. At the same time it shows in its accuracy of latitude and longitude that, like some of the other maps, it can only have been drawn originally with the aid of spherical trigonometry. It is therefore a scientific product in the true sense of that term'.

The feature which is so different from modern maps is what looks at first glance to be a bad representation of the Baltic. The Baltic today runs nearly north and south. But on the otherwise so scientifically correct map it is shown running east and west. The Baltic was very well known in 1508, the date given to the map. For three hundred years before this date it had been a highway of commerce. A federation of north German states, the Hanseatic League, is said to have dominated trade in this region. What then could be the reason for the ancient draughtsman depicting so different a coast line in the far north of Europe whilst so meticulously accurate when depicting coastlines in other parts of Europe? It seems to me that the explanation for this strange northern feature is clearly given in the *Oera Linda Book*. It says that the whole of the far northern coast was altered when the mountain vomited fire and tremendous mass of land heaved and collapsed, where valleys heaved up into hills, then sank beneath the sea. The coastline of the greater part of the far north underwent a great change, along with the climate.

It would not have been possible for the British Isles to pass unscathed through the geological fury. The north of Scotland is shown on these two maps with unfamiliar shape, a further indication that the coastline of the far north at the time of Atland or immediately after the catastrophe, when the Gulfs of Bothnin and Riga did not exist and the shape and the position of the Baltic was vastly different to what it is today.

The Oronteus Finaeus Map also shows the broad level north coast of Ancient Scotland, extending almost to the Shetland Islands. Some of the islands shown north of Scotland have since submerged. The east coast of Scotland covered what is now the Dogger Bank, and the extension of Cornwall includes Lost Lyonnesse.

246

GLOSSARY OF NAMES, TITLES AND TERMS
USED IN THE '*OERA LINDA BOOK*'

Note: Many of the characters, place-names and terms used in the *Oera Linda Book* will at first be unfamiliar to the majority of readers. This glossary should prove useful for easy reference and guidance.

ADEL: Son of FRISO.

ADELA: Queen of FRYA'S people; three years a BURGT-MAAGD, or chief of the Council of Virgins. Writer of the first narrative of the *Oera Linda Book*. Wife of APOL.

ADELBROST: Son of APOL and ADELA; co-writer, with his sister, APOLLONIA, of the second narrative of the *Oera Linda Book*.

ALDERGAMUDE: Ouddorp, home of the old sea-king STERIK, near Alkmaar, a town 20 miles NNW of Amsterdam.

ALDLAND: See ATLAND.

APOL: Husband of ADELA; male chief of 'Linda' country; 'three times a sea-king'. Grevetman of Ostflyland and Lindaoorden, in charge of the towns of Lindgarda, Linda-hem and Stavia.

APOLLONIA: Daughter of APOL and ADELA; co-writer, with her brother ADELBROST, of the second narrative of the *Oera Linda Book*.

ATHENS: Old Frisian word for 'friends'. The name which the descendants of ATLAND gave to the Greek capital. It is significant that, apart from its obvious connection with the Greek goddess Athena (See MIN-ERVA), the word has no meaning in Greek.

ATLAND: Seafarer's name for ALDLAND, literally, the 'Old Land'; home of FRYA'S people, a land mass to the north and east of the British Isles, which sank in some cataclysm in 2193 B.C.

BEEDEN: Grandson of FRETHORIK and WILJOW; writer

of the fifth section of the *Oera Linda Book*.

BURGTMAAGD: Literally, 'borough-maid'. Chief of the Council of Virgins, in charge of 21 maidens and seven apprentices, custodians of the eternally-burning lamp (See FODDICK); dispensers of law and advice, answerable to the EEREMOEDER.

EEREMOEDER: Earth-Mother; Overall Chief of the BURGTMAAGDEN, or borough-maids.

EVA (or EVIN): An innate spirit of justice in every man, derived from the great God, WR-ALDA. Also means, tranquil or smooth.

FASTA: The first EEREMOEDER, appointed by FRYA; later became the Roman goddess of the hearth, Vesta, under whom six Vestal Virgins were committed to maintain the eternal flame. (See FODDICK.)

FINNS: Descendants of FINDA, yellow people, who came out of the East.

FLYLAND: Vlieland, a 'refuge or asylum' to the west where FRYA gave her TEX, or laws.

FODDICK: The perpetually-burning lamp with magical powers, maintained by virgin-priestesses of FASTA; symbol of FRYA'S religion of the eternal light. The original was at the Citadel in TEXLAND; from it, all other sacred lamps had to be kindled.

FRANA: EEREMOEDER of TEXLAND, murdered *c.* 589 B.C. by the MAGY, king of the MAGYARS.

FRETHORIK: Co-writer of the third narrative of the *Oera Linda Book*, the text being taken over on his death by his widow, WILJOW.

FRISO: A king-prince of Frisian origin who returned to Europe with the fleet of Nearchus, an officer of Alexander the Great, from a Frisian colony which settled in the Punjab fifteen-and-a-half centuries before Christ.

FRYA: Mother of the fair (white) races in Atland mythology. Probably the prototype for the Norse goddess of love, Freyja, sister of Frey, god of peace and fruitfulness.

GEERT: Priestess under whose guidance FRISO'S colony settled in the Punjab.

GEERTMEN: Frisian colonists of the Punjab, named after

248

GEERT.

GODASBURGT: Gothenburg.

GOLEN: Druids; missionary priests of Siden. (See TRIU-WENDEN.)

GREVETMEN: Burghers.

HEERMAN: Commander.

IFKJA: Wife of ADEL.

INKA: Admiral, nephew of STERIK. He sailed west in search of remnants of Atland which had not been sub-merged and doubtless landed in South America where he founded the Inca Dynasty of Peru. 'Inca' to the Peruvian Indians, meant 'king'.

IRTHA: The Earth in Atland Mythology.

JUULFEEST: Midwinter celebration of FRYA'S Day, when cakes were baked in representation of the Juul, or wheel of the sun. It was from the Juul that FRYA formed letters to write down her laws, probably the origin of runes. JUULFEEST is doubtless the origin of the so-called pagan Yuletide, upon which the later festival of Christmas was grafted.

JON: A sea-king who, with MIN-ERVA, sailed to Tyre and later established John's Islands, or the Pirates' Isles.

KADHEMAR: Phoenicians; literally, 'dwellers on the coast'.

KALIP: BURGTMAAGD at WALHALLAGARA (Wal-cheren), c. 1188 B.C. So-named because her lower lip pro-truded. She received Ulysses when he came in search of the eternally-burning lamp and was probably the original model for Homer's Calypso.

KALTA: A renegade BURGTMAAGD after whom the Kelts or Celts were named.

KAT (or KATERINE): High-priestess who, by jumping over-board from a ship between Jutland and Sweden, gave her name to the Kattegat.

KONERED: Son of FRETHORIK and WILJOW, writer of the fourth part of the *Oera Linda Book*.

KREKALAND: Frisian name for Greece.

KRETA: Frisian name for Crete.

LYDA: Mother of the black races in Atland mythology.

LUMKAMAKIA: Embden, home of WODIN.

249

MAAGDEN: Maidens.

MAGY: Priest-king, head of the MAGYARS.

MAGYAR: Descendants of FINDA'S people who, with the FINNS, invaded Northern Europe from the East.

MARSATEN: Swiss Lake-Dwellers, visited and observed by APOLLONIA *c.* 540 B.C. and ADEL, *c.* 250 B.C.

MIDDELBURG: City in Walcheren, ruled by MIN-ERVA in 1630 B.C.

MIN-ERVA: (surnamed NYHELLENNIA): A Frisian BURGTMAAGD, princess of FRYA at WALHALL-AGARA. She became the Roman goddess of wisdom; Greek – Athena, in whose honour the Acropolis was built at Athens.

MINNA: EEREMOEDER of TEXLAND at the time of the MAGYAR invasion, *c.* 2012 B.C.

MINNO: Frisian sea-king, born at Lindaoord, between Wieringen and Kreyl. Became the Cretan law-giver, Minos.

MIS-SELLJA: Marseilles, bought from the Frisians by the Phoenicians.

NYHELLENNIA: Surname of MIN-ERVA; probably the origin of the adjectives Hellenic, Hellene, etc., of the Greek classical period.

SCHOONLAND (or SKENLAND): Scandinavia.

STERIK: Old sea-king of ALDERGAMUDE; uncle of WODIN, TEUNIS and INKA.

TEUNIS: Sea-king, nephew of STERIK. He led his people to Phoenicia *c.* 2000 B.C. and founded Tyre. Also known as Neef Teunis (Cousin Teunis), from which the Roman Neptune, sea-god of the Mediterranean (Greek – Poseidon) derived.

TEX: The 'law' of FRYA. Compare with 'lexigraphy' meaning a system of writing, from the Greek, *Lexikon.*

TEXLAND: Place named in honour of FRYA'S laws where a citadel was built and the TEX inscribed upon its walls.

THYR: Finnish god, son of Odin (Scandinavian – Thor; German – Donar; Anglo-Saxon – Thuner.)

THYRISBURGT: Tyre, ancient Phoenician city, founded by TEUNIS.

TRIUWENDEN: Druids; literally, 'abstainers from the truth' which was what the Frisians called the GOLEN, missionary priests of Sidon.

VOLKSMOEDER: Queen; literally, 'Mother-of-the-people'.

WALHALLARAGA: Walcheren, where MIN-ERVA was BURGTMAAGD. Compare with Valhalla, the 'heaven' of Norse warrior-heroes.

WILJOW: Widow of FRETHORIK; she took over the writing of the third section of the *Oera Linda Book* on her husband's death.

WODIN: A king or leader who was STERIK'S nephew; later, a Norse god, Wodan, Odin.

WR-ALDA: The eternal, unchangeable, perfect, almighty essence of all things; in Atland cosmogenesis, the equivalent of an unknowable God. Literally, 'the Old Ancient', or 'Oldest Being'.

Someone Else is on Our Moon

GEORGE H. LEONARD

Revealed – the astounding facts about intelligent life on the Moon.

AN EXCAVATING MACHINE AS BIG AS A CITY –
ON THE SURFACE OF THE MOON!
And that's just one of George H. Leonard's sensational, shocking revelations

Few people noticed the secret code words used by astronauts to describe the Moon.
Until now, few knew about the strange moving lights they reported.
Or were aware of the huge mechanical contrivances seen working in the craters of the Moon.

George H. Leonard fought through the official veil of secrecy and studied thousands of NASA photographs, talked candidly with dozens of officials from NASA and listened to hours of the astronauts' tapes. Here he presents the stunning and inescapable conclusion of his work:

THE SPACE AGENCY – AND MANY OF THE WORLD'S TOP SCIENTISTS – HAVE KNOWN FOR YEARS THAT THERE IS INTELLIGENT LIFE ON THE MOON.

'Truly mind-boggling' *Publishers' Weekly*

'The most provocative piece of celestial detective work since the books of Charles Fort' Joseph J. Goodavage, author of *The Comet Kohoutek*

(Startlingly illustrated)

COSMOLOGY   £1.25

0 7221 5486 0

How to be More Psychic

IVOR POWELL

Your guide to developing the hidden powers within you

It's astonishing but true – we all possess awesomely effective hidden psychic powers. And this unique book tells us how we can discover and unlock the vast potential imprisoned beneath the surface of our conscious minds.
In a down-to-earth, rational and systematic way, the well-known clairvoyant Ivor Powell provides a practical manual of:

* Clairvoyance
* Dowsing
* Psychic healing
* Divination
* Dream interpretation and prophecy

Culled from knowledge ancient and modern, HOW TO BE MORE PSYCHIC divulges methods that have hitherto been restricted to a select group of practising psychics.
IT IS A BOOK THAT WILL AMAZE AND FASCINATE YOU – AND IT COULD CHANGE YOUR LIFE!

OCCULT/COSMOLOGY   85p

0 7221 6976 0

A selection of Bestsellers from Sphere Books